BATTLEFIELD

BATTLEFIELD

Farming a Civil War Battleground

Peter Svenson

Burford Books

Printed in the United States of America.

10 9 8 7 6 5 4 3 2 1

Library of Congress Cataloging-in-Publication Data is on file with the Library of Congress.

CONTENTS

PREFACE

——————

THERE IS A GENERATION come of age that really digests movies and videos—watching them over and over, ruminating upon the meaning of every scene, every line of dialogue. Such a method of viewing imparts a delicious familiarity with events and personalities as a story unfolds, making it seem as real as the life of the watcher.

So I would like my humble offering to be digested, if not by my generation then by another, for this story is a recollection of one small niche of Americana, peopled with real individuals and placed in a real setting. Such an encapsulation includes detail that is most beneficially absorbed by a tortoise-paced, repetitive reader who is in no rush to ever finish, or forget, the lessons of history.

Cross Keys, Virginia
May 1992

ACKNOWLEDGMENTS

I WOULD LIKE TO THANK the following people for their help during the many stages of this writing project: William I. Bennington, Kemper Jarrels, Ellen H. Layman, David W. Lowe, Jeff Mellott, Melvin Miller, Margaret Neumeister, Donald E. Schwab, and Colonel Richard B. Smith. I would also like to thank numerous other individuals who assisted in meaningful ways, as well as staff members of the Rockingham Public Library, the James Madison University Library, the University of Virginia Library, the Virginia State Library and Archives, the Harrisonburg-Rockingham Historical Society, the Virginia Historical Society, and the New York Historical Society. A special note of gratitude is extended to my editor, Betsy Uhrig, who singled out my voice amid the babble over the transom. Lastly, I would like to thank Becky and Hope and Van for the steadfast balm of their love.

FOREWORD
TO THE 2017 EDITION

I~T HAS BEEN TWENTY-FOUR YEARS~ since *Battlefield: Farming a Civil War Battleground* was first published. Being my first nonfiction book project, it took several years to write, including hundreds of hours of old-fashioned research in libraries and archives, as well as a rewriting process that seemed, at the time, interminable. Not only this, but the finished manuscript was turned down by eighteen publishers, until one editor at Faber and Faber, in Boston, saw its potential as a marketable work of nonfiction.

My aim in presenting the book was simple: to weave the present with the past. I had the good fortune to purchase forty acres of farmland in Virginia's rural Shenandoah Valley, forty acres with a largely unknown, and certainly unheralded historical dimension. I was also fortunate to possess the wherewithal to delve and describe, a wherewithal I wouldn't exactly call a gift, but more an unquenchable curiosity. The forty acres had a story to tell; I merely became its mouthpiece.

As I familiarized myself with two completely different spheres—the local impact of an episode in the 19th century American Civil War, and the demands of present day farming—I saw a way to connect the two, and this book was the result.

Now, from the vantage of nearly a quarter of a century, I realize that my book still holds a certain appeal to readers who want something more than a mere dry recounting of facts, or, conversely, a fictionalized account that takes liberties with the truth. What I wrote is neither the stuff of movies, nor doctoral theses. This is what happened, why it happened, and where it happened.

My ten years of living on a Civil War battleground and relating to it from an agricultural perspective was, in hindsight, an experience I will always cherish. It involved a lot of hard work, from manually lifting hay bales to restoring, repairing, and operating farm machinery. Yet I found the work both physically and mentally rewarding. And as I grew involved with the facts of the 1862 battle itself, an added dimension quite took over, although the research—before facts were finger-tipped—was time-consuming, and the writing—first in longhand until I learned word-processing—went just as slowly.

This Burford Books edition expands the original book with pages of photographs that serve to bring the Cross Keys battleground even closer to the reader, making her or him acutely cognizant of how things were for the Union and Confederate combatants, and, much later, for me.

Peter Svenson
Fayetteville, New York
September, 2017

ONE

Down a honeysuckle-margined right of way leading to a forty-acre expanse of rolling hayfields, there is an antebellum farmhouse on the left, behind a pair of silver maples and a low retaining wall of purplish river rock. From May 1985 to May 1986, this was our home. We were a family of four, embarked upon the uncharted waters of a second marriage: an artist, a college professor, and two children who were shuttled along the interstate to join the household on weekends and school vacations. Although my two children, Hope and Van, have grown to high school and college age, respectively, and are rarely at home with us anymore, my wife, Becky, and I still drive past the farmhouse every day and think back to that year of our uncertain voyage both forward and backward in time.

We were renting the farmhouse by the month, having purchased the forty acres beyond for the purpose of building a dwelling of our own and Starting Over. Geographically speaking, this property lies on the plain just south of the headland of the Massanutten range in Virginia's Shenandoah Valley, in a farming community called Cross Keys, named for an early nineteenth-century tavern which displayed the sign of crossed keys above its door. The quarter-mile right of way opens onto a heavily trafficked highway, Port Republic Road, that runs for eleven miles between Harrisonburg, a city of 35,000, and Port Republic, a village that flourished in the bygone days of river commerce, but is now little more than a bedroom community. Our tract, four miles distant from Port, as it is called, is indistinguishable from similar acreage in the populous countryside divided into farms and residential lots except in this respect: it borders a ragged, hundred-acre historical preserve that is held in private trust. A battle was fought here in the American Civil War: the Battle of Cross Keys.

In 1985, to my inexpert eye, the locale appeared relatively untouched since the 1860s. I equated forty acres with privacy, a prime ingredient in the living of an artistic life. The immediate improvements I was contemplating for the property—fixing up its bank barn and machine shed (both stood in the field nearest the farmhouse, having originally belonged to a single farmstead), expanding one end of a creek into a pond, and building a new house flanked by two studios in which Becky and I would pursue our separate careers—would be minimally disruptive; but then again, I was minimally informed. Like everyone else, I was ignorant of the historical particulars.

Over the past hundred and twenty-three years, the battle had been reduced to five words mouthed in an inconsequential slur: The-Battle-of-Cross-Keys. Sites of Civil War action are all around the Shenandoah Valley, and they trip off the tongue with notorious ease. The-Battle-of-Cross-Keys is like a password, a name to drop during conversational forays, a demonstration of sensitivity to the past. It can be counted on to pop up from time to time, although no one seems to know precisely where the battle was fought, or when, or by whom, or what happened.

The property to the south of the rusted barbed wire fence belongs to the Lee-Jackson Foundation, a nonprofit organization headquartered in Charlottesville, some fifty miles across the Blue Ridge mountains. Founded in 1953, the Foundation is dedicated to, as their letterhead says, "our history, education and national heritage"—suspect words, I thought when I first read them, considering the wild condition of the acreage. To me, it was a buffer zone pure and simple, an enlargement of our privacy that we would not have to pay taxes on.

As an abstract painter, I like to think of myself as a cultural refugee from Progress with a capital P. In most respects, of course, I am a very ordinary minion of materialism, harboring typical expectations of home and vehicle ownership, of increased earning capacity, of food and frivolity aplenty. The American way has been good to me, I cannot complain. Still, I feel brutalized by the late twentieth century, and, try as I might, I can never quite get in step with it. I paint and paint, but the better my work gets, the harder it is to sell.

Rockingham County, Virginia's largest in gross receipts of agricultural sales, and Harrisonburg, its seat, are growth areas of broad definition. Their economic and demographic horizons appear to be limitless. The county was settled, i.e., wrested from its nomadic Native Americans, in the early eighteenth century by an influx of middle- and northern-European immigrants who carved out farmsteads in the fertile valley plain. Today, what is old is torn down with regularity and without remorse to make way for the new. Ever expanding, the city nearly tripled in square mileage when it annexed land from the county in 1983. Shopping centers and housing developments continue to jostle for elbow room. Interstate 81, a major artery of commerce along the eastern corridor of the nation, intersects the city, pumping the lifeblood of retail goods, services, and tourism into the regional economy. A thriving guarantor of this vitality is James Madison University, where Becky teaches art, a state institution of eleven thousand students, which acts upon the same blueprint for expansion and looses an endless crop of young consumers upon the local mercantile establishments.

Rockingham County welcomes new industry with brash public enticements; signs along the interstate proclaim that the traveler is entering a "Certified Business Location." Factory sites are numerous. There is an excellent labor pool, a copious water table, a plethora of tax incentives. Good roads radiate in all directions. The county is proud of its long-held reputation as a safe haven for the establishment of corporate roots. By being industry-friendly, the county planners are shifting the preponderantly agricultural base into the higher gear of the twenty-first century. The landscape of the future will be shared by agribusiness and industry —vistas of cornfields and poultry barns (the county calls itself the "Turkey Capital of the World") interspersed with rectilinear eruptions of manufacturing plants and parking lots and residential clusters. This was why I welcomed the protection of the adjacent, unused hundred acres. Battlefield or not, it was the best kind of neighbor I could hope for: no neighbor at all.

The Lee-Jackson property was purchased in 1960 through the efforts of Jay Johns, a self-made millionaire in the coal industry, an acquisitive and autocratic figure bent on preserving several battle sites crucial to the Shenandoah Valley campaign of his boyhood hero, Major General Thomas J. "Stonewall" Jackson. Elderly and with glaucoma, but hardnosed as ever in his business dealings, Johns had tendered low, take-it-or-leave-it bids on three contiguous farms, buttressing his appeal with speeches about patriotism and sympathy for his blindness. (At the end of his long life, Johns was to employ a similar persuasiveness to secure a final resting place for himself alongside his hero in the Jackson family cemetery in Lexington.)

Two of the farmers succumbed to Johns's offers, which included lifetime rights to their farmhouses, but the third refused. The gamut of Johns's hard sell didn't alter the fact that prime farmland would be taken out of production. The third farmer wasn't necessarily immune to the

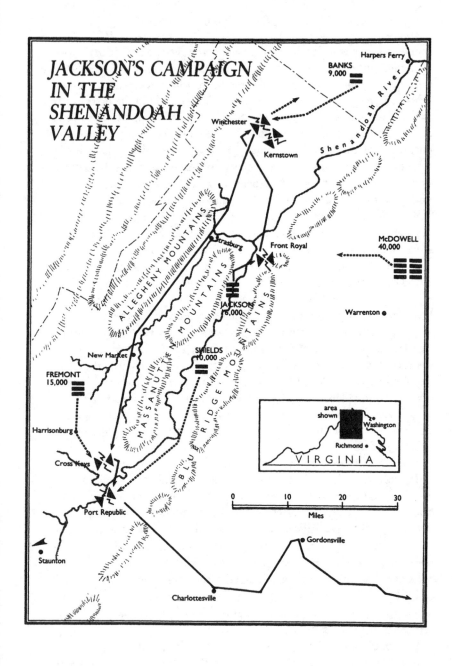

JACKSON'S CAMPAIGN IN THE SHENANDOAH VALLEY

BANKS 9,000

Harpers Ferry

Shenandoah River

Winchester

Kernstown

ALLEGHENY MOUNTAINS

Strasburg

Front Royal

McDOWELL 40,000

JACKSON 6,000

Warrenton

New Market

SHIELDS 10,000

FREMONT 15,000

MASSANUTTEN MOUNTAINS

BLUE RIDGE MOUNTAINS

Harrisonburg

area shown

Washington

Richmond

VIRGINIA

Cross Keys

0   10   20   30

Miles

Port Republic

Staunton

Gordonsville

Charlottesville

SOURCE: *A Battlefield Atlas of the Civil War*, The Nautical and Aviation Publishing Company of America.

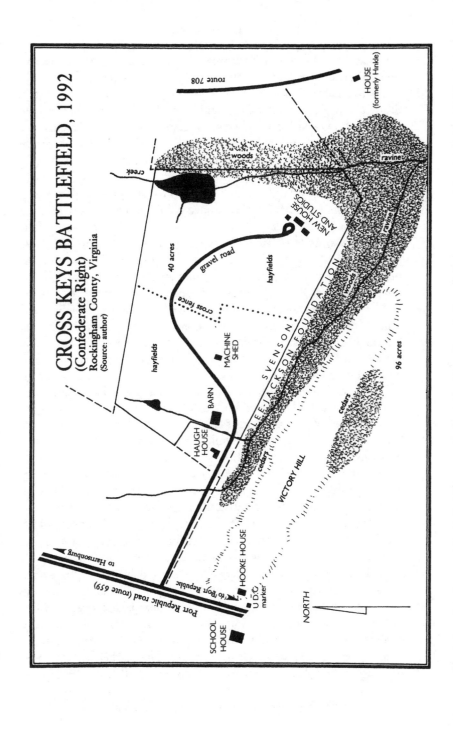

CROSS KEYS BATTLEFIELD, 1992
(Confederate Right)
Rockingham County, Virginia
(Source: author)

route 708

HOUSE
(formerly Hinkle)

woods

ravine

creek

ravine

40 acres

NEW HOUSE
AND STUDIOS

gravel road

hayfields

cross fence

hayfields

LEE-JACKSON FOUNDATION

MACHINE
SHED

woods

BARN

96 acres

HAUGH
HOUSE

cedars

cedars

VICTORY HILL

HOOKE HOUSE

to Harrisonburg

Port Republic road (route 659)

to Port Republic

U.D.C.
marker

NORTH

SCHOOL
HOUSE

prerogatives of history or wealth or personal handicap. It was just that no city slicker was going to talk him out of his livelihood for the sake of a battle that took place a hundred years earlier. The farmer knew that disuse and neglect would follow, and he was right; from a farming perspective, the Lee-Jackson land went to waste as soon as it entered a state of preservation. Now, cedars choke the fields, honeysuckle obfuscates the fencelines, and between them broomsedge and ragweed sprout in the nutrient-leached topsoil.

The farmhouse on the nearest of the two tracts stands beside the public road at the crest of a long flat-topped hill known as Victory Hill. An asbestos-shingled, two-story structure with deep soffits and mournfully tall windows, its latest face-lift has rendered it an innocuous yellow. Johns had a notion to turn the house into a battlefield museum, the proprietors of which would be the former owners, now tenants. During the course of one year, a collection of papers and dirt-encrusted artifacts were displayed on tables in the front parlor, but there were frequent episodes of thievery. The tenants moved out, and what remained of the collection was donated to Washington and Lee University. The house was rented to a succession of short-term occupants until, becoming too burdensome to manage, it was sold with a three-acre lot and outbuildings.

On the other tract, a quarter of a mile in back, stands the wrecked shell of an older house, abandoned since the early 1970s, mute testimony to the durability of its rusting roof and rotting weatherboard. Nearby, a bank barn deteriorated along a similar path of neglect until it was blown down in a summer storm in 1987.

After the museum closed, the Lee-Jackson Foundation decided to try a more passive visitor facility: a drive-through park and battle diorama, to consist of concrete benches around a ring of raised-letter tablets. Plans were abandoned, though, when the state highway department, which had been counted upon to provide matching funds, backed out of the project. There remains one battle marker, a substantial stone plinth capped by a plaque with a misspelling, erected in the 1920s by the United Daughters of the Confederacy. Originally standing across the field along an older stretch of road, it was reinstalled squarely in front of the short-lived museum, but when the house was sold, the new owners objected to passersby who, stopping to read the bronze inscription, looked directly into their living room. The marker was uprooted once again and placed in the farthest corner of the yard, beside the highway.

Johns's lasting legacy is not the cultural and historical attraction he envisioned; it is the land itself, still whole (with the exception of the three acres) and rampantly nonproductive, and this is no small victory in the War against Progress. With the passage of time, the property has not been transformed into a shopping mall or a condominium sprawl. Rather, it declines along nature's slow curve, neither glorified nor diminished by humanity, decaying as naturally as the Sphinx in the Egyptian desert. (But the metaphor needs amending, for what wonder has not been deleteriously affected by the march of civilization? In the case of the Lee-Jackson property, the discarded shotgun shells that litter the thicket are prime evidence. Then, too, the fast-food wrappers that blow in from the highway and lodge in the underbrush cannot be ignored, nor can the old tires that mysteriously wind up in the creeks.)

The cedars that blanket the hillsides are encroaching on the formerly cultivated fields like prickly, dark sentinels with a Christmas scent. Birds thrive in the sanctuary – great blue herons, wild ducks, crows, blackbirds, blue jays, cardinals, finches. In the clearings, myriad blooms of wild vegetation sparkle chaotically – goldenrod, ironweed, marguerite, Indian paintbrush, daisies. By overlooking the indicators of the twentieth century, it isn't hard to go back in time. Imagination adds the thunder of a cannonade, rattling rifle fire, and the tramping of infantry. A similar modicum of fantasy reconstructs the quietus after the gun smoke has drifted away: the calmer orders and subdued conversations, the moans of the wounded and the strange silence of the newly dead.

Across the fence, the fields are in hay – the legacy of the previous owner – excluding a margin of deciduous woods sloping to a ravine that wraps around the eastern corner of the property. When we bought the land, I suspected the forty acres held secrets that would eventually be brought to light, for I was genuinely curious about the battle. Who among hundreds of millions of Americans is not captivated, at least momentarily, by the Civil War? Some 90,000 books and articles are testimony to the ever-widening ripples of the nation's most traumatic social and political aberration. My problem was lack of time. In starting over, I would be occupied on a daily basis for months on end. My curiosity would have to be satisfied in increments.

Still, my interest began to percolate. When I had a spare hour, I visited the county courthouse to look up deeds. I canvassed old-timers in the neighborhood. My initial findings astonished me: the land Becky and I bought was none other than the tract the millionaire preservationist coveted a quarter of a century earlier, but was denied.

How did we get it? When I had been cruising around, looking for those few mythical acres of privacy, I happened to notice the tangled, unfarmed Lee-Jackson property at a remove from the road. In my innocence, I inquired of a local farmer if it was for sale.

He assured me it wasn't and proceeded to tell me why. The longer I listened to his disinterested account, the more precious the property seemed. It was out of reach and I was a fool to have gotten my hopes up. In exasperation I said, "Well, do you know anyone around here who's got land for sale?"

"*I'll* sell you forty acres," he said.

TWO

THE OLD FARMHOUSE, our temporary quarters, sits in a sheltered draw between pastures and cropland next to the lane that runs along the Lee-Jackson fence. Many of the surrounding farms have residences that were built during the previous century, just as their mailboxes still bear the old family names—Germanic names like Diehl, Landes, Jarrels, Miller, Myer, Rodeffer. Yet these farms are implacably modern, with wide fields of corn and sorghum, pastures for grazing stock, or loafing lots for Holstein dairy herds.

A hundred and twenty-odd years earlier, a family named Haugh had been in residence in the house we rented. The Haugh farm had comprised our forty acres as well as most of the adjoining land on the flat-topped hill. Mid-nineteenth-century farms in the Shenandoah Valley were largely self-sustaining; cleared land was cropped for the purpose of feeding the family and its farm animals, and the balance of forest was raided for its timber and firewood. The principal crops were small grains (wheat, buckwheat, rye, oats, barley), hay (timothy, timothy-clover), and corn. If a farm produced an excess of pork, butter, eggs, huckleberries, and the like, that excess was bartered for goods or services within the farming community. At the time of the Civil War, the Cross Keys area had a gristmill, a sawmill, a drygoods store, a blacksmith, a carriage shop, and a cider press. The biggest farms raised wheat for export out of the Valley and utilized slave labor, but an average sized farm of a hundred acres, more or less, was run only by its family members.

Cross Keys had been predominantly a Brethren, or Dunker, community, reflecting the old-world heritage of its first and second generation American families. The Dunker church was located at Mill Creek, equidistant from Cross Keys and Port Republic on the market road. A smaller Presbyterian congregation worshipped at Union Church, a peaked log structure at the junction of the market road and the

Keezletown Road to the north. The heart of the Cross Keys community was the old tavern and stagecoach stop half a mile to the west along the Keezletown Road that had been there since 1802. In 1823 the Cross Keys Tavern was enlarged to include a drygoods store and renamed for its second proprietor. Rodham Kemper, who ran it until 1845. By the 1860s, an owner by the name of Yager had taken over, and the business expanded anew, whereupon it became known as Yager's Store.

Yager's Store served as a link to the outside world for the farming community of several hundred people. The news of Virginia's secession, the progress of the rebellion, the rise of a man named Jackson—all this had been spread from the store. Then the war came to the community itself.

On the morning of June 8, 1862, a Sunday, as Mary Haugh and her daughter were at home watching formations of Confederate soldiers through the windows, a panel of the front door was splintered by a bullet. The family hurried to the cellar just before a booming, shrieking artillery crossfire enveloped their farm. It must have sounded like the end of the world. A percussive shell struck the house, tearing through the roof and setting fire to the shingles and the rafters, before crashing through the attic and ripping a wall partition on the second floor, then landing with a damaging dent on the stairway to the entrance hall. The fire burned for hours.

In the left uppermost pane of a second floor bedroom window, there remains to the present day a neat hole where a minié ball passed through. After the battle, someone had had the presence of mind to preserve the pierced glass between two unbroken panes.

Stories of civilians trapped in the midst of warfare rarely survive in oral history. Despite my inquiries, few members of long-standing local families remembered any tale that had been handed down from the day of the battle. After being told the story of the Haughs, I uncovered three others. One concerned a young farm wife who disguised herself as an old woman when Union officers quartered themselves in her home on the Keezletown Road. She took out her false teeth, dirtied her face with soot, and covered her blond hair with a ragged shawl. The second tale related how another family, living a mile to the south in the direction of Good's Mill, hid their silver under a newborn baby in a cradle just before the Yankees burst through the door. The soldiers were so hungry that they sucked raw turkey eggs and devoured flour right out of the sack. Upon leaving, they took every valuable they could find, but they never thought to look beneath the baby. The third tale concerned a

German-speaking woman whose house had stood just north of our hayfields, in the path of an invading regiment of German immigrants. When she heard the Union soldiers speaking her native tongue, she leaned out her window and yelled in German words to the effect that she hoped each of them would catch a Confederate bullet.

Luckily for the Haughs, the battle was over by late afternoon. As the gunfire died away, the family dared to climb out of the cellar, which must have been uncomfortably damp, perhaps filled with several inches of water, for it had been raining heavily until two days earlier. Suffice it to say, the chaos of war descended one Sunday morning after breakfast, and lingers today in charred rafters, disfigured woodwork (under many layers of paint), and a sandwiched pane.

It is easy to peel away the additions and modifications, and picture the plain log structure as it stood in the 1860s with its summer kitchen, its well, its privy, its barn and chicken coop. The old place breathes history, not just of the Civil War, but of a generation before and half a dozen generations since. The original log house – architecturally classified as a two-story, double-parlor Greek Revival – was built in the 1840s on a limestone foundation with a dirt cellar, flanked by two exterior limestone chimneys (long since disappeared). Its layout is fully symmetrical, with front door, entrance hall, and stairway placed squarely in the center. A two-story wing was attached to the back around the turn of the century, and further refinements such as electricity, indoor plumbing, and a bay window were added over the years until the house acquired its present configuration, not unlike many farmhouses of its vintage.

Several generalizations are common to old farmhouses: (1) they are drafty; (2) they are impossible to heat; (3) they are full of wasted space; (4) the floors creak, the windows are painted shut, the wiring and plumbing are inadequate, there is a lack of closet space, etc.

Our decision to occupy the Haugh house for a dozen months had been made reluctantly, for we were used to up-to-date living quarters. We had moved here from a comfortable, contemporary house, one I had built several years earlier on an elevated ridge not three miles distant. There, an unhappy situation had developed. We were barely settled in when a poultry-farming neighbor gave notice that he would be erecting a barn against our common boundary. No ordinary poultry barn, this one was slated to stretch almost a fifth of a mile, and because it would generate odors, dust, noise, and feathers in quantities beyond what we thought we could tolerate – and we had no legal recourse to prevent its construction—we had put our little farm up for sale, and sold at a loss. Luckily, we were gone before the turkeys moved in.

I was determined not to suffer another self-eviction. The forty acres were in the shape of a rhomboid, amply wide and deep, with one corner bitten off where the Haugh house stood. Our property lay between and behind two roads, Port Republic Road to the west and Route 708 to the east, so roadside building lots would forever be at a remove—or so we hoped. In addition to the buffer of the Lee-Jackson tract and the ravine along the creek, farmland stretched without interruption for the better part of a mile.

But the undulating countryside, with its proximity to Harrisonburg as well as its views of the Massanutten headland and the Blue Ridge, was just the locale to make a real estate developer salivate. Were it not for our timely land grab, "Battlefield Estates" might have been in the offing. Likewise, the acreage would have suited a poultry operation or a manufacturing plant, or any other commercial venture that needed to be distanced from the noses, eyes, and ears of persnickety neighbors.

The farmer who sold us the land had kept the major portion of his farm intact. Lopping off forty acres, now that he was advancing in years, was a practical thing to do, and he wasn't too concerned with what happened to it. The planning and zoning commission of Rockingham County didn't care, either, for there were no historical districting statutes on the books. The land was zoned for general agriculture, which meant that just about anything in the way of commercial or residential development was permissible—apartments, shooting ranges, convenience stores, gas stations, garages, even junkyards and airports. The only restrictions applied to subdividing property within a limited number of years, restrictions that could be circumvented by grandfather clauses and permits for special use.

We had no ulterior motives—no commercial intention and certainly no plans to subdivide. My immediate goal was to situate a modest home for a family of four somewhere on the forty acres. Although a dozen places were suitable, my conscience was beginning to whisper about the perils of desecration. Moreover, common sense told me to keep the hayfields as undisturbed as possible. With Becky's approval, I decided to build off to one side. At the time, this location seemed reasonable, since it left the fields intact for farming and oriented the house toward the woodlot, away from the traffic on Port Republic Road.

The ground where I drove the first stake to delineate the foundation of the house was on a gentle incline at the southeastern corner of the property, close to the ravine and the woods along the Lee-Jackson boundary. I knew locating the house here would necessitate a driveway about six-tenths of a mile long, and many truckloads of gravel to make it accessible in bad weather, but it fulfilled my most important requirement: it was off to one side.

As my plans went through their stages and shapes, I began to reflect upon the rôle of a battlefield's caretaker. Not just co-owner, but caretaker. The battle loomed as a vague imagining, a stirring of blue and gray that always seemed to be fading. After more than a hundred and twenty years, the battlefield needed someone to look after it if it was to remain meaningful in the onslaught of a future that all but dismissed its noncommercial value. It needed a personal input, something akin to love: the surest method of preservation, but by no means the easiest or the cheapest. Ultimately, it required a commitment of magnanimity so that others could see why a battlefield of the Civil War mattered. For here was not a reference in an appendix, or a passing mention on a page of text. Here was the actual place, still unspoiled and unimproved to the extent that if one wanted to run two armies through here again, one could, even if it was only in one's mind.

Was I up to the challenge? Already, the possibilities were making me dizzy with a new sense of purpose. I had discovered few actual pieces of the puzzle, just some old deeds, disfigurations on a farmhouse, and an uncorroborated story or two. Somehow my ideas were being raised to a level where they seemed important enough to be broadcast to the whole world. It wasn't art, it was reality. It was a novel experience. The point of no return had been the morning Becky and I signed the deed, making the forty acres our own.

That very morning, I had climbed over the fence (there was no road yet) and set out on a pinching-myself-to-see-if-we-had-really-bought-it ramble. As I crested the first hill, I saw two souvenir hunters systematically scanning the fields with metal detectors. One man was walking north-south, the other east-west, and neither took notice of my arrival.

I accosted them with closer and closer hallos. At length, they heard me and ambled over, removing their headphones. Genial fellows they were, both from northern Virginia, a pair of Civil War buffs down for the day, and more than willing to tell me what they were looking for and how they were going about it. One said he had unearthed nineteen different types of projectiles here—something of a record, he thought, which illustrated the extent of the artillery exchange. Both carried topo maps and sported multipocketed vests that could have been worn by lunar astronauts for the collection of moon rocks.

I asked them if they had permission from the property owner to dig for relics. Nope, they'd just wandered across the fence from the Lee-Jackson property. Did they know that recently enacted laws made it illegal to hunt for artifacts on Civil War battle sites? Nope, they'd never heard of such laws. As casually as possible, I informed them that, as of an hour ago, my wife and I were the new owners. They reacted to my announcement in a low-key manner. In that case, they said, they'd just cross back over the fence and not bother anybody.

Right then, as if on cue, one man's headphones bleated its proximity to buried metal. Conviviality took a nosedive. Both hunters eyed me warily. I mustered what could pass for signeurly aplomb. "Go ahead and dig," I said.

I wished I had never said it. The quarry was a minié ball, dirt-burnished and undeformed. It could have been dropped by a soldier, fumbling as he attempted to reload in the heat of battle. It could have fallen through a hole in a pocket, or lain within an ammunition pouch long since rotted away. It looked as perfect as the fake ones in plastic trays on the countertops of antique emporiums.

The men gave me the bullet and I never saw them again. Later, I could have kicked myself for not demanding that they fork over anything else they might have found on this side of the fence. By leaving so compliantly, was it possible they had walked off with major booty? A black mood grew within me; it was our first day of ownership, nay, our first *hour*, and already I had borne witness to a theft. What was more, I had been an accessory to the crime. But my anger was pointless. Since the dawn of the electronic age, the environs had been subjected to thorough, unhurried hunts. In all probability, these visitors had taken nothing—or at least nothing of consequence.

Now, the prospect of slim pickings is reason enough to discourage treasure seekers, but my experience of that morning congealed into a deeper feeling of regret. Stripping artifacts from a battlefield is a strange hobby—a plunderer's pastime, like robbing graves. Morally, it is indefensible. What gives an electronic circuit the right to sniff out that which time and the elements have buried? As insignificant as these artifacts may be, surely they lose their final iota of meaning as soon as they're lifted from the soil.

I know the arguments to the contrary, the ones that postulate how educational an exhibit in a glass case can be. Fine, I say. Let that which has been already culled or plucked or stolen or sequestered be put on public view. Let schoolchildren gawk as they pass in front of the case. If a curator wants to arrange artillery shells in descending height on an artfully rumpled scrap of velvet, that's okay, too. Admission can be charged, if necessary. And if a marble mausoleum is needed to convey the properly reverential tone, it's all right with me if they build one.

The trouble is, ninety-nine percent of all battlefield treasure that trickles back into the present winds up in jars or dresser drawers. An acquaintance of mine has a long shelf of gallon jars, each filled with leaden relics, broken bayonet tips, buttons, buckles, knives, nails, coins, and the like. The jars are labeled with masking tape and magic marker—"Kernstown," "McDowell," "Winchester," "Cross Keys," "Port Republic"—and are meant to be perceived as a quantification of the detritus of Jackson's Valley Campaign. Just looking at the jars (and feeling their individual weight, if I care to) puts me in awe of the effort that was expended on the collecting.

But when my thoughts return to the actual ground from which these hundreds of items have been removed, I cannot help but visualize the little divots that, before they are flattened by heel or spade, serve as transitory memorials to what has been taken for all time, and I do not think the shelf or the jar or the dresser drawer is as fitting a memorial.

Back in the old days, however, before artifacts were exhaustively hunted, they simply appeared underfoot. I learned that spent shot and shell were readily discernible on the Cross Keys battlefield as recently as fifty years ago. The creek that ran through the woods at the bottom of the ravine was a favorite wading place for children because of the cannonballs that turned up in the mud. Back then, youngsters thought nothing of discovering rusted projectiles, objects of no more interest than river stones, just heavier. Cannonballs were things to pick up and heave as far as possible. They fell with mighty splashes—themselves subtle lessons in history, mini-reenactments of original trajectories.

The families who farmed this land routinely exposed battle artifacts during spring and fall plowing. A brass buckle or button might have been worth stopping for, occasioning a respite from the tedium of the furrow, but when commoner bits of iron, lead, or crockery clanged on the plowshare, they were plowed under and forgotten.

Some years back, a neighbor had stumbled upon an intact, unexploded Parrott shell about eight inches long. He assigned it the usual place of honor on his mantle, even though it was a curio that might explode one day and blow his living room to smithereens. During the course of an introductory visit, I was invited to step inside and have a look at the thing. It was not the kind of object a person could examine without wanting to touch. Something about an artillery round of any vintage – its heft, its shape, its nipple of fuse – endowed it with an almost sexual magnetism. No wonder there had been pilferage at the museum. My neighbor handed the shell to me with the offhand remark, "Careful, it's live."

I cradled it in both hands. It was heavy for its size, with an antique aerodynamic design that looked threatening and harmless at the same time, like an ungainly paperweight that, conceivably, could roll off a table and onto a person's foot.

As I held it, taking excessive precaution not to drop it, I summoned what scant knowledge of explosives I had. At what age did the chemicals become unstable, or were they inert? Was the fuse still viable? What were the odds (astronomical, I hoped) of the projectile just going *kaboom* while it nestled in my sweating palms? It had no visible deformation, which meant it had never been fired, right? Or had it been a dud that came in for a soft landing?

I remembered reading about how the authorities still swept for unexploded matériel from World Wars I and II, from the Korean and Vietnam conflicts, from harbors and shipping lanes that were once mined, from assorted no-man's-lands between the good guys and the bad guys around the unneighborly globe. Once in a while, I came upon the odd news item about someone being maimed or killed while digging a hole in a backyard, accidentally unearthing a live bomb.

It occurred to me that the bomb I was on the verge of exploding was my overheated imagination. Call it intuition, call it paranoid delusion – that rusty, hundred-and-twenty-some-year-old conversation piece was giving me the creeps.

I handed it back to him and he put it back on the mantle.

18

THREE

Excited as I was by the prospect of house-building while staying there, I couldn't fail to observe throughout the Haugh house the handiwork of the nineteenth-century carpenter and the materials at his disposal: heart pine planking, beaded board, poplar (faux oak) trim, and hand-wrought hardware. Every dimension was generous by contemporary standards – the width of doors, the breadth of stair treads, the wainscot, the baseboard. Each mullioned window retained panes of original "bubble" glass. There was so much to appreciate aesthetically, it sometimes overwhelmed me, and when it did, I tended to focus on the defects – the gritty, decayed varnish or the telltale powder of termites.

Grudgingly, we tolerated the old house's inconveniences. The toilet flushed inadequately, the water pressure was negligible, the roof runoff that collected in the cistern was undrinkable. The floors rebounded underfoot at the sagging center of each room. The chimneys didn't draw properly. One cold evening when the living room stove was really cranking, a creosote fire flared up with a horrendous roar – a near tragedy that taught us to be wary of weakened mortar joints in old brick. Also, the lights flickered, fuses blew, and in damp weather the whole place emanated an odor of animal decay, the result of rat poison distributed by a previous tenant.

We had pretty much thrown our belongings in the door. Camped there and counting the days, we were ill at ease, keenly anticipating a more comfortable future. Over the winter, we burned five or six cords of wood just to heat the living room, dining room, and kitchen (a third of the house). When the bedrooms got below forty degrees Fahrenheit, we made our bedrolls in the living room alongside the stove. Van and Hope became expert at burrowing into sleeping bags and remaining there until they were pried out with threats and promises.

During the worst of the winter, we fought frozen pipes and the urge

19

to chuck it all and move into an apartment in town. Walls and floors were like cold stone slabs. Windows frosted over. Heat from the woodstoves was best captured by standing only inches away, then rotating slowly. The heat seemed to radiate not more than a foot or two before it dissipated into the chilly corners.

Locked out of housebuilding by snow and ice, I passed the time reading about the Civil War. From the beginning, I felt like an observer from another planet. The nineteenth century was light-years away. It was not easy for a modern American, a baby boomer, to fathom the ordeal and upheaval of the 1860s. I was ignorant of the direct pain of warfare. Moreover, I seemed to be incapable of sorting out facts, figures, and dates to the point where the big picture came through with any degree of clarity. All my life I have been envious of people who retained knowledge like a sponge soaked up water. I could only relate my meager gleanings to an intuitive perspective: imagining life as it was then and contrasting it with life as I lived it now. The differences flabbergasted me. On occasions when I picked up a fact or two, truths that just wouldn't quit my imagination, I let them settle slowly until they left an indelible impression.

Take the humble minié ball, for example. This low-velocity .58 caliber lead bullet, designed in 1849 by French army captain C. E. Minié for long rifle use, was responsible for ninety percent of the battle casualties in the Civil War. (Only eight percent of the casualties were caused by artillery fire, and the remaining two percent were presumably inflicted in close combat with pistols, bayonets, pikes, and swords.)

The beauty, or terror, of the one-ounce minié ball lay in its deadly accuracy. Upon detonation of the charge, the three rings cast into the bullet's hollow base expanded to lock into the rifling grooves of the gun barrel. This made for a tight fit as the bullet was propelled the length of the bore, enhancing muzzle velocity and spin. Within firing range, the bullet went exactly where it was aimed – remarkable accuracy for that time.

Eyewitnesses related that when a soldier was hit by a minié ball, his first reaction was to undress sufficiently to examine the wound. Depending on this self-assessment, he either bandaged himself to return to battle, or resigned himself to certain death. Minié ball wounds other than grazes were almost always massive and grievously traumatic. The large, impact-deformed bullet fragmented bone and tissue in its path, and entrance and exit holes brought on septicemia, the control of which was poorly understood. Medical evacuation and field surgery were primitive by twentieth-century standards. One glance at an army surgeon's pannier, or field medical kit, told the whole story: the most prominent item was the amputation saw, followed by the carving knives of diminishing size, then the pincers and the clamps. To my eyes, it was a sadistic assortment of instruments, a mutation of a carpenter's toolbox. Nothing was sterilized, anesthesia was maintained with a chloroform-soaked rag, and painkilling was best accomplished with whiskey or inexact dosages of opium, heroin, and cocaine.

By the end of the war, the Confederate states mustered in one million men, while the Union army swelled to two million, three hundred thousand. Six hundred eighteen thousand soldiers lost their lives in the conflict, yet only one third of these deaths was battle related. Two thirds, or 412,000 deaths, were due to disease. This terrible fact, so incredible in the light of present-day hygienic advances, illustrated for me the true horror of the war.

The primary fatal illnesses were intestinal infections and inflammations of the lungs. These were caused by a lack of sanitation, contaminated water and food, and inadequate clothing. In 1861 alone, fully a third of the Union army was on sick call at any given time. The decades that preceded Pasteur and Lister were especially deadly for people engaged in the harsh and stressful military campaigns.

The best picture I could summon, overall, was of two lurching armies —one larger and aggressive, the other smaller and defensive—as they clashed not only with each other, but also with an unseen army of viruses, parasites, and bacteria. It was a scene of unsurpassed tragedy that the passage of time tended to glorify in fabulous code—the blue and the gray, brother against brother, *Gone with the Wind*, and so forth.

Even burdened as I was by horrifying facts, only when I left the shelter of the farmhouse and, bundled against the cold, walked the battlefield could I bypass the platitudes, insofar as I could focus my imagination backward in time. War was hell, but the Civil War had been an especially perverse hell because it divided a constitutionally unified body politic. The optimism of the youthful nation had been enervated by the delineation of two drastically different interpretations of the Jeffersonian promise of freedom. On the one hand there were states' rights and slavery; on the other, indivisibility and abolitionism. The clashing of the armies exposed the raw nerve of long festering regional and cultural differences. In the minds of ordinary citizens, duty and honor had no choice but to rise to the occasion. The political fireball exploded at Fort Sumter and burned brilliantly until Appomattox.

A century and a quarter later, the nation was still healing, but the fields southeast of Cross Keys were profoundly at peace. No bullets whistled, no shells exploded. There were no more wounds, nor sickness, nor deprivation of any kind here. The battlefield was like an island with the commotion of the twentieth century, exponentially greater than that earlier time, pressing from every side.

As our year in the farmhouse drew around, and the daffodils were blooming again – each one like a gift from the Haugh family that seemed to say, "See, it wasn't so bad, was it?" – the mild weather led us out of the bitter winter. Smiles of nostalgia would repeal our frowns. Swifts were building nests in the unused chimneys, and lengthening afternoons filled the musty rooms with sunlight. Belatedly, the old place exuded a cheerfulness that made me happy to come home at the end of a day's work on the new house. Now I counted the weeks with regret, knowing that the old was soon to be replaced by the new, and that I would never live long enough for the new to become old, even half as old as the old had been.

Meanwhile, in my spare time, I continued to read about the Civil War. I was trying to get some idea of the way battles were fought and what the soldiers on both sides experienced under fire.

Military events during the Civil War were classified in terms of their size, purpose, and organization. In descending order of size they were: campaigns, battles, engagements, combats, actions, assaults, skirmishes, operations, sieges, raids, expeditions, reconnaissances, scouts, affairs, occupations, and captures. In the twenty-nine campaigns that were waged, seventy-six battles were fought. Virginia, the leading theater of war, had half again as many military events (2,154) as the next state, Tennessee (1,462). Statistically, in the entire war, nearly a third of all military events occurred in Virginia.

There was no generic battleground of the Civil War, no place or event that could be classified as typical. Battles were fought on plains, in woods, on beaches, on bluffs, along rivers and roads – anywhere two opposing armies touched one another by design. The size of battles varied greatly, and the extent of the casualties did not necessarily correlate with the available manpower, or the outcome in terms of victory and defeat. Some battles were fought in the course of a few hours, others went on for days. Sieges lasted for weeks, even months. A battle was the formalized collision of two fairly equally codified bodies of combatants, governed by commanding generals, with orders disseminated by the general's staff. The chain of command, from corps to division to brigade to regiment to company to individual soldier, was responsible for carrying out specific goals. At the very top of the chain, the commanders-in-chief (Abraham Lincoln and Jefferson Davis) and their advisors concerned themselves with overall strategy. At the bottom of the chain . . . well, everybody knows what happens at the bottoms of chains.

Some battles began as simple confrontations; others started with intermittent, increased applications of force that grew or shrank with the turn of events. Some battles were single, protracted firefights; others gained momentum as reinforcements came on the scene. Still others were a series of bloody sideshows. A battle could encompass a wide land area of several square miles, with room for remote artillery duels and infantry maneuvering, or it could crowd itself into a corridor-like setting, where the opposing armies could only push each other back and forth.

In one respect, though, all battles were alike: before they were fought, they didn't seem particularly scary. The young men on their way to the front for the first time cheerfully anticipated the fine figures they would be cutting in battle, the brevity of the engagement, and the shameful cowardice of the enemy. As the crowded railway cars approached a theater of war, inexperienced soldiers partied as they had never partied before. Newly drilled, in newly issued uniforms (perchance with recent letters from loved ones burning in their breast pockets), they sang songs of nonsense and sentiment, steeling themselves for the moment of glory.

"Seeing the elephant," the phrase used in the 1860s to describe combat duty, was the ultimate test of a soldier's mettle. From the moment he was within range of enemy artillery, to the bloody hand-to-hand melee, a soldier mustered what coolness and confidence he had, and if he didn't have enough of either, he panicked.

Battle management during America's nineteenth-century civil rebellion had its roots in eighteenth-century European military theory. Ideally, a battle was fought with the decorum of a game of chess. Artillery batteries were unlimbered and shelling was synchronized along the front. Cavalry units were thrown in for lightning strikes of terror-inducing speed. Infantrymen were positioned shoulder to shoulder in long rows, one following the other, depending on the battle order and regimental strength. A line of soldiers closed up, or "dressed center," as its individual members fell. Commanders were critical of a poorly executed drill. Holding the battle line straight and unbroken as far toward the enemy as possible was tantamount to courage.

Rules of engagement, practiced by both the Union and Confederate armies, were defined in the texts of West Point training manuals. A conservative approach to victory was preferred. In a textbook battle, the greater force prevailed. Most of the maneuvers were effected broadside to broadside, the orderly troops marching to the accompanying "long roll" of the snare drums.

On the individual soldier's level, there was great psychological reinforcement in doing what everyone else was doing. This is a premise that remains at the core of military theory to the present day. A century after the conclusion of the Civil War, I was in boot camp at the Great Lakes Naval Training Center, where I learned firsthand the exhilaration of being one of a hundred people marching, exercising, eating, and sleeping as a unit. While the cadre mentality produces obedience, it also produces harmony and selflessness, the whole being much greater than the sum of its parts.

Yet, *theory* was the key word in my boot camp experience. I was but a theoretical sailor, a willing participant in drills and exercises. My life wasn't on the line, and I knew it. At chow call one evening toward the end of the sixteen weeks of basic training, I was jarred out of my complacency. A rumor had spread in the mess hall that the Chinese were bombing the U.S. – preposterous hearsay, considering the uninterrupted Muzak and silent sirens. Nevertheless, panic could be read in the eyes of every recruit. Boot camp regulations precluded access to newspapers, radio, or TV, so nobody was in a position to gauge the absurdity of "the skinny." For the moment, we were all scared believers.

Once the soldiers in the Civil War had seen the elephant, their theoretical soldiering was over. Tall tales and rumors were supplanted by witnessing, and hopefully surviving, actual combat. Naïveté and optimism flew out the window, too. The gruesome odds of receiving death before receiving a discharge from service were almost one in six, and the discrepancy between nineteenth-century weapons and eighteenth-century tactics made the odds hard to beat.

The rebel yell, a bloodcurdling scream of fear and fearlessness, was a Confederate soldier's personal talisman against the odds. Soldiers from both sides yelled as they advanced upon each other (as soldiers have always done), but the rebel yell was different. It was a combination of baying at the moon and cussing without words: a white man's war whoop.

To my mind, the rebel yell signaled the obsolescence of those eighteenth-century tactics in that it functioned not only as a war cry, but also as an expression of pure terror, a soulful reaction to the deadly science of gunnery. To maintain courage in a hail of lead that pierced the body with holes the size of a dime and exited with holes the size of a fist, to maintain courage against the pressure of canister shot that clipped huge gaps in battle lines—to keep one's mind amid the din and smoke of the carnage—it was necessary to scream at the very top of the lungs. It had nothing to do with valor.

The familiar litany of the largest, bloodiest battles and campaigns was a string of names to me: Shiloh, Antietam, Fredricksburg, Chancellorsville, Gettysburg, Chickamauga, Spotsylvania, Second Cold Harbor. The names signified losses to life and limb on a scale that few civilians, then or now, could comprehend. Regimental casualties as high as eighty-two percent were reported in Antietam and Gettysburg. In separate engagements throughout the war, 115 regiments from both sides sustained casualties of greater than fifty percent. I was soon to discover that one such regimental devastation occurred at Cross Keys.

The will to fight in the face of such danger was indistinguishable from the will to survive. After the infantry ranks had advanced in formation, and fired at the outermost range, they tended to close upon each other in disarray. The cumbersome rifles were useless in point-blank battle (as were bayonets) unless one grasped their muzzles with both hands and swung them like clubs. Hand-to-hand combat was in actuality a stabbing, choking, smashing, slashing, stomping, gouging, pounding, kill-or-be-killed free-for-all.

Patriotic sentiment was far from the mind of a young Ohioan who described Antietam two days after the battle in a letter to his father:

> The smell was offul . . . their was about 5 or 6,000 dead bodes decaying over the field and perhaps 100 dead horses . . . their lines of battle Could be run for miles by the dead they lay long the lines like sheavs of Wheat I could have walked on the boddes all most from one end to the other.

An investigation after the battle at Gettysburg, Pennsylvannia, revealed the extent of the individual soldier's confused, hyper-emotional state. At Gettysburg, 27,500 single-shot rifles were retrieved from the field after the fighting. Twelve thousand guns held two unused loads in the barrel, 6,000 guns held from three to ten loads, and one held twenty-three. In other words, as many as 18,000 men had been overstuffing their rifles in the grim charade of loading and capping, aiming and firing. The plugged-up rifles were as useless as the wooden sticks some of the men had shouldered in drill when they had been green recruits.

Now, toward the end of the twentieth century, combat weaponry has been refined to the point where it all but eliminates such misuse under stress. A modern assault rifle can be operated by a baby. A pull of the trigger, a flick of a lever, and bullets fly wherever they are directed. The chilling effectiveness of today's firepower gives distance and impersonality to the making of war; what front and rear sights were to the Enfield rifle, electronic rangefinders and laser targeting devices are to the modern firearm. In the not-too-distant future, small arms will probably be capable of firing death rays and particle beams. The science of war is Progress personified. It is no longer necessary to see the enemy to destroy him. In bunkers, the punching of buttons does the trick. War has become like surgery. Goals are set and tools are chosen. Operative risks can be limited, or chances can be taken on winner-take-all initiatives. If an initiative gets out of control, it can be stitched up with diplomacy and/or propaganda. And once the battle is over, the enemy — now the patient — can be placed on a life-support system: a Marshall Plan.

Like the major in *Dr. Strangelove* who rode an A-bomb out the open hatch, combatants will continue to yell the rebel yell, or something that approximates it, but nobody will be listening. Technology does not have ears or a soul.

FOUR

W<small>HEN THE SPRING RAINS CAME</small>, the cellar of the farm-house filled with a foot of water that stayed for weeks. All we could do was shut the door at the top of the stairs and ignore the subterranean flood, hoping that mosquitoes wouldn't breed. Around this time, we had to deal with the simultaneous expiration of the water heater, the kitchen range, and the clothes washer. The winter had been harsh, and now, with a full-fledged mud season and three crapped-out appliances, spring was shaping up to be just as difficult.

But this second round of hardships evaporated in the push to finish projects on the new property. Besides steadily working on the house and studios, I had completed some extensive repairs on the barn and machine shed. Both structures had called for differing approaches to their mending. The machine shed—of indeterminate age, perhaps thrown crudely together in the 1950s by a farmer temporarily turned carpenter—had taken some quick scabbing and reroofing. The barn, because of its size and significance, had been awarded more patient ministrations. It was built in 1921, as I determined from numerals incised in concrete on the rainwater reservoir beside the foundation.

Bank barns, so called because they are situated against an earthen bank, or bridge, that gives entry to the main floor (also called the thresh-ing floor), hearken back to the days before fully mechanized agriculture. During the Civil War, nearly every farm barn of consequence in the Shenandoah Valley was burned to the ground, not only by the maraud-ing Union troops who obeyed the general directive to cripple the bread-basket of the South, as the grain-cropped valley was known, but also by the Confederates themselves who regarded the barns' contents as poten-tial spoils of war to be kept from falling into enemy hands. By the end of 1864, after Ulysses S. Grant had ordered Major General Philip H. Sheridan to devastate what remained in the Valley, only one or two antebellum barns survived amid hundreds and hundreds of square miles of farmland.

During Reconstruction and later, as the Valley population swelled with more European immigrants, new barns were built by master carpenters, many of them newly arrived from Germany and Switzerland. These itinerant craftsmen traveled from farm to farm, offering their services in exchange for room and board and a modest cash fee to be paid upon their departure. A typical tenure at a farm lasted from several weeks to several months, depending on the size of the building project. The master carpenters directed the construction of the huge barns without plans of any kind, yet they managed to achieve a precision that fitted peg to hole and notch to notch in massive framing timbers sawn to their specifications by the local sawmill. They also orchestrated barn raisings, when entire communities turned out to assemble the soaring framework, once the foundation and flooring were in place.

Traditional bank barns (dating from the end of the nineteenth century through the first decades of the twentieth century), while subject to variations and size differences that custom-fitted the barn to the individual farm, have a comforting sameness based upon time-tested design. The long side of the barn opposite the bank is cantilevered about six feet to provide an overhang that shields a row of stalls at ground level where draft animals were kept. (Barn cantilevers originated a century or two earlier when farm buildings were taxed for the square footage their foundations occupied.) A corncrib is built into one ground corner on the bank side and lined with hardware cloth tacked against closely spaced lath to keep rodents at bay. A long wooden trough runs the length of the stalls along the barn's centerline. This is supplied by feed drops at either end, through which loose hay can be pitched from above. A rudimentary set of stairs leads up to the main floor.

The cavernous main level of a bank barn is divided into three sections: a left and right mow (rhymes with cow) in which hay was piled, and between them, a central, heavily planked floor where wagons were driven up, unloaded, and later stored. On this floor the threshing machine was positioned, driven by a long belt connected to a stationary engine that sat outside. In earlier times the harvested small grain had been threshed (the seed separated from the hull) on the barn floor by hand-flailing, and the strong draft through the barn carried off the chaff. To the sides, the mows are floored with loose scrap lumber to allow ventilation of the hay from below.

Entering the barn from the bank side means pushing open the big doors that roll on an overhead track. There is an isolated room sheathed in tongue-and-groove pine built into the catty-corner opposite the top of the corncrib. This is the granary, which is divided into bins for the various feed grains. In some granaries, the bins are permanently in place; in others, the walls of the bins can be rearranged for different configurations of storage. Because grain was the most valuable commodity in the barn inventory, every precaution was taken to preserve it from the depredations of thieves—insect, animal, and human. The granary is provided with a tight-fitting, locking door that scrapes the floor as it closes. Most granaries have a second door that opens to the outside of the barn, and a little window with a hinged shutter to admit air and sunlight.

The size of the barn determines the number of doors on the bank side. Our barn has four main doors. There are several six-door barns in the neighborhood. A larger barn usually has a second granary and corncrib located in opposite corners. There are at least two big rolling doors on the cantilever side of the main floor to facilitate the threshing draft and for pitching out hay. Below these doors is a ten-foot drop to the ground.

High on the side walls of the mows are ventilation louvers. The quantity, size, and arrangement of these louvers serve as a signature of the master carpenter. Occasionally, the louvers are decorated with a fancy trim to enliven the expanse of weatherboard. The builder of our barn must have been a staid fellow, for he incorporated three plain, louvered rectangles on each end wall, the topmost situated right under the apex of the roof. Another signature is discernible in the design of the narrow ventilation band that runs longitudinally, just beneath the eave on the cantilevered side. (In our barn, it is a utilitarian crisscross lath.) A barn can never have too much ventilation, assuming it is provided in ways that keep out the weather. The orientation of the structure is important in this respect; the bank side usually faces in the direction of the prevailing wind, not only for the purpose of threshing, but also, with the big doors shut, to insure that no ventilation areas will be exposed to a driving rain.

By the mid-1920s, with the application of the internal combustion engine to farming, bank barns were essentially obsolete. Their stalls for draft animals went empty, as did their corncribs and granaries when corn and grain were processed in the field by combines. Their mows, which had been designed for loose hay, were adaptable enough to baled hay, but the posts in the barn framework and the angled hip bracing tended to get in the way of the new equipment.

Still, the barns were built to last. Barring a fire or rare tornado, their oak framing stands firm season after season, while their oak or heart pine siding, painted or unpainted, maintains a lasting integrity. As long as the roof stays in place, a barn can be useful for generations. Many farmers have expanded their barns by adding silos and forage sheds. Nowadays it is common to glimpse the original outlines of a bank barn deep within a conglomeration of sundry roofs and cylindrical towers.

The roof of a bank barn is steeply pitched, not only to allow headroom for stacking hay in the mows, but also to repel water quickly and minimize snow loads The galvanized, standing-seam roofing used on the later barns has an unlimited service life if it is painted once in ten years, assuming the cleats that hold it to the roof sheathing continue to grip the wood. Lightning rods are spaced every dozen feet along the apex, with each spire attached to a braided copper cable that extends down the side of the barn to a ground rod. Snow guards are fastened to each seam a few feet up from the gutters, thus reducing the possibility of a damaging avalanche. Downspouts divert the rainwater into a collection system for watering the animals. Next to our barn, the concrete reservoir looks like a bomb shelter without a roof. Cracked by seventy years of side pressure from the earthen bridge it abuts, the reservoir has long since lost its ability to hold water.

The last bank barn to be built in the neighborhood (the barn that had stood on the Lee-Jackson property) was the first to fall down. Forty years of unrepaired wind damage to the roof had finally exacted its toll. The coup de grace of an August thunderstorm wiped out one of my favorite watercolor subjects, but I was mentally prepared for its end. Since I had been coming to it, a third of the roof had disappeared and the exposed planking on the main floor was slippery with neon-bright moss. Because the guttering no longer channeled rainwater away, the earthen bridge, swollen by repeated saturations, was gradually pushing in the foundation. With the underpinnings on the verge of collapse, the joints in the weathered timbers were slowly working loose. The barn swayed noticeably in any breeze. Each time I dared to venture inside I was poised to leap out at the first crack of warning, before the whole structure came crashing down.

When it was built, it must have been regarded as a Parthenon among bank barns. It boasted six main doors, two granaries, and a trolley track up under the roof ridge that had carried a dump fork for moving large clumps of hay. It had five ornately trimmed louvers on each mow wall, as well as a sliding door on the lower level. Stenciled on the walls of both granaries in three-inch-tall black numerals was "1923," along with the signature of the master carpenter, Wm. Meyerhoeffer, in flowing pencil script.

The proud builder could not have foreseen the neglect that was to follow. Herr Meyerhoeffer numbered among the last in a line that seems to have vanished forever. Builders don't carry plans in their heads anymore. A modern agricultural building is fabricated in a factory, strapped together in a kit of fiberglass and aluminum and epoxy-clad steel, and shipped halfway across the nation. It is delivered to the site by flatbed truck, and erected in a day and a half with the aid of a telescoping crane. And anyway, up-to-date farmers don't even store hay in barns anymore. If the hay isn't chopped up for ensilage, big round bales are wrapped in plastic and left, like giant marshmallows, in rows at the edges of fields.

Our barn was well along the path to decrepitude when I began to work on it. Its roof was red with the rust of a dozen years beyond when it should have been repainted. The sheet metal had been pocked by bullets and birdshot when farmboys plinked at pigeons as they preened above the mows. A downspout lay in the grass where it had fallen a decade earlier; the siding at the corner was disintegrating from the sluicing of the disconnected gutter.

The barn doors had been bashed and broken by ornery livestock or clumsy tractor operators. Long ungreased, the rollers on the overhead track squealed resistantly. Louver boards were askew or missing. The main floor was layered with fifty years of crud: decomposed hay, cattle manure, rat turds, pigeon droppings, dried mud. I had to pick my way over bald tires, bottomless buckets, torn feed bags, skeins of baling twine, and assorted machinery parts—the sad remains of a farm that had bloomed and gone to seed.

We needed the barn for storage. Construction materials, unsold artwork, the excess household inventory that we didn't want to clutter the farmhouse with—these things belonged in the barn, but first I had to strap on a dust mask and shovel the floor clean. It was a task unlikely to be forgotten in my annals of personal distaste. I brushed away ancient cobwebs festooned with a particulate of hay and dirt. I cleared out nests of vermin, small skeletons, snakeskins, foul caches of grain and corn. I hauled at least five pickup loads of rusty junk to the county landfill, and twice as many loads of organic matter to spread on Becky's garden.

When the dust finally settled, and the cracks and holes at the sides of the dark interior emitted a firmament of pure light, I understood why people compared the inside of a barn to a cathedral. So it was, a shrine to agriculture past, a place to meditate upon sweating horses and clanking chains, the rasp of the plowshare and the creaking spoke wheel. I could see, now, that a barn readily transcended its utilitarian function by being a place to sit away from furnishings and hearth. The barn eased my preoccupation with civilization's tempo. There was no clock staring from the bureau or bookshelf, no imperative that told me to fix meals at certain times or rush away to appointments. The painter Arshile Gorky hanged himself in a barn. In Virginia. Countless others had, too, I supposed, although quiet contemplation never led me to thoughts of self-destruction. To the contrary, I found the barn a good place to laugh. Its somber confines, pinpricked with luminosity, seemed to chide good-naturedly, "Don't take things so seriously. Lighten up!"

Whatever a barn interior does for the psyche, it tends to force the abandonment, if only momentarily, of the material quest. Like any tabernacle, it shuts out the world of Mammon the thickness of a wall away. Vaulting space, subdued light, brooding architectural forms that jut in all directions—it's a formula, really, that perfectly suits the human need for detachment. I could sit in the barn (having placed an old chair for this purpose) and look out at the headland of the Massanutten, hanging behind the hayfields like a local Mount Fuji. Thus at ease, I was reminded of the utterly appealing beauty that wove through life, if only I followed the thread.

But even while absorbed with these contemplations, I was mindful of the task of fixing up and reversing the damage to the barn's exterior. Accordingly, I mended the broken doors and greased their rollers and track. I hooked up the recumbent downspout and fitted new weather-boards into place at the bad corner. I straightened or replaced the louver boards that pigeons and wind had knocked asunder. I hired a college student to scrape and paint the barn, an undertaking that lasted the greater part of a month. He, too, became an acolyte of the spiritual dimension of the old structure, and he did a conscientious job. The gleaming white paint and dark green trim restored the pride that time had dimmed.

As for the roof, I fully intended to patch and paint it myself until I actually climbed an extension ladder and poked my head above the guttering. Only then did I realize how seriously I had underestimated the steepness of the pitch. There I was, twenty feet above the ground with the ladder planted precariously on the barn bridge. My worm's-eye view was of a sheer cliff, and my latent acrophobia sprang to the fore with a blatant "Nosiree!" It didn't seem right to risk the college student's life and limb, either.

So I looked in the yellow pages and hired a professional barn roof painter. He scampered up the rungs and proceeded to walk the sheet metal as though he were strolling along a sidewalk. He even straightened up the four lightning rods, two of which pointed so obliquely that my children referred to them as sundials. The roof was patched and spray-painted in an hour and forty-five minutes.

The barn reverted to full-time agricultural use several seasons later when I actually began making hay. It was an unlikely pursuit for an artist, but it fitted right into the scheme of things. Once again, the mows are filled and the main floor is crowded with farming equipment. There are concessions to modernity, of course: the hay, no longer loose, is stacked in bales, and the equipment is pulled by tractor instead of horses. The barn still shelters its ongoing complement of pigeons and assorted rodents, as well as litter after litter of wild kittens, and in the stalls below, swallows still suspend their nests on the sides of floor joists. The swallows indulge in their aerobatics during the summer months only, while the pigeons coo upstairs all year long, mating and dropping, mating and dropping. Their nuisance factor is obvious (perhaps the gun-totin' farm boys were usefully employed, after all), but I cover the haymaking equipment with plastic sheeting and focus my mind upon other diversions. That way, at least, the roof won't leak.

FIVE

Not long after we moved into the farmhouse, I hired an acquaintance of mine named Earl, who operated heavy equipment, to start the excavations for the pond as well as the house and studios. It was my goal to complete the pond first, since it could benefit from being filled by the spring rains.

Earl and I had worked together before; he understood how important the pond was to me. Although I was no neophyte to the designing and siting of artificial bodies of water, my last pond had amounted to little more than an oversize puddle. The fault had not been entirely my own. I had wanted to expand a silted-up livestock watering hole at the base of the slope on my previous lot, so Earl had scooped out the basin and enlarged the dam, adding extra ditches to capture more runoff. But because the hillside was dense with honeysuckle and loblolly pines above an absorbent carpet of pine needles, the runoff remained minimal despite my additional diverting measures. The water simply soaked in as it ran downhill, never reaching the bottom. The pond resembled an empty, steep-sided basement excavation except after a prolonged rain, when it filled to a depth of three feet. A watering hole it had been, a watering hole it would remain.

In frustration, I had fantasized a number of unworkable solutions, including paving over the hillside and erecting windmills to pump water from a series of wells. I even considered lining the pond with ferroconcrete or butyl rubber, which are used for lining cooling pools for spent fuel assemblies at nuclear reprocessing facilities. Fortunately, I had been wise enough, or rather, poor enough, not to sink another penny into the project. Yet, when we moved away, I carried with me an unfulfilled desire to build a large, successful pond that would be brimming full year-round.

There was an established runoff pond at the northwest corner of the forty acres, a frog-filled reflection pool that had been dug to replace the nonfunctioning reservoir at the barn. The place for the pond of my dreams, though, was at the property's northeast corner, in the wooded ravine where the creek flowed under the barbed wire fence from the pastures that still belonged to our neighbor, the farmer who sold us the land. In normal weather, the creek maintained a slight but steady flow. In a drought, the creek went dry, although water continued to seep along its muddy bed. After a heavy rain, however, the creek rose quickly, and its current packed a wallop.

Our neighbor spoke of a failed pond he had built a hundred yards upstream. The dam had washed out twice in high water. With a nod of his head, he indicated the remains — a tufted hummock between sharply eroded cuts in the creek bed. He was convinced it couldn't be rebuilt successfully without a major capital outlay, and he illustrated his belief with a verbal picture of something that resembled the Grand Coulee Dam. If he were me, he said, he would forget the whole idea. There were plenty of recreational ponds nearby that were open to the public.

To further discourage my ambition, he mentioned that the highest water he'd ever seen in the creek had been running at the top of the fence. Now that was a lot of water. The more he spoke against my idea, the firmer my resolve became. How could he understand that I was intent on redressing an old failure? His description of the bench mark gave me a starting point for my calculations. I pictured the same volume of water at the depth of one foot, slowly running through an emergency spillway. A big earthen dam would be needed, but nothing gargantuan. The solution to the problem was a spillway of sufficient width to divert the floodwater around the dam and back to the creek bed downstream.

With a homemade transit fashioned from a sighting level and a camera tripod, it didn't take me long to stake out a dam and spillway across the ravine. In addition, I planned for fifteen-inch corrugated culvert piping to carry the normal outflow beneath the dam at creek level. The pipe came in twenty-foot sections that connected together with bolt-on collars. I had one section welded into a T, to be installed upside-down so that the top of the pipe, or standpipe, determined the water level of the pond. (The spillway level would be six inches higher to bear away excess water when the standpipe was already draining to capacity.) The base of the T that opened into the pond was fitted with a hinged valve for draining the pond during construction. After the pipe was set in place, I would build a dock thrusting out from the dam directly over the standpipe, with a trapdoor in the planking to facilitate maintenance of the pipe.

When the actual earth-moving began, both the dam and spillway were deliberately over-engineered to accommodate the stress of high water. With the patience of a sculptor, Earl put his front-end loader through its paces, creating what resembled an elongated mountain at one end of a vast ditch. As he added earth to the dam, he rolled the loader back and forth to tamp the surface with the weight of the machine.

We suffered our share of setbacks. The loader broke down repeatedly, and wet weather kept turning the project into an unworkable, slippery morass. Just when we seemed to make a little headway, a hydraulic hose would rupture, or a spring storm would drench the raw ground and cause the creek to become an implacable hurdle. Nevertheless, the sun periodically returned to dry the mud, and Earl had a knack for fixing his loader on the rainy days. In three weeks, our work was completed. It was time to shut the valve at the base of the standpipe and wait for the pond to fill.

But it had stopped raining. Days, weeks went by and not a drop. Lawns turned brown, spring gardens withered, vehicles stirred up dust on the secondary roads. The creek, seasonally lethargic, contributed negligibly to what was shaping up to be another glorified puddle, only this time, the empty basin surrounding it was enormous—at least twenty times the size of my little folly on the hillside. Daily, I visited the empty pond with gathering thoughts of desperation. Where was the fabled torrent? Had the naysaying farmer been talking about a once-in-a-century phenomenon?

The dock, designed to extend over the water at thirty inches, loomed twelve feet above on cross-braced stilts, as though a madman had erected a diving platform for a circus act. It reminded me of the "airmail" boxes perched atop high poles that rural wags placed beside their mailboxes. Had I created a dock for the purpose of catching flying fish?

Although I had seeded the dam and spillway, birds were the beneficiaries because the newly graded soil was too dry for grass to germinate. Meanwhile, the plucky creek inched up the water level to the three-foot mark. At the suggestion of my children, we held a wading party one warm afternoon in the shadow of the dock. While I cooled my heels in the tepid pool and pretended to be enjoying myself hugely, I resigned myself to the thought that it was better than nothing. The pond *was* filling. These things took time. And anyway, as Becky reminded me, I needed to be weaned from a deepening dependency upon instant gratification.

But my weaning never took place, for the drought ended with a thunder-boomer that poured cats and dogs. Shielded beneath a wind-beaten umbrella, I stood on the dam and watched. Loose branches, roots, bark, and leaves were lifted from their muddy repose and borne along the surface of the rising water. From bank to bank, the virgin pond had the variegation of a hearty bowl of soup. There was no doubt in my mind that the pond would fill. The question was: would the dam hold?

The rain continued, and around noontime two days later my question was answered by the sound of the standpipe taking water to capacity with a greedy, sucking roar. The spillway was under almost a foot of water, bearing away the excess flow. Behind the dam, the frothing flood-water rejoined the creek, now a rapids that coursed out of its confines, inundating the bases of the trees in the ravine.

The pond was full and the dam was holding. From beneath the umbrella, I peered through the deluge at the fence posts upstream. Sure enough, the water was cresting just beneath the top strand of barbed wire.

SIX

—————

THE BOOKS, THE CONVERSATIONS, the walks, the figuring out over and over made the truth sink in. Our forty acres were indeed a battlefield. They weren't next to, or near, or in the vicinity of one—they were the battlefield itself. The fact settled into my consciousness like a weight. I began to harbor streams of thought about soldiers—about dead soldiers, particularly.

From time to time, people ask me if I have ever seen ghosts on the battlefield. No fewer than 150, and possibly as many as 350 men, Union and Confederate, perished here on that fatal Sunday. Death struck each soldier, here as in any other battle, in a straightforward way. The trajectory of a piece of metal ended upon a target of flesh, the odds of good aim and bad luck coinciding perfectly. For the soldiers who looked death in the face and died, the experience could not have ended without a metaphysical transformation of some sort.

As mortality passed forever in the midst of searing pain, I believe that souls must have been left hovering. There is no other way to say it. Of life after death I know nothing, or next to nothing. Like anyone else, I theorize and build soaring arches of faith, but my conjecture about the moment of corporeal dissolution remains difficult to put in words without veering into the realm of Special Effects. The farmboy in butternut who was reluctant to abandon his kinfolk, or the blue-uniformed immigrant who cherished memories of the old country—each dying individual was transformed in some incomprehensible way. Body and soul separated. The body lay inert. Is it wrong to surmise that the soul flew up and away?

My thoughts are not without precedent. Every religion in the world speaks of death as a departure from life. "He gave up the ghost," they say, meaning that his spirit was liberated when his body ceased to function. I often found myself multiplying one soul by several hundred as I tried to envision the mortal remains lying on the fields and in the brushy woods. Seen or unseen, ghosts must have been here.

But to answer the question: no, I have never seen ghosts on the battlefield. I have never seen ghosts anywhere—in a cellar, on a stairway, or in an attic, and I never want to. This is not to say I am unmoved in the presence of departed spirits, for I am. Most people are, in one way or another.

The very first time I walked on the battlefield, there seemed to be a faint emanation that may have been germane to these considerations. It was nothing I could put my finger on. For lack of an answer, I dismissed it as a product of my imagination. I soon realized, however, that it had nothing to do with me, no matter how susceptible my brain was to the power of suggestion. The overgrazed pasturage, with its barn and machine shed, was adding up to more than the sum of its physical characteristics.

Granted, it was a comely quarter, distanced from the blur of traffic, peaceful as any forty acres could be. The pastoralness set me aquiver, to be sure, but there was more to it. In the lengthening shadows of that first afternoon, as I perambulated the fields among the skittish cattle that fled my approach, yet followed from behind as though I were a Pied Piper, I pondered the evidence.

And then, Eureka! I understood. The thing I sensed was that people had been here before, en masse. At times, I have noted a comparable intimation after a public auction, when the last item of furniture has been carted off and the last pickup truck has driven away. The grass is patterned with tire tracks and footprints. The buzz of the crowd, the auctioneer's warble still echo in my ears. A whiff of humanity lingers, a subtle indefinable something, but it is not an olfactory sensation. It, too, is an echo, a reverberation of the auction-goers who were convened an hour earlier. A similar presence lingered in these pastures a hundred and twenty-three years after the battle. After that length of time, I would not have thought it possible to stand at the heart of a battlefield and pick up its living pulse.

Later, during the months of construction when I sat in a lawn chair at the end of the day and unwound in the silence that so closely followed my noisy agenda, the faint pulse returned. My toolbelt lay at my feet like a bristling assortment of armaments. Two kittens were asleep in the chair next to me. I sat there until I fell into a kind of trance. My plans and executions receded to the point where my perceptions cast about for deeper themes. Again, that reminder or remainder of humanity wafted on the air, and it startled me. I thought I might be going mad.

Having respect for the dead means that future generations don't pave over cemeteries for parking lots. Cemeteries are paved over, on occasion, but it is the exception rather than the rule. There is no law, however, that says cemeteries can't be tourist attractions. A headstone, plain or fancy, reminds onlookers that so-and-so existed within the confines of two dates. If the carved numerals are decipherable, a moment of mental arithmetic ensues, a calculation of how old so-and-so lived to be.

In Harrisonburg, there are more than 250 Confederate graves in a quadrant of the oldest cemetery. Each small marble marker reads like a word in a chilling sentence, or a sentence in a numbing chapter. The regularity with which the markers are placed, row upon row like a marching battalion, suggests an orderliness, a solidarity of purpose. The Southern Cause is given shape and substance. I know it was an act of practicality, the organizing of corpses in a limited space, but still the geometry of the graves disturbs me. Death for any cause, lost or won, is not quite so cut and dried as a cemetery layout.

There are Union mass graves on the Cross Keys battlefield, but no one knows precisely where. A likely location may be the woods along the Lee-Jackson boundary, not more than a hundred feet from our new house. John W. Wayland's *History of Rockingham County, Virginia* recounts a letter written in 1912 by William N. Jordan, a ninety-one-year-old native of the county, then living in Frankfort, Indiana.

I bought me a home near Cross Keys, and lived there until the Civil War commenced. I was assessor of that district in '59 and '60, and I was captain of the Cross Keys and Mt. Crawford cavalry. I had about 100 men in the company, and we were mustered into service of the Confederacy on the third day of June, 1861, and were in a number of battles. Among them was the fight at Cross Keys. We were on the left flank of Gen. Ewell's army during the fight.

My farm was just outside of the line of battle. The Yankees broke open my corn crib and took corn to feed their horses, but did not disturb my family. This was on Sunday . . .

They [the Yankees] had made a hospital of a very large two-story house, and set it afire when they left. It was thought by the old people that lived close there that there was a large number of dead and wounded in the house at the time, for they heard some of them calling for help. And they left their dead lying all over the battlefield; and we had to make a big circuit to cross the river to get on the battlefield.

Major General Richard S. Ewell, commanding a division comprising slightly less than half of Stonewall Jackson's army, had engaged the army of Major General John C. Frémont here on Sunday. On Monday morning, the Confederate division marched to rejoin Jackson at Port Republic, four miles to the southeast, where a second battle was fought against another Federal force en route from the north, commanded by Brigadier General James A. Shields. A rear guard had been ordered to burn the covered bridge that entered Port Republic, thereby impeding Frémont's army coming from the direction of Cross Keys. The loss of this strategic bridge hampered Jordan's return to the battleground three days later.

We did not get around there until Wednesday morning. Gen. Imboden, who was in command of the cavalry, detailed me and my company to gather up and bury the dead. At one place we buried 81 bodies, and at another 21. They were mostly foreigners, from the looks of them. It has been so long ago that I don't remember how many we lost in that battle.

In the aftermath of Civil War battles, mass graves were dug with shovels and by horse-drawn scraping pans that sliced into the ground with repeated passes. Corpses were covered with less than two feet of earth. At Gettysburg and elsewhere, heavy rains exposed the bones of the dead during the weeks and months following interment. Given the passage of time, it seemed odd that treasure hunters had neither discovered nor plundered the mass graves at Cross Keys. There were several explanations. Since the ground was softened by days of rain, perhaps the excavations had been deeper than usual. Also, the corpses may have been stripped of metal—buttons, buckles, ammunition, and so forth—prior to burial. Whatever the reason, far more than a century has passed, and nobody has stumbled upon the evidence. Once in a great while, sheer forgetfulness accounts for the survival of places and things. In this case, the abandoned Union dead were thrown together in unmarked ditches, their final camouflage as unknown soldiers, and they are still resting there.

SEVEN

FROM TIME TO TIME, I brought home picture books about the Civil War to show Van and Hope. On a Sunday afternoon, we'd sit on the subfloor of the new house, a sawdust-carpeted plane a few feet above the battleground, and thumb through the pages. The unfinished construction that penned us in was displacing two thousand square feet of lethally contested field. The only clue to the war was the book I was holding on my lap.

Engravings and photographs from the turbulent 1860s presented the subject of war in two distinct manners: engravings illustrated the Civil War, and photographs burned it in the memory.

Engravings tended to be stylized compositions, scenes of the war depicted as if on a grand canvas, replete with heroism and action in the traditional beaux arts formula. Many engravings began as sketches on the spot, drawn by field artists who followed the war campaigns. The finished sketches were relayed to engravers, who duplicated reduced versions, more or less faithfully, for printing and distribution in daily and weekly newspapers, as well as monthly magazines. The rules of good picture-making were adhered to: centrality of composition, differentiation between foreground and background, left to right balance, and strong value contrast. Most of the field artists kept their work before the public for the duration of the war, and were paid handsomely for their efforts. It was the dawning of the age of picture journalism.

But photography had not yet been incorporated into the printing process. As products of an infant science, photographs were created without prolonged artistic manipulation. Cameras were positioned and pictures followed. Cameramen who took the war as their subject were haphazard technicians, fumbling with crude equipment, aiming their lenses with the finesse of stevedores. What resulted were prints of provocative reality, peeks at the human condition that often trespassed beyond polite convention. Portrait sitters' hair was greasy with pomade. Epaulets sagged, frock coats were unbuttoned. Some sitters were bow-legged, others plainly showed hunger, mistrust, misery. The photographers bore witness to the unadorned spectacle of destruction, too.

No photographic record was made of the campaign in the Shenandoah Valley in the spring of 1862. Visual coverage was achieved by a handful of sketch artists, some working in the field, others working in the studio from descriptions supplied by campaign participants. The only artist to actually witness the action at Cross Keys was Edwin Forbes, a former art student from Philadelphia. At Cross Keys, the youthful Forbes saw his very first battle, having been assigned to the command of Major General Frémont by *Frank Leslie's Illustrated Newspaper*, a weekly journal that was among the first to introduce the American public to pictorial coverage of current events by way of page-long engravings.

At the start of the Civil War, *Leslie's Illustrated* had a press run of almost 100,000 copies. Its printing plant in New York City was staffed by 130 craftsmen, who revolutionized the engraving process with technical breakthroughs and round-the-clock employment. The time between receiving an artist's original sketch and distributing the finished journal was shortened to as little as forty-eight hours, depending on the newsworthiness of the event.

As an impoverished but dedicated student, Forbes had fully intended to embark upon a career in oil painting, but the lure of a steady job with Frank Leslie's organization overpowered his fine art ambitions and coincided with his love of adventure. With enthusiasm, he joined the army's southward march on his chestnut mare, Kitty, packed with sketch pads, pencils, pens, brushes, and watercolors. Describing his experience at Cross Keys in *Thirty Years After, An Artist's Story of the Great War*, Forbes wrote, "I fully expected when I started for the front to accompany troops into battle and seat myself complacently on a convenient hillside and sketch exciting incidents at my leisure."

The artillery crossfire on the morning of June 8 came as a surprise. In his languid, if not genteel, introduction to the Union rank and file, Forbes had been supplying sketches of camp life, compositions which depicted individuals or small groups keeping busy in the best Army tradition. (A popular maxim stated that for every ten hours of battle, there were ten weeks of drudgery.) But as Forbes rode forward to document the active Union batteries, he realized to his dismay that even at a distance of half a mile, he was exposed to enemy fire. The danger unnerved him. At once he saw "how greatly reality differed from imagination," as well as the fact that "to be a spectator was nearly as dangerous as being a participant." He galloped back to the brow of a hill at the rear, where, remaining on horseback to facilitate a quick exit, he sketched the scene before him with the aid of binoculars.

A hundred and twenty-six years later, while browsing in an antique store in Harrisonburg, I came across an engraving based on one of Forbes's battle sketches of Cross Keys. The yellowed print had been torn from a *Leslie's Illustrated* by a dealer who regularly dismembered old periodicals. (Matted and framed, an antique print fetched more than the periodical itself.) The Forbes engraving was a bravura depiction of the long and sinuous Union lines in reserve. Overhead, gun smoke billowed from bursting shells. In the distance were accurately rendered contours of the Blue Ridge. It was an overview of the army's extensive logistical sprawl, stylistically toned in blacks and whites by the craftsmen in New York.

Forbes was remembered by his peers as a gentle, highly imaginative person who had no stomach for casualties. Reflecting on his abrupt retreat from the guns at Cross Keys, Forbes said it had been due to the sight of "the desperately wounded who were being carried to the rear." A little more than a year later, in the aftermath of Gettysburg, the (by then) veteran field artist was no less unhinged during an inspection of the silent front:

> The sight was ghastly, everything bore the mark of death and destruction . . . the whole slope was massed with dead horses . . . the earth was torn and plowed by the terrible artillery fire, and under fences and in corners, and anywhere that slight shelter offered, the dead lay in dozens . . . it was difficult to tread without stepping on them.

Small wonder Forbes resorted to the power of optics to distance himself from the murderous confrontation at Cross Keys. His first taste of action was a harbinger of bloodier battles to come. In the course of the war, he often resorted to sketching in the saddle, through binoculars. The subscribers of *Leslie's Illustrated* saw his close-up views of the battles, not realizing that the artist had maintained a safe distance for the sake of his sanity. The intimacy and detail of the engravings earned Forbes a well-deserved acclaim.

Elsewhere and later in the war, photographers compiled their frank record. In camps, troops stood at attention, patently uncomfortable in ill-fitting uniforms, their rifles with fixed bayonets taller than themselves. Staff officers lounged in folding chairs at the entrances to cavernous tents. A soldier sat on a three-legged stool, transfixed in the act of washing his clothes. Another soldier posed with a pet squirrel. Then, as now, military service had little to do with heroics and much to do with coping from day to day.

The photographers who followed the war were often frustrated by their inability to capture "action." The development of true portability and versatility in photography was nearly fifty years away. Men like Mathew B. Brady and Alexander Gardner and their assistants hauled their cumbersome equipment by mule-drawn wagon, and received little compensation for their efforts. In most instances, they were disparaged by field commanders and jeered at by soldiers. An informal censorship resulted, brought about by a lack of officially sanctioned purpose or usefulness, so the photographers kept to the sidelines where they plied their craft in a vacuum of indifference. Little did anyone realize that every time the shutter clicked, an archive was in the making.

What is it about photographs from the Civil War that so captivates the modern viewer? Is it the documentation of a time no person alive is old enough to remember? Is it the motion-freezing imperative of slow shutter speed and emulsion-coated glass? Or is it the sensuality of war itself—as in the half-thrilling, half-horrifying testimonial found in the work of war photographers from the present era?

Photographs from the Civil War fall into three broad categories: pre-action, post-action, and portraits. Photographs of pre-action illustrate the social and military organization that fueled the war effort. These pictures include, but are not limited to, diverse products of technology: munitions, means of transportation, buildings, bridges, clothing, furniture, supplies, and the like. Quaint as these subjects appear by today's design, they reflect the dynamism of American society in the first blush of the industrial age.

The photographs of post-action illustrate the havoc wrought by the military application of this technological dynamism. Forests become wastelands of tall, splintered stumps. Once stately mansions are reduced to piles of brick and plaster. Chimneys are landmarks—obelisk-like, detached. Railroad tracks have been twisted and torn, engines wrecked, cars derailed. The ubiquitous "twelve-pounder" cannons sit mired in mud, useless and abandoned amid breached fortifications.

And the dead. Corpses are strewn about the uneven ground, some covered with rough blankets, others not. Some are bloated in death, some shriveled or skeletal. Many are without shoes. There is a famous picture of a dead Confederate soldier at Fort Mahone in Petersburg, Virginia. He lies face up in the mud on the bank of a muddy creek, with his mud-caked arm and pointed finger upraised, as if he is midway through a yarn about his own muddy end. Other photographs show the dead awaiting burial. In some, a semblance of order has been restored; the corpses are laid out in neat ranks—the cemetery syndrome. A few are fitted into rude coffins, as if to imply that the paperwork has been completed.

Another famous photograph: Dr. Bunnell's Embalming Establishment near the Fredricksburg battlefield. The good doctor's banner, draped on the side of his commandeered barn, proclaims services that will render fallen soldiers "free from odor or infection," a preliminary to the long, slow journeys in the baggage cars back to their hometowns.

And finally, the pictures of the burial grounds, backfilled with a plowed urgency. Row after row of temporary markers, wooden boards that may or may not have been inscribed with relevant data, are stuck in the earth like garden stakes until the stonecutters' more durable craft makes them no longer necessary.

The third category of photographs, that of portraits, is largely the work of unknown studio photographers and daguerreotypists in the cities and small towns. In order to pose for a portrait, a sitter had to remain inert and wide-eyed for tens of seconds at a time, often aided by a brace to the back of the neck. The dreamily extended exposure somehow captures the essence of the brusque warrior, so recently the peace-loving civilian. More than anything else, the act of posing signified a willingness to die in the defense of one's country. The pose and the props were chosen with care.

From the youthful exuberance of a conscript, with pistol in hand and dagger in belt, to the gravity of a two-star general, with braided arm relaxed upon a tasseled armrest, the portraits trumpet a logic and ardor common to both sides. The sitters' attitudes are not concealed by their frozen expressions. Grand expectations read like large print. Why sign up? To preserve the Union, of course! To free the slaves! To defend states' rights! To whip the the Yankee invader!

The portraits were framed under glass, bordered by ornately stamped and gilded tin, or enclosed in wooden cases clad in tooled leather. Oval formats were popular. Mothers, fathers, siblings, wives, and lovers clung to these keepsakes when they could no longer cling to the real person. Intangible symbols of glory and honor, the portraits too often became tangible reminders of abbreviated youth and luckless demise.

EIGHT

THIS WAS MY FOURTH home-building project in fifteen years, and I sincerely hoped it would be my last. Three times I had tried to settle down and failed. Here I was with three strikes against me, advancing into my forties, making a fresh start at it, this time on forty acres of history and hay. Becky and I needed a house to grow old in—a house that would be spacious yet affordable, pleasing yet practical, a house I could construct for the most part by myself.

In preparation for the project, I struggled to recapture a mindset I had not tapped for several years. I pored over the latest construction literature at the public library, reviewing plumbing and wiring manuals, noting changes in the building codes. Visiting lumberyards and construction sites, I updated my knowledge of materials and methods. Last, but not least, I devoted hours to financial calculations, hours that convinced me to forgo most of the frills. Tile baths would be eliminated on this go-round, as well as hardwood floors and skylights.

But no Thoreau was I when it came to the finalization of my plans. Owner-building in the postmodern era has strayed from its traditions of economy and self-reliance. Values like these are not only discouraged, they are forbidden. A present-day Thoreau will have serious supply problems if he attempts to build without dimensional lumber, serious financial problems if he purchases construction materials without a bank loan or at least a line of credit, and serious legal problems if he ignores the building codes. If he is civilly disobedient, he will face a stretch in prison in lieu of a whopping fine, which a present-day Emerson may not have the wherewithal to pay. After all, one can't build a house without a bathroom anymore.

In my previous housebuilding experience in Rockingham County, I had run afoul of the building inspector because a floor wasn't level. It had been an error on my part, but it hadn't seemed worth correcting at

47

the time. (Had Thoreau placed a spirit level on his floor before he deemed his cabin livable?) I compounded the error by questioning the authority of the county official, and there had been hell to pay before we were granted a certificate of occupancy.

This time around, I was determined to mind my p's and q's. There was a marked surliness in the inspections office when I applied for the new building permit. My credibility was on the line. It was up to me to prove to the inspector that I could be architect, carpenter, mason, concrete finisher, roofer, plumber, electrician, insulator, drywall contractor, and landscaper rolled into one. I had no intention of kowtowing, but it didn't seem wise to lock horns with him either, so I took my time and did everything in a manner that would meet his approval. The better part of a year passed as I wore these various hats, but I persevered, mainly because I had done it all before and I knew there was an end in sight.

The joys of construction were akin to the joys of driving: I glimpsed them now and then as I navigated through a maze of rules and regulations, ever mindful of the safety factor. In construction, the biggest reward was reaching a stopping place, the feeling of accomplishment at the end of the workday—the courses of masonry perfectly plumb, the studs in knotty rank. The obverse of this reward was the physical fatigue and the incremental jump in the construction loan as the cost of the day's materials were added to the tally.

Owner homebuilding was expensive, despite what was said in the journals printed on recycled paper. The price of construction materials, those unitized configurations of cellulose, stone, glass, plastic, and metal, had risen precipitously since my earlier experience. Then, I didn't understand how completely the multinational forest product corporations ran the show. Smarter now, I resented their monopoly, but felt more ensnared than ever—a lumberyard addict. Their diversified products, many of which were byproducts of byproducts once considered worthless, had proliferated in supply as well as demand. At the local level, the suppliers peddled their chip-, particle-, beaver-, wafer-, whatever-board at prices commensurate with the inflationary spiral.

Few can beat the system. I know only one person who really tried, a friend of mine named Rick, who is a self-employed machinist and well driller—it was he who welded my standpipe. Rick rigged up an antique sawmill to process his own trees, and it was a kinetic treat to watch his sawmill in action, to follow the log carriage as it rammed the wood into the whirling fifty-two-inch blade while an auger heaped the sawdust into

48

a fragrant dune and a chuffing Farmall turned the long drive belt that flapped like a living creature. Yet Rick's enterprise was a quixotic venture at best. If he sawed (then dried and milled) lumber for me, he'd have charged twice the price of the lumber companies in town.

No, a person in his or her right mind can't escape the incentives of conformity. Across the Blue Ridge fifteen years earlier, when I had been a greenhorn to the construction trade and heavily influenced by counter-cultural trends of the sixties, I had designed and built a home of three interconnected geodesic domes. Like many others, I had been swayed by Buckminster Fuller's siren song to the point where I entertained visions of domed communities, even domed cities, in a new world of harmony. My first house still stood, a leaky anachronism inhabited by a family of aging New Agers, but that was another story.

My rebel days were over. Everyone's rebel days were over, it seemed. Now, I merely followed an approved plan from start to finish. The fact that I designed and built houses demonstrated no great feat of ingenuity or acquired skill. It only showed my intransigence toward the accepted wisdom that exempted the intelligentsia from common labor. It showed that I had a fondness for planning things in my mind and executing them with my own two hands. It showed that as an artist, it didn't matter if I put my career on hold for twelve months while I picked up the shovel and hammer and saw and did the dirty work.

In addition to my tool belt and power tools, I took two kittens to the construction site every day. They brought me companionship, and the contrast between their playfulness and my industriousness was a source of ongoing comic relief.

Hope and Van called the kittens Bonuses, because they were unanticipated extras, litter mates donated by a neighboring family that had moved away. Bonus One and Bonus Two were orange twins, hard to tell apart, but as they matured, their differences became manifest. One was an instigator, a quicker study at chase and play, while Two developed the personality of a lap sitter. Later it was observed that One had a squarish nose and Two had a round one, so we started calling them "Square Nose" and "Round Nose."

I had trained the kittens to jump into the cab of the pickup each morning as I left and each evening as I returned. They sat beside me like proper little passengers during the half-mile ride across the hayfields. It was an early indication that both were suckers for a soft seat. As my work advanced, and the frame of the house was under roof, I placed a

49

couple of webbed lawn chairs beside a woodstove in which I burned lumber scraps from the interior partitioning as fast as I produced them. The kittens favored the chair nearest the stove because it was bolstered by a foam cushion. "Favored" is too weak a word: they *adored* the chair and were glued to it for hours. When I lifted them out of it at the end of the workday, their claws carried the cushion right along.

My sawhorses were set up not five feet away from the chair, where I trimmed two-by-fours with the circular saw. The piercing saw-shriek, against which I wore hearing protectors, didn't faze the felines. I spiked together doorjambs and corner posts, hammering home the hefty sixteen-penny c.c. sinkers with a racket that would raise the dead, but the kittens quietly wrestled with each other, or licked their paws, or snoozed.

In the beginning, I wondered if the kittens were deaf, or extraordinarily stupid, but I soon realized they were merely content. The foam cushion — its reflected heat, its smell — must have been a kind of surrogate mother. Witnessing their peace as I toiled made me feel undignified, but it elevated me to a happy-go-lucky state of mind. My rattlesome quest for self-aggrandizement was quite beyond the scope of the kittens' concern. I was there to work; they were there to play and groom themselves and sleep. Supposedly, my work gave meaning to my existence, but their existence had a meaning of its own that quite excluded the human notion of usefulness. In a prison of my own making, I was tripping over extension cords, bumping my shins against stacks of unused lumber, caged by skeletal stud walls between the subfloor and the bottom chord of the roof trusses. The unfinished shell of the house had a long way to go before it could rightfully be called a home, yet it was already home to the kittens. They had their warm chair. They had each other. They didn't mind the incessant commotion of their solitary master.

And so, the most noteworthy alteration to the forty acres came into being: a single-family residence and its adjacent studios. A man and two cats witnessed the day-by-day journey to completion. I marked my accomplishment against the indifference of the cats. I knew that when the house was finished, I, too, would be indifferent. At that point, it would be home to me as well.

Half a year after pounding that first stake into the ground, I was roughing-in the plumbing and wiring. With my power tools, I notched and drilled pathways for the pipes and cables through the walls, over the ceiling, and under the floor. A couple of work lights illuminated the dark corners. Periodically, I used a vacuum cleaner to clear away the shavings and sawdust. A radio played. I took for granted the electrical service that had been so hard won only a few months earlier.

Back when I had begun mixing mortar for the concrete block foundation, I needed electricity to pump water from the newly drilled well, but no service, either overhead or underground, had been officially supplied to the forty acres. At one time, a jury-rigged wire had carried current from the farmhouse to the barn, where a single, naked bulb had illuminated the main floor, but the wire had been severed years ago. The electricity I would use was more than a drop cord could provide, and the distance alone made this unfeasible.

Upon making a formal application at the Shenandoah Valley Electric Cooperative, the branch of the Rural Electrification Administration that supplied the farmhouse, I was surprised to learn that the other side of the forty acres lay within another supplier's jurisdiction. On a power distribution map for the county, the jurisdictional divide ran right through the center of our property, approximating the path of an extant cross-fence. The R.E.A. representative said he could electrify the barn for me, "but the other folks have to run the juice to 'way over yonder," unless they gave contractual permission to the co-op to do it.

Wasting no time, I paid a visit to the other folks — Virginia Power, known as Vepco — to secure what I thought would be a rubber-stamp approval. A distribution engineer pulled a map from a file drawer. It showed the same division along the cross-fence, the western twenty acres belonging to the R.E.A. and the eastern twenty acres belonging to Virginia Power. The engineer shook his head. He was polite, but adamant. Competitor utilities did not service each other's territory. Vepco would be ready and willing to accommodate me from its poles on Route 708. A clear-cut, herbicide-maintained forty-foot right of way across the ravine would be required. An alternate right of way could bring the wires directly over the pond. Either way, there'd be no charge for the service installation.

Well, both proposals were unsuitable. The last thing I wanted was a cleared right of way through the wooded ravine, which would serve as a privacy screen as well as a source of winter fuel. As for the pond route, I had always abhorred ponds in the paths of utility easements. There was something dreadfully degrading about the way wires marred the reflection of the sky — black lines forever bisecting the water's surface. I had even seen ponds with utility poles planted in the middle of them, as if the engineers had thumbed their noses at anything that impeded the regulation distance between poles or their arrow-straight vector across the countryside.

By contrast, the R.E.A. cooperative offered to run our primary service underground (also free) all the way from Port Republic Road if Vepco would cede the territory. How could I help but prefer this proposal, and why couldn't the folks at Vepco understand? It dawned on me that I was up against more than an inflexible rule; I was challenging a tenet of economic survival. A utility company was loath to relinquish even one customer whose lifetime of rate-paying would add tens of thousands of dollars to its coffers.

My persistent preference for the service from Port Republic Road sparked a battle of its own. Fighting for the disputed territory were engineers and public relations officers, their supervisors and *their* supervisors, commanded by members of the board in ironic uniform of blue blazers and gray flannel trousers. I must have talked with two dozen people on various levels of both utility hierarchies. Engineers descended on the battlefield with measuring wheels, steel tapes, and transits. Big shots arrived in company cars. Some of the visitors reconnoitered the ground so quickly that they left without opening a door or rolling down a window. The ones who stayed showed no rancor, but freely admitted that it was an unusual situation. On sunny days, linemen came out to sunbathe on company time, or at least eat a leisurely lunch. For them, it was a good fight and a relaxing one. The two-way radios in their trucks squawked intermittently, adding to the polyphonic chirping of the insects and birds.

With a view to ending the battle, which was dragging on for weeks with no compromise in sight, Becky and I made a personal visit to Virginia Power's regional headquarters in Charlottesville. It was late on a Friday afternoon when we got there. The offices were empty; receptionist, secretaries, and staff had all gone home for the weekend. An executive attired in blue and gray—the head honcho himself—strolled out to greet us. We were ushered into his inner sanctum, seated on luxuriant leather chairs, engaged in the smallest of small talk. Then, with a patrician tilt of his head, he got down to business: we were invited to plead our case.

We began with the prerequisite flattery about how we had been Virginia Power customers for years, and had only praise for the company's dependability, consumer-conscious attitude, etc. We proceeded to discuss the historical nature of our property, pointing out the arbitrary jurisdictional divide which must have been a long-overlooked fluke of distribution planning. We mentioned the hassle of having to pay two utility bills were we to electrify a building – the barn, for example – on the other half of the property. We reiterated the desirability of underground service coming from Port Republic Road, versus the undesirability of overhead service coming from Route 708. Becky underscored the point by saying that if it were *his* house, he would think the same.

We concluded our remarks by emphasizing that *we did not want* Virginia Power's electricity. Nothing would change our minds. We would go to court to get the R.E.A. juice, if necessary. He stiffened perceptibly, squinting at us over pressed fingertips. He stood up. Becky and I stood up. We parted with amicable handshakes. He said he'd look into it.

A week later, a convoy of mustard-green R.E.A. trucks rolled down the lane. A ditching machine with a cable vibrator like an upside-down shark fin was unloaded, along with an enormous spool of underground primary cable. The battle had been won.

Nine months later, the house and studios were nearing completion. As I was nailing up siding boards on the outside, professional drywall finishers were inside smoothing the sheetrock. I admired their ability and they admired mine. We agreed that trading places would not be a good idea. Both our jobs required expertise, but to be truthful, neither job was as hard as it looked, despite the amount of practice it took to get good at it. In the long run, skill is tedium – a repetition of muscular and mental coordination that becomes second nature. A skilled worker can't help but do the job right, and he or she isn't even trying. Usually, a skilled worker isn't even *thinking*.

Take the simple task of hammering a nail. I had had access to a hammer and nails as far back as I could remember. In Rhode Island, during my elementary school years, my father belonged to a social organization called the Tavern Hall Club. Every June the club held its annual picnic, an event I looked forward to above all others because it included a nail-driving contest. An eight-by-eight-inch pine beam lay on the ground, along with a sixteen-ounce hammer and a lard can full of twenty-penny spikes. I can still picture the portly, retired carpenter who was in charge – his granny glasses, his engineer's cap, his striped coveralls. He started each nail in the beam to prevent any mangled thumbs. The person who drove a spike with the fewest hammer blows won a prize, the nature of which I've long forgotten because I never, ever came close to winning it.

I remember grasping the handle of the claw-hammer with both hands, exerting the greatest mental effort to strike the nail squarely on its head, but somehow glancing every blow and eventually bending the nail so badly that it had to be flattened on its side. While I nursed my embarrassment at the end of the line, awaiting another turn, I marveled at the prowess of those older than me – the teenagers, who seemed so much taller and stronger. Five hammer blows, six – the nail slid into the wood like a skewer into soft cheese. Then, several adults took turns. Three blows, even two, and the head of the nail drew flush with the dinged and dented pine. Would I ever learn to wield a hammer that way?

Over the years, I must have risen to the challenge of the Tavern Hall Club picnic, for as an adult, I take exceptional pride in my ability to hammer a nail. I have absorbed the physics of it from repeated practice during carpentry projects both large and small, for myself and others. I have learned how to hold a hammer so its heft and velocity are put to maximum use. I know how to start a nail so that it goes where it is supposed to go – straight, or at an angle, even an oblique angle – and I can modulate the force of my hammer blows from furious pounding to nudging taps. My aim is flawless, too, although it is decades too late to claim a prize.

I can straighten bent nails, pull or break hopeless nails, countersink, and dimple. I can space nails to conform to an appropriate "schedule," and I know which nails to use for different applications. I am prescient about whether a nail is going where it should or shouldn't. I can drive brads right up against a pane of glass. In short, I can do just about anything there is to do with a hammer and a nail, and I do it uncommonly well.

I have even gained insight into the subtle distinctions between Korean and Polish nails, between Hungarian and Taiwanese nails. There are differences in the sharpness of their points, the ductility of their shanks, the shape of their heads, and the composition and color of their cement or vinyl coatings (c.c., v.c.). How do I know? By going through box after fifty-pound box.

So when I appreciated the drywall finishers' sculptural aptitude as they slathered the joint compound over the seams in the ceiling and smoothed them by troweling – all the while balancing on stilts – my wonderment at their skill was tempered by my awareness of the essential mindlessness of their toil. The drywall finishers were somewhere between a coffee break and lunch, cranking out another job in fulfillment of another paycheck at the end of another week. They were getting the job done.

"Getting the job done"—a phrase that bespeaks motivation, a purposeful expenditure of effort toward an end result. What motivated me as I put the finishing touches on the house? No paycheck awaited me, and I had no illusions of a life of ease once the project was over.

I had been working on the house exclusively for months and I was tired of it. Our cash resources were negligible. It had taken almost fifty thousand dollars to get the house to a point where it could pass the final inspections. To fail was to court disaster, not only for my reputation as a builder, but also for our line of credit, which had been stretched to the breaking point. The Permit of Occupancy, that chit of pink foolscap, was a precious diploma; we needed to graduate from the School of Endless Debt, and soon.

Despite its antique ambience, the Haugh house was a poor substitute for the state-of-the-art dwelling that was being readied across the fields. We were like moths before the flame. Potable water, insulation, counter and cabinet space in the kitchen, built-in closets, more than one electrical outlet per room—these were enticements most citizens of the late twentieth century would succumb to. Having engineered these features and others, I was eager to live in their midst and take them all for granted again.

What about the Thoreau in me? Where was that frugal spirit, that holdout from the mainstream of consumerism? And what of the war against progress? Was I not complicating the earth with yet another structure to pay taxes on and run services to? Another house to besmirch the sky with its chimney, to foul the ground with its septic field? I had no excuses. The middle-aged person is to blame for every wrong turn away from the young person's idealism. I guess it was the anticipation of comfort that drove me on. Comfort and change. I had ridden the white horse far enough, and now I was ready to dismount. Even in the Walden woods, old Thoreau himself broke camp one day and never returned.

When the lease ran out on the farmhouse at the end of that second May, we, too, decamped. By tractor and pickup, we moved our household to the far side of the battlefield, heaping the cart and truck bed high in flagrant violation of the laws of reason. It didn't matter—we owned the road. Each load was like a caricature of an Okie family's worldly possessions—chair legs akimbo, odds and ends stacked precariously—but our material wealth filled load after load, and our destination was a lot closer than California.

Resettling in a pristine dwelling that smelled of acrylic carpet and latex paint was a luxury akin to sitting in a brand-new car and driving off into the sunset. Once again, there was trust in the future, trust in material satisfaction, trust in the standard-issue promises we were indoctrinated, as children, to depend on. The inevitability of mortgage payments, of electric bills, of real estate and personal property taxes (which all jumped precipitously) hadn't sunk in. The *now* of newness pervaded our life, like the new smells. Days were heady with nest-feathering projects such as planting flower beds, choosing drapery patterns, rearranging furniture.

Two weeks after we were settled in, I scheduled the building inspector's final tour. Technically, we weren't supposed to be living there yet. It remained for me to hang a bathroom door, install a railing on the steps to the basement, put up smoke detectors—details the building code spelled out quite specifically. A nitpicking official could have declared us a public nuisance and fined us a hundred dollars a day. Oh, and I was supposed to put a vacuum breaker on each outdoor spigot. A vacuum breaker is a small brass contraption designed to prevent contaminated water in a garden hose from siphoning back into the house plumbing. Usually it is discarded as soon as the inspector drives away, because it requires some fiddling with each time the spigot is turned on in freezing weather.

I am reminded of an electrician's advice, a house or two back, when he had been watching me drive an eight-foot ground rod from consecutively lower steps of a stepladder. Conscientiously, I banged away with the sledgehammer, but the steel rod hit rock before half its length was in the ground. I pounded and pounded to no avail. Wordlessly, the electrician handed me a hacksaw. I expressed concern that the building inspector would disapprove, knowing that the rod wasn't buried a full eight feet.

"Pshaw," the electrician spat. "He ain't got X-ray vision. Just be sure you throw the cutoff way over in them bushes."

NINE

THE VIEW FROM the new front porch was of hayfields and sky. Though the house was somewhat unfinished with respect to interior trimwork, my attention had shifted away from carpentry. Generations ago, when settlers had come to the heavily forested Shenandoah Valley, they must have thought along similar lines: having built a shelter, it was time to turn their attention to making a living off the land. But the twentieth century left me too educated to consider an instinctive approach to cultivating my land. I knew little about farming, and the artist in me recoiled from wading in without cerebrating, without agonizing. How was I to deal with this huge expanse? What was I really looking at, and what should I be learning?

During the excavation of the basement, I had been brought face to face with the geological stratum beneath the battlefield. It was an Ordovician shale that had been deposited about 455 million years ago, a friable, predominantly burnt-orange sedimentary rock referred to as the Martinsburg Formation. It lay beneath most of central Virginia and between the mountains that bordered and interrupted the Shenandoah Valley. In the vicinity of Cross Keys, it was manifested in a sinclinal fold of shale and siltstone, deeply weathered to a taupe-colored topsoil on the surface. Topsoil depth varied between eight and twelve inches. Below that was a paler layer of shale and fine-grained sandstone, some with quartz grains, which gradually hardened to rock consistency within three feet.

Groundhog holes had furnished the raw data for me even earlier. The excavated material at the mouth of a den consisted of fragmented shale, some of it in long slivers, dun-colored and coated with dust.

Since the basement extended seven feet into the hillside at its deepest point and covered an area of two thousand square feet, Earl had been kept busy, and when he wasn't carving out the basement, he was digging the septic field and hauling gravel for the driveway. The hardened teeth of his loader and backhoe ripped into the Martinsburg Formation with relative ease. Tons of hydraulic pressure applied with lever-flicks made the rock seem softer than it was, for when I manually dressed the footer troughs in preparation for pouring concrete, I could only make headway with a pickax. Dislodging the shale chunk by chunk was hard labor, the kind that led to fantasies of pneumatic drills and dynamite.

The relative impermeability of the subsoil meant that the drainfield needed to be about twice as large as normal. This was ascertained by a grizzled functionary from the county health department, who managed to lose his way three times before stumbling onto our lane. Together, we searched for percolation areas near the house site. I was armed with a two-handled posthole digger and an iron buggy axle sharpened on one end for splitting rocks. He was armed with a straw fedora and whiskey breath. The health department required three test holes, each a minimum of four feet deep, observed as they were dug.

Judging by the shale at the basement excavation, I had already suspected that the property wouldn't pass a "perk" test with flying colors. We were dealing with compacted hardpan and rock right beneath it. With two feet down and two feet to go, it felt as though I was punching a hole through the Rock of Gibraltar. Only by pounding repeatedly with the buggy axle could I crumble the shale sufficiently to extract it. For such tremendous effort, the progress was negligible, and to make matters worse, my overseer's patience was wearing thin.

As I rested to catch my second wind, I wondered about the fertility of the hayfields. Farming was on my mind. The land had been farmed for at least a hundred and fifty years, maybe longer, and a glance across the Lee-Jackson fence reaffirmed the ravages of soil depletion. There was no need to be digging so deeply. What I really wanted to be doing was collecting soil samples for analysis. Mentally, I tried to give the old bureaucrat the shove. Go watch someone else sweat his fool head off, I suggested via my brainwaves. The inspector eyed me with concern, as if heatstroke was responsible for my hostile stare.

Yet, conveniently, he gave a thumbs up on the very next hole. Had he seen enough of the Martinsburg? After he left, I proceeded to extract shallower core samples from six additional areas. Later, I mixed them together in a bucket and filled three small cardboard boxes and sent them to Virginia Polytechnic Institute in Blacksburg. A few weeks later, V.P.I. sent a printout to the effect that the soil was viable, and in good pH balance, too. It was more than an official stamp of approval; it was a positive prognosis, and I took it to be an invitation. The forty acres were inviting me to farm.

The grass, acre after acre of green grass, held a special appeal. Grass is a generic term that encompasses, as my dictionary states, "any of a large family (*Gramineae*) of monocotyledonous mostly herbaceous plants with jointed stems, slender sheathing leaves, and flowers borne in spikelets of bracts." Gramineae flourishes everywhere—on plains, prairies, deserts, savannas, jungles, mountaintops, marshes, even polar regions. Seeds ride the wind four thousand feet above the earth, as well as using lowlier means of transportation like digestive systems and fur or feather coats. Human commerce has been responsible for seed dispersal in unexpected ways. For example, the introduction of African grasses such as guinea-grass and molasses-grass occurred wherever slave ships made ports of call. (The tropical grasses had been the slaves' bedding on the voyage as well as feed for the animals carried with them.)

In the Shenandoah Valley of the 1860s and earlier, native grasses grew in the margin between the forests and cultivated fields. From the rocking chair on the front porch, I was surveying the descendant of native grasses, a modern blend of orchard grass mixed with fescue and red and white clover. Such an expanse of pasturage did not exist in the nineteenth century when livestock with bells around their necks foraged in the margin of tree stumps. It was impossible for me to tell how that margin had been distributed on the Haugh farm; fencelines had changed as cropland expanded, and the last of the great stumps had long since disappeared.

In the twentieth century, forage crops have been reinvented by seed geneticists. Strains are developed to combine the greatest nutritive value with the shortest growing season and the least cultivation. Crops are engineered for their resistance to the interference of insects and pests and competition from weeds. By and large, native grasses have become a nuisance, a throwback to the days before American agriculture began pumping iron. Competitive farmers demand stronger fertilizers, bigger machinery (for tillage, seeding, and harvesting), and freer use of chemicals. In 1986, the Farm Bureau in Cross Keys stocked seed for five fescues, five orchard grasses, three ryegrasses, eight clovers, four timothys, and eight alfalfas, as well as bluegrass, herdgrass, sorghum, millet, and sudangrass.

But I had a more limited agriculture in mind. The undersized hay operation that I was beginning to envision didn't need to be a test plot for miracle hybrids. Already, the fields were thickly thatched. By the conscientious application of low-input farming methods, I could keep the land productive, and keep it so indefinitely. The hay could be marketed directly from the barn to passersby who saw the Hay for Sale sign at the end of the driveway.

In former years, according to the farmer who sold us the land, the forty acres had been cropped in a three-year rotation of corn, wheat, and timothy. Such a rotation was commonly used to retard nitrogen depletion, especially prevalent with the growing of corn. A decade had passed since he had reseeded the fields in their current hay/pasture mix. Weeds such as Johnson grass, broomsedge, foxtail, and chicory were beginning to establish themselves, but a small percentage of weeds did not harm the forage value of the stand, he said. Certain weeds actually improved the palatability of hay, and this fact dovetailed quite nicely with my plans. I wanted to farm the battlefield in a way that would not change its gestalt, or turn it into something over which I would have to exert chemical control.

But when I shared my ideas with the county extension agent, I was summarily returned to the twentieth century. He recommended that I eradicate *all* extraneous plant matter with spot spraying of herbicides. An even better thing to do, he said, was to "Roundup" the fields (Roundup being a commercial herbicide) and start over. Moreover, he urged me to apply nitrogen fertilizer twice a year. I declined his advice because the fields were still reasonably productive and the overabundance of nitrogen in the runoff was responsible for algae growth in the ponds and creeks. Why be constantly jump-starting nature? Low-input farming sought to break such accreted regimens, even if it meant lower yields. I considered my refusal a pro-nature fusillade in the war against progress.

Maintaining a good hayfield, though, would mean more than driving a tractor over it at harvest time. During the year I was building the house, I was aware of my unavoidable contribution of neglect. Cedar seedlings sprang up in the sod. Thistles and nonnutritive, invasive weeds such as burdock and milkweed colonized broad areas. Groundhog holes appeared all over the place. Fences were breaking apart. A field thus booby-trapped by time and indifference was the nemesis of haymaking machinery. If I didn't get started soon, the option to make hay would simply disappear.

One of the first problems I tried to deal with was the groundhog overpopulation. On the forty acres, forty groundhogs must have been making an appearance on any given day, and their excavations were worrisome. These were not just gopher holes; some were more than two feet across, and almost as deep. The hard, unexpected jog of a tire rolling into one could actually throw a person right out of the tractor seat. Then, too, the damage to farm equipment that suddenly ran hard against the ground could be difficult and expensive to repair.

In a swale near the cross-fence, at the very center of the property, was the mother of groundhog dens. Its multiple entrances, with excavated shale mounded beside each one, implied generations of digging rodents, as well as numerous seasons during which tractor-drawn equipment had bumped over the uneven ground. When Earl was finishing a job in the neighborhood with his front-end loader, I saw the opportunity to get rid of the groundhogs and level the irregularities once and for all.

Earl pushed the ground flat in two passes, and I thought no more about the groundhogs for several weeks. Meanwhile, the orchard grass I had reseeded began to sprout. Then one day, a new entrance hole appeared, interrupting the greening like a taupe navel. It was business as usual for the den dwellers.

At this point, nine out of ten farmers would have reached for their high-powered rifles. The lone dissenter might have considered deploying a gas cartridge, or smoke bomb, which was what I did. The trick was to light the fuse, shove the cartridge underground, and block the hole with shovelfuls of dirt before the cartridge exploded. It meant working fast. If the fuse wasn't damp and the cartridge didn't malfunction (and the groundhogs were at home), they would die from sulfurous asphyxiation. I had used gas cartridges successfully on other field pests. It was a farmerly kind of eradication; lighting a match didn't bring out the blood lust that aiming a rifle did. But in this instance, my attempt failed miserably. The entrance hole reappeared after several days, just as wide, just as deep. Busy paws had excavated a fresh pile of shale, with the burnt cardboard cylinder of the spent cartridge on top.

Meanwhile, the Fourth of July was coming up. Mad with revenge, I concocted an improved weapon, one that fifteen-year-old Van heartily endorsed. To one end of a stick about five feet long, we taped a gas cartridge *and* a string of firecrackers recently acquired on a trip through South Carolina. With sewing thread, we bound the two fuses together. This would have the effect of a double whammy, a stun bomb. A better father-son project hadn't come along in months.

Before breakfast on the glorious Fourth, while the grass was silvered with dew, we carried our device to the swale. As we marched across the field, I envisioned a two-hundred-word submission to a farm journal, a testimonial about an inexpensive method of enhancing the reliability of a gas cartridge. Really, it was a clever idea, maybe even deserving of a patent. In high spirits, we began the countdown, but as soon as I lit the combined fuse and jammed the stick down the hole, even before Van could follow with shovelfuls of dirt, the firecrackers went off with a deafening blast. With my hand still on the stick and my head not more than two feet from the hole, it was I who was stunned.

The explosion blew the fuse right out of the cartridge, so we pulled out the stick, reinstalled the fuse (what was left of it), reignited the fuse, then pushed the stick back in the hole. The cartridge fired before the stick was fully inserted, but we managed to seal in most of the gas. The end of the stick thrust obliquely into the air and we left it that way. We were hungry for a holiday breakfast.

Over the next two weeks, periodic inspections confirmed that the stick was still standing and the hole remained plugged. With conspiratorial chuckles, father and son recounted their bumbling deed in farmer-ese: "Popped them li'l boogers' eardrums, fer sure! Almost popped our own, by gum!" But had we succeeded in killing the groundhogs? We assumed the odds were growing with each passing day.

And then, one morning, the stick lay flat on the ground and there were *two* newly dug entrances. Our efforts counted for naught. We were witnessing firsthand the time-worn truism that critters could (and would) outsmart farmers.

Well, that very morning, a synchronized attack was initiated — two shovels, two cartridges, two fuses, and two matchbooks — but why prolong the account of our futility? Suffice it to say, a generation of sulfur-sniffing groundhogs may have been in residence under the battlefield, and if so, I should have been reaching for my rifle weeks earlier, with a bow of obeisance to the wise majority.

I had better luck with eradicating plants. Thistles were a particular nuisance. Their seeds blew everywhere. Once a field was overgrown with them, it was all but useless except for minimal grazing. There were cattle farmers in the neighborhood who did exactly that, who paid no mind to the proliferation of their thistles. If a farm wasn't producing hay, it didn't matter if thistles took over. And if the farm was sold to a developer, the developer's first act would be to strip the land of its topsoil. Then, nothing at all would grow.

Anticipating no such future for our forty acres, I made a belated commitment to getting rid of the thistles that were on the verge of multiplying out of control. I enlisted the aid of Van and Hope, who both understood the need for decisive action and were eager to help. We began our anti-thistle campaign in the cool mornings of early June, right before the blooms went to seed. We dug thistles, and we dug them with a vengeance.

The trick was to use a good, sharp shovel. We couldn't just clip the stalks. The bulbous taproots sent up new shoots almost overnight unless they were mortally damaged. Taking seven years to mature, the prickly plants grew to six feet and taller, with root tendrils radiating almost as far into the hardpan. Thistles were the assertive survivors of primitive eons; they didn't come out of the ground without a fight. When one was severed and ready to fall over, the digger was glad for the protection of long sleeves, gloves, and a hat with a brim.

As we worked, I couldn't help but think of an easier way—herbicidal spraying. Americans rarely farm with hand tools anymore, except as a last resort. Silo unloaders, skid loaders, blowers, conveyor belts—and most prominently of all, chemicals—do the work formerly done by two hands and a strong back. When had I last seen a farmer in a field with a shovel?

But herbicides are double-edged swords. On too many fields, the evidence was plain: killing one type of weed only enhanced the growth of another. Thistles readily succumbed to poison, but equally problematic weeds sprang up in their place. Some farmers poured salt on freshly chopped thistle stems, a plausible option in a confined area. A neighbor on the other side of the Lee-Jackson property used a weighted hoe that added momentum to his chopping stroke. My children and I found that a direct attack with the blade of a shovel worked best. I drove the pickup in first gear, while Hope and Van sat on the opened tailgate, ready to jump off. The sighting of quarry, tall as an adult and topped with violet blooms, sent us into action. We were hungry for the kill. We exhibited strong herbicidal tendencies. Taproots were sliced with well-aimed stabs. Often, it took some hacking at the tendrils, plus hard leverage—bending the shovel handle almost to the breaking point—before the offending plant toppled to the ground.

The thistle-digging scenario varied with the terrain, but in the course of a morning we eradicated them by the hundreds. By noon we were flushed with exertion, our fingers cramped from gripping our weapon-tools so intensely. At field corners we planned to rest, but didn't because there were always a few more thistles ahead. When we finally reached a stopping place, we flopped down in the tall grass shaded by fenceline cedars, the shovel blades shiny at our side.

As we reclined, the pungent odor of catnip rewove the fabric of our equilibrium. We gazed out across the hayfield, a playground for butterflies. Birdcalls and breeze mingled with the drone of honeybees. The green grass broiled brilliantly in the heat-shimmer. On a not dissimilar morning in an earlier June, one army advanced toward another over this very ground. Later, shovels were carried across the fields, but not for the purpose of digging weeds.

TEN

In the vicinity of Cross Keys, it isn't easy to gain a sense of orientation as to what actually happened on June 8, 1862. The bronze inscription bequeathed by the United Daughters of the Confederacy isn't much help. The blue lines and gray lines, red lines and white lines of the Virginia Department of Transportation's battle map on the Keezletown Road look like something for a military cryptologist to decipher. Still another public reminder of the battle, an equally obscure map on a peeling plywood panel outside the Cross Keys–Mill Creek Ruritan Hall – formerly Union Church (no connection with the Yankees) – is remarkable only for its weathered appearance.

In terms of size and stimulation, none of these compares with the Jackson Electric Map, on display at the Harrisonburg-Rockingham Historical Society in downtown Harrisonburg. This is a floor-to-ceiling depiction of the entire Valley Campaign. Like a shrine, it stands in a room of its own.

Dating from the early 1960s, the map has been recently overhauled and computerized. It shows the route taken by Stonewall Jackson's army as it marched for three months up and down the Shenandoah Valley, and made forays into and across the mountains to either side. The surface of the map is in garish green bas-relief, studded with blinking lights that illuminate the army's progress, accompanied by a twenty-minute voice-over and musical dub. As the battles are described one by one, the lights at the battle sites flash like cockpit warnings. At intervals, the whole map is lit up like a marquee.

The audio component adds insult to injury. A narrator with a style just short of buffoonery works the windy script. The first time I heard it, I recognized the voice of countless training films and nature videos, a gentleman so soothing, so authoritarian that it was difficult not to imbibe his every word. Although his elocution was impeccable, there was a pained overlay to his purse-mouthed diction that crept under my skin. His tone was too sincere. And in the background swelled the music of old Warner Bros. cartoons: the coyote stalking the roadrunner, the pirate scheming the downfall of the duck. Storm clouds gathered, weary marchers tramp-tramp-tramped, ignorant armies clashed by night. As the recitation unfolded, it was impossible to keep a straight face.

I have sat through it three times. The first was for my own edification, the second and third times were in polite escort of relatives and friends visiting from out of town. My negative assessment may be simply the result of overexposure.

The story of the Valley Campaign is a fascinating one when shorn of mawkishness and febrile high drama. Thomas Jonathan "Stonewall" Jackson matured from history professor to army general in a matter of weeks. His daring stratagems of mobility and speed utterly confounded Lincoln and his war cabinet. Many of Jackson's own subordinates thought he was crazy (Major General Richard S. Ewell, a division leader in Jackson's corps, said, "I never saw one of Jackson's couriers approach without expecting an order to assault the North Pole"), and there were times when his march-weary troops frankly hated him, yet Jackson could always rally his army when battle action was imminent. As he privately pondered, then implemented maneuvers of attack and retreat, he focused both the empathy of his compatriots and the precious manpower resources of his enemies. Single-handedly, he controlled the defense of the Shenandoah Valley in the late winter and spring of 1862.

The year had begun quietly enough for both armies, with the majority of both Union and Confederate forces bivouacked in winter quarters. The South was just beginning to experience the shortages that were resulting from the ever-tightening naval blockade, but morale was high. The North was still clinging to the idea that the war would be brief, although major military victories had been few and far between. Major General George B. McClellan, the "Union Napoleon," was recovering from typhoid fever and giving President Abraham Lincoln the runaround with respect to the proposed movement of his vast Army of the Potomac out of its camps around Washington and in the direction of the capital of the Confederacy at Richmond. Determined to get the war effort moving by spring, Lincoln issued his General War Order No. 1 on January 27, 1862, calling for an across-the-board advance of land and naval forces against the Confederates by Washington's birthday. McClellan's army slowly migrated southward by the longest and safest route, by water to the Virginia Peninsula, from where he planned to move northwest toward Richmond. In Kentucky and western Tennessee, Brigadier General Ulysses S. Grant saw the chance for action against the Confederate front at Fort Henry and Fort Donelson along the Tennessee River, and took it. His success in the first weeks of February earned him a hero's reputation and a promotion, and the eastern flank of the Mississippi was no longer in Rebel control.

By March, the Confederate War Department deemed it necessary to empower Major General Albert Sidney Johnston with 40,000 troops to move northward from Corinth, Mississippi, in order to crush Grant before he could be reinforced. At Pittsburg Landing, Tennessee, on April 6, the Confederates launched a surprise attack and gained a temporary victory, but Johnston was killed, and in the confusion of the change of command, Grant, now reinforced, was able to take the field the following day. This bloodbath was Shiloh, a two-day fight that resulted in more than 23,700 casualties.

Back to the east, the Union leadership was especially concerned with the vulnerability of its coastal cities, the navy yard at Norfolk having been abandoned almost a year earlier. On March 8, the Union fleet anchored in Hampton Roads was attacked by the Confederate ironclad *Virginia*, fashioned from the scuttled hull of the former Federal warship *Merrimack*. The next day, John Ericsson's innovative *Monitor* steamed up the channel, and the standoff between the two low-profile gun platforms changed the course of naval history.

In early April, having gained the Peninsula by the sea route, McClellan's 100,000-man force got bogged down before Yorktown, where he encountered an entrenched Confederate position. He requested reinforcements of Major General Nathaniel P. Banks, who was operating in the northern Shenandoah Valley with 38,000 men. Banks was kept busy by his brushes with–and losses to–Jackson's much smaller force of less than 4,000 and Jackson's cavalry of 600, under the command of Lieutenant-Colonel Turner Ashby.

Banks complied with McClellan's order, and began marching two of his three divisions toward Fredericksburg. The division that remained, commanded by Brigadier General James A. Shields, was charged with holding the area around Winchester, Virginia, a town that was considered to be strategically important because it was only seventy miles west of Washington, north of the northern end of the Massanutten Range with easy access to the capital. Jackson struck hard against Shields's 9,000 troops several miles south of Winchester at Kernstown on March 23. Although the Confederates were driven from the field with high casualties (455, which included many men missing), Jackson managed to inflict even higher casualties (568) on the Union troops. The battle focused strong attention on the Shenandoah Valley from Washington and Richmond. Banks was detached from McClellan's command and sent back to Winchester. Jackson was able to learn from his tactical mistakes and go on to win battles at McDowell (May 8) and again at Winchester (May 25) as well as numerous smaller events.

From the west, Banks was reinforced by Major General Frémont with 15,000 troops, and from the east, Major General Irvin McDowell's corps added an additional 20,000. Jackson was reinforced too, most prominently by Ewell's division of 8,500, eventually bringing his troop strength to 16,000. The forces Lincoln was converging against him posed an overwhelming danger. The trap was set, but never sprung, for Jackson's superior mobility enabled him to slip away to the south. By early June, only the two Union armies of Frémont and Shields, with an attrited force of 11,000 and 8,500, respectively, were pursuing Jackson southward, each along one side of the Massanutten Range, potentially positioned for a pincer if they could join forces at the end of the mountainous divide. Jackson's knowledge of military history may have enabled him to relate his predicament to Napoleon's during the Second Italian Campaign of 1800. Two Austrian armies, separated by a similar mountain range, had been bearing down upon the retreating French army, but Napoleon had chosen to fight each of them in turn, and defeated both.

Jackson's plan was to keep Frémont and Shields apart, so that each could be dealt with individually by his army, which by this time had shrunk to 12,500 (Jackson's rapid marching always left stragglers). As the electric map illustrates, Jackson parked most of Ewell's division astride the road to Port Republic near Cross Keys to hold Frémont in check while he proceeded with his own troops four miles southeast, across the North River bridge to Port Republic. This was a prime defensive locale, for just below the town the North and South rivers converged to form the South Fork of the Shenandoah. There he intended to meet and defeat Shields, then wheel back on Frémont with his combined force.

The plan was well-conceived, even though it didn't materialize quite the way Jackson thought it would. Frémont engaged Ewell in the terrifying artillery duel at Cross Keys. On the Confederate right, Brigadier General Isaac R. Trimble met an inept offensive with a surprise rebuff and countercharge. Frémont fell back, thus failing to join forces with

Shields. Upon hearing of the success at Cross Keys, but plagued by an unanticipated incursion from Shields's advance forces as well as logistical problems while fording the rain-swollen South River (a temporary bridge of wagons placed end to end then planked over was singularly ineffective), Jackson called for Ewell's troops to rejoin *him*. Trimble's brigade, the last of the Confederates to cross over the North River, destroyed the bridge so that by the time Frémont's troops arrived, they were prevented from coming to the aid of Shields's struggling army.

The battle at Port Republic was equally fierce. Heavy casualties were inflicted on both sides as the lines of engagement wavered. The commanding Union artillery position overlooking the plain of battle was lost and retaken two times before it was captured by the Confederates and turned to their advantage. At length, the smaller Union fighting force under the command of Shields's subordinate, Brigadier General Erastus B. Tyler, was overpowered and pursued in retreat northward toward the town of Conrad's Store, now called Elkton, twelve miles back on the Luray road. After a few days' hesitation (fearing a renewed offensive by Frémont that didn't materialize), Jackson allowed his victorious soldiers an extended respite three miles to the south near Weyer's Cave, now the town of Grottoes (the present Weyer's Cave was reincorporated five miles to the west), until June 18, when Lee's Southern Command ordered him to march toward Richmond. The Valley Campaign was over. It hadn't been quite the linear, goosebump-raising whupping the electric map portrays; rather, it had been a meandering, improvisational march, plotted against the threat of an uncertain and blundering enemy.

So when the lights blinked on and off at Cross Keys, and the syrupy voice-over trembled with stage emotion while the music reeled from climax to climax, I closed my eyes and ears momentarily. I refused to be taken hostage in that darkened, airless room with two dozen folding chairs and a donation jar on a pedestal in a corner. Instead, I was home on the battlefield, where the birds sang and the grass grew and there was nothing to restructure my feelings except the heat of a June morning—the dazzling brightness of sun bordered by somber patches of leaf-cast shade.

ELEVEN

O<small>F THE DOZEN OR MORE HOUSES</small> in the vicinity of the
battle at Cross Keys, every one was pressed into service as a makeshift
hospital, with the willing or unwilling cooperation of the inhabitants.
Bloodstains on the floor are reported to be visible in several of the houses
and outbuildings that are still standing. To the north and west were
hospitals for the Yankees; to the south and east were the Rebel hospitals.
One or two houses, it was said, held wounded from both sides.

The tavern at Cross Keys filled quickly with Union casualties. As
many as eighty soldiers were evacuated there in the course of the battle,
and one by one, they either died or healed as the days and weeks passed.
Today, the old building is still there, and still inhabited, but due to the
straightening of the highway in the present century, it is located directly
behind the low brick edifice of the Cross Keys Farm Bureau, the successor to Yager's Store.

The former tavern and its collapsing front porch convey nineteen decades of wear and tear. Home to a poor family whose discards are strewn
about the front yard, the old place looks ten shades of gray, from its unpainted weatherboard to its broken second-story windows stuffed with
blankets. Even the scraggly bushes against the limestone foundation look
ashen.

Dogs scavenge from the Farm Bureau's trash dumpster, a pungent blue
cube anchoring one corner of the yard. The proximity of the dumpster
to the house suggests the obvious: the old eyesore is ready to be thrown
away. So what if it was a way station on an early Valley thoroughfare?
So what if it was a battlefield hospital? Today, its history counts for
naught. Its propinquity to the loading and dumping zone of the agricultural cooperative renders it superfluous and isolated – a worthless piece
of real estate, a slum.

From the earliest days, there had always been one thriving store in

Cross Keys. In recent years, the Farm Bureau was scaled back from a general merchandise outlet to little more than a convenience store, although it still sold farm supplies and feed until it closed in 1991. On a typical visit, I drove in, pumped ten dollars of gas, exchanged pleasantries with the person behind the cash register, and left. As I backed out of the parking space, I'd catch a glimpse of the tavern, a backdrop to the bulk feed tanks and the dumpster. At times, it looked so weatherbeaten, so forlorn, it could have passed for a mirage.

In eighteenth-century England, the sign of crossed keys stood for hospitality, hostelry, and safe haven. When I served in the Navy twenty-five years ago, I wore a sleeve-patch of crossed keys, the designation of ship's storekeeper. There may have been a religious significance to the symbol as well.

In a pictorial directory of county landmarks, published some years ago, the tavern rated a full-page black-and-white photograph which hinted at its former prosperity. It had been a bustling alehouse, post office, and stagecoach depot for the better part of the nineteenth century. After Yager took it over, the drygoods store was installed in a newer frame building next door (also extant), the immediate forerunner of the Farm Bureau.

The tavern has a symmetry similar to that of the Haugh house, although it was built earlier and is somewhat larger. Like the Haugh house, it is a two-story, full dovetail-notched log structure (sided with clapboard) abutted on both ends by chimneys, the difference being that the tavern chimneys are flush with the siding. The wide masonry that accommodates both an upstairs and a downstairs fireplace provides additional structural integrity as well as an elegance quite beyond that of a traditional farmhouse. Though at first glance, the tavern appears to be about as run-down as an old place can get, a closer inspection reveals a subtle perpendicularity, thanks to the limestone on the end walls.

Still, time hovers over the building like a bird of prey, waiting to swoop down and claim it with the full approval of the local populace. Its rusted, sagging roof looks bad, bitten at the eaves by corrosion and stained with ochres and siennas like a Morris Louis canvas. Even as the roof stays in place, the old house is being devoured from within; evidence of termites and borers is manifest at corners and siding laps—dribbles of digested wood, wiggly incisions. If the structure is soon to fall in a heap of lacy wood and chinking, its chimneys will succumb, in turn, only to the brute force of a bulldozer.

In the meantime, it remains a viable abode, a survivor of an earlier point in commerce when there were hitching posts instead of parking lots. Between its front porch and the windowless rear wall of the Farm Bureau, an expanse of dandelions, empty gallon jugs, plastic dairy crates, and flattened cardboard boxes bridges the span of almost two centuries. It would be a picturesque scene to the watercolorist in me seeking to wring sentiment from substance, but to my history-conscious self, it is a cruel portrait, a reminder that the past is often nobler than the present. Only a conspiracy for expediency leaves relics such as this in society's midst. The old house *is* Cross Keys. It needs no pedigree or plaque – it is the original. But to the people inside and next door and down the road, it is a meaningless antique. Nobody wants the responsibility of tearing it down or fixing it up. It has stood in a landscape of change for so long that nobody, not even its inhabitants, takes notice anymore.

At the very least, the Cross Keys Tavern belongs on the National Register of Historic Buildings. Why is everyone looking the other way? Is there no echo of the stagecoaches as they lumbered to a halt, of boisterous travelers and local revelers quaffing the foaming brew? Is there no reverberation of the screams of an amputee, the moans of a dying farm boy, a feverish prayer whispered in German, or muffled sounds of battle to the southeast?

On a larger scale, if a person cares to think about it, the old tavern mimics the degraded environment of the entire region. I have lived here long enough to be acutely aware of the ravages, although few people publicly share my sentiment. To resort to overly lush prose while describing the Shenandoah Valley is a not uncommon practice among writers. Fabled in song and verse, valleys are the geographical haunts of peace and prosperity, fertile clefts between inhospitable hills. This particular valley has been touted time and again for being akin to the original Eden. "This is such beautiful country!" visitors tell me on more occasions than I can remember. "You are soooo lucky!" I nod my head, and let them keep their rose-tinted illusions. It is easier for me to nod my head than to enumerate the complaints and qualifications I harbor within it.

To be sure, there is much in these environs worth waxing enthusiastic about – the history, the climate, the agrarian community that still functions to a large extent. I do not wish to dwell on the negative, but for the sake of the un-technicolored truth, I cannot overlook the aspects that corrupt the quality of life here, to which I have grown so accustomed that I hardly note their presence, much less their insidious magnification.

Visitors to the battlefield often remark about the purity of the air. Compared to the atmosphere of Washington, D.C., or another choked metropolis, it is indeed pure. On most days, visitors can inhale draughts of the rural ether and view the wonders of the locale without their eyes and lungs smarting from airborne irritants.

There are days, though, when the air literally stinks. Farmers fertilize their fields with hog sludge and poultry litter, the former smelling like the rawest of cesspools, the latter smelling like a gagging, ammoniacal issue from hell. Proximity is critical to the tolerance level. During our tenure at the Haugh house, windows had to remain shut on days when our nearest neighbor rolled by with his "honey wagon." The fertilized field extended to within ten feet of the farmhouse, and sludge was spread on a biweekly basis.

Our earlier experience with the turkey farmer on the hill should have acclimatized us to the odors of agribusiness. Prior to erecting the world-class poultry facility, he had dumped tons and tons of poultry litter alongside our fence and right of way. Although he failed to build up our tolerance for the smell to come, he was only doing what hundreds of other poultry producers in the vicinity have done and will continue to do—he was expanding his operation. His waste management (or mis-management) program affected everybody within a mile. We just happened to be at the epicenter, but our plight was commonplace. The feed mills in Harrisonburg are responsible for its reputation as the city that smells like dogfood.

There are other odors to contend with. The damp air of a Valley night is fraught with the errant molecules of industry. Every tall stack which protrudes above a local industrial plant is emitting, likely as not, a corrosive, a caustic, or a carcinogen. Illegal venting under cover of darkness is a routine practice; why else would those smells be noticeable at all? The Valley is no industrial corridor, no Bayonne-to-Wilmington, yet its skies carry the same crepuscular smogs. On nights when the industrial odors are especially sharp, I lie awake, wondering how much more abuse the old planet can take. When hundreds of millions of insomniacs pass the night with similar thoughts, perhaps something will be done. The science of ecology is in its nascent stages, and attempts at planetary cleanup seem faddishly inconsequential, like pinpricks on the behemoth. Yellow slickers and rubber boots, measuring devices and pointed fingers are clinical reactions to very unclinical situations. What is needed is an overhaul of the greedy corporate heart.

As mentioned earlier, the use of fertilizers—specifically nitrates in organic and inorganic compounds – has left its mark on the bodies of water in the neighborhood. Our new pond immediately began clotting over with bright green filamentous algae from June through September, thanks to the overrich runoff from a hog farm upstream. In places, the algal growth was so dense we couldn't wedge a canoe through it. But how was I to tell our pork-producing neighbor that his livelihood was fucking up our recreational pond? The land was zoned A-1. There was no way to alleviate the cause, short of breaking the law. Instead, we tried to deal with the effects.

Van and Hope and I attempted to rake out the algae with garden rakes, but we only succeeded in breaking the rake handles. We waded in with an old tennis net, but the algae-clogged net became too heavy to pull. We grabbed great armloads of green and heaved them ashore, but the job was too disgusting. We flung paddlefuls from the path of the canoe – too tiring. As a last resort, we dumped in a bag of outrageously priced algicide, which killed a few fish before a rainstorm flushed it down the standpipe. It would have taken fifty bags to kill the algae.

In the end we just gave up. Like everyone else, we accepted that the algae was there to stay. Now it comes and goes in various seasonal amounts – a color, a texture, a presence that owes its origin to competitive farming.

Another kind of pollution garners less attention because it is easier to tune out, yet, unarguably, it is the most pervasive of all. Rare is a moment devoid of human-generated sound. It suffuses the countryside like smoke, varying in density between a whisper and a roar. Even in the dead of winter, when the snow is falling and the fields and woods are absolutely still, the reverberations of human restlessness go on – the scraping of a snowplow, the throaty purr of a farm tractor, an airplane high above the clouds. During the rest of the year, noise pollution reaches significant levels, culminating in a daily barrage of gunshots at the approach of hunting season, when our neighbors on Route 708 sight-in their weaponry.

One summer afternoon, having nothing better to do, I logged two minutes of invasive noise, a record that was typical of a much longer span of time. The following transcription proves that stillness, absolute stillness – excluding the constant of nature's background symphony – is as remote a possibility as a meteorite landing on the roof of the barn.

1) Borne upon the wind from the northwest, a repetitive crescendo and diminuendo of traffic whoosh on Port Republic Road.

2) From somewhere – can't pinpoint exactly – an agricultural motor, perhaps a silo unloader.
3) Airplane flying overhead. Faint enough to be a commercial jetliner at 35,000 ft.
4) Throaty vibration of heavy equipment to the north. Must be bulldozing for the poultry barn near the crossroads.
5) Gunshots, distant. Groundhog eradication?
6) Popping of metal roof as sun comes out from behind cloud – but this doesn't count.
7) Small airplane SE to NW, directly overhead.
8) Another airplane.
9) Barking dog and man's voice, SW. Calling cattle?
10) Another airplane.
11) Automobile horn.
12) Truck passing on Rt. 708.
13) Hammering to the east.

The continuous overlay of human-generated sound was as much a part of the environment as the grass and the trees – a paean to the complexity and diversity of the twentieth century. Everyone contributed, and rightly so. There was no escaping it, not even in one's dreams.

Later that afternoon, I added my own drum to the ambient hum by driving to the mailbox on Port Republic Road. Without thinking, I caused the drivetrain to whine in varying frequencies as I shifted gears. Tires crunched on the gravel, and the suspension of the old pickup creaked as it jounced over the potholes. On the way back, I stopped at the barn to do some maintenance on the tractor. Add door slam of truck. Add screech of barn door rollers. Add tractor.

I remembered the first time I walked the battlefield at night, not long after my initial contact with the farmer who sold us the land. Before concluding the deal, I had wanted to find out what the forty acres looked, sounded, and smelled like after dark, and I wanted Becky to experience it, too.

It was a mild evening, and we were in a celebratory mood. We carried a chilled bottle of champagne and two plastic cups over the fence to the crest of one field (where Union artillery had been positioned, as I was to learn later). Uncorking the wine, we drank a toast to the splendor of the country night, and to our good fortune in finding for ourselves what no realtor had been able to find for us.

Over our heads, amid the stars, artificial satellites were orbiting and airplanes were blinking. On the horizon, at least twenty dusk-to-dawn security lights shone from neighboring farms. Behind them, the reflected glow from Harrisonburg was a pale, inverted bowl to the north. At all points, the pungent aroma of agriculture wafted on the night breeze, mixed with chemical scents I could not identify. In the distance, a stereo played. And the traffic, the monotonous highway traffic passing half a mile from where we sat, was amplified by a directional wind that made it seem as if we were curbside to a freeway.

All of a sudden, I began to have my doubts. Actually, I was a little embarrassed to have raved about the property so, to have insisted that Becky come out with me to this cosmically disturbed field to bear witness to the polluted night.

"I really love this place," she exclaimed.

TWELVE

The peculiar journalistic slant of *Leslie's Illustrated*, while strongly sympathetic to the North, described the Battle of Cross Keys in a way that explicated the page-long engraving from Edwin Forbes's sketch of the battlefield. Captioned "Opening of the Fight," the longitudinal copy across the right side of the page went as follows:

> By one of those singular chances which have made the conventional day of rest the day of famous battles, on the morning of Sunday, June 8th, 1862, the advance of General Frémont's army came up with the Confederate forces at Cross Keys, about six miles to the south of Harrisonburg. The enemy were posted among wood, and their position was much strengthened by the uneven surface of the ground. Before the Federals was spread an open amphitheatre, not of level ground, but of rolling hills skirted by forests, which completely shielded the enemy. General Stahl, who, with his brigade had the left, advanced, driving the enemy's outposts through a thick belt of timber, and over an open wheat field into quite a thick wood. It was while crossing this wheat field in pursuit that his own Eighth New York Regiment suffered much loss. The enemy, ambushed in the wheat on the edge of the field, behind the fence, and in the woods, suddenly revealed themselves by a terrible fire that cut down nearly the whole of the two companies in advance. In accordance with their usual tactics they then gave way, and Stahl drove them back at the point of the bayonet until he found his brigade with its batteries nearly surrounded. They pressed around the guns, but the pelting storm of grape and canister, with the rifles of the brave Bucktails, who were detained to the support of the batteries, held them at bay. Stahl's command then fell back, at first in some confusion, but finally in good order, and took position on the open ground, expecting the enemy to follow; but *they* preferred the woods, and made no pursuit.

Forbes's sketch portrayed the Union reserve awaiting orders to advance. A train of ambulances was parked in the immediate foreground, although its corpsmen succored no casualties, for Forbes's tender sensibilities censored any effects of the near side of the artillery duel. Instead, shells burst in the air like fireworks, nonlethal and illuminating.

The artist's point of view, like the copywriter's, implied a moral judgment against the defensively positioned Confederates. Unlike the Yankees, in resplendent abundance to the left and right on the open plain, "they" took pot shots from behind trees and bushes. "They" didn't have the guts to come out and fight.

But in 1862, forests were the predominant feature of the landscape. The road between Harrisonburg and Port Republic was bordered by thick woods, a far cry from the modern artery that leaves Harrisonburg in a welter of convenience stores and condominiums. Today, the vicinity of the mile-wide line of battle has become a panorama of cultivated fields, farm buildings, and paved highways, not to mention the multitude of single-family dwellings that nibble away at the road frontage. The ground chosen by the Confederates still dominates the countryside, so that even the most nearsighted student of the battle will not fail to see the advantageous lay of the land, but now field margins ghost the deciduous fullness of the past. Only a rim of woods outlines the bluff at the center and left of the Confederate line, and to the right, a few oaks and hickories remain where Trimble's brigade stood.

In 1865, Frémont was requested by the War Department to submit a general report of his operations from March 29 through June 27, 1862, the period during which he commanded the Mountain Department of the Union Army. The report was an apologia for his modus operandi three and a half years earlier, and in it he described the situation as he had arrived at Cross Keys:

> The enemy occupied a position of uncommon strength, commanding the junction of the roads to Port Republic. He had chosen his ground with great skill and with a previous full knowledge of the localities. His main line was advantageously posted upon a ridge, protected in front by a steep declivity, and almost entirely masked by thick woods and covered by fences. Near his center, and on the summit of a marshy creek, he had massed, in addition to his guns elsewhere, three of his best batteries . . . It was almost impossible to force this position by a regular attack in front, which would have exposed us to cross-fires and flank attacks, and to have attacked him irregularly and

at random on either of his flanks would have carried us off the roads into wooded and broken ground of which I was entirely ignorant, and would very certainly have resulted in disaster.

In Ewell's report, submitted to Jackson the week after the battle, the description of the topography was identical, if briefer:

The general features of the ground were a valley and rivulet in my front, woods on both flanks, and a field of some hundreds of acres where the road crossed the center of my line, my side of the valley being more defined and commanding than the other.

The South never had an indigenous weekly newspaper with the impact of *Leslie's* or *Harper's*. While Forbes and other artists contributed visually to the Yankee civilians' appetite for news of the war, Southerners relied on word-of-mouth reports from the front and their own sparsely illustrated dailies. The telegraph link to Richmond was frequently nonfunctional, unlike its counterpart to Washington, which usually relayed messages within a day, or two at the most. This was not to say that the illustrated weeklies weren't perused, when available, in the South; its public thirsted for news from any source, however dated. The Northern slant only challenged Southern civilians to read a little more carefully between the lines.

To be evenhanded, therefore, in understanding the battle at Cross Keys, I had to study it as an event in and of itself, not as a polemic for the shortcomings of John C. Frémont or the brilliance of Thomas J. Jackson, or vice versa. Jackson wasn't there, and Frémont, though he was most definitely there, could just as easily have been absent. On that fateful Sunday, the foibles of human nature were as responsible for the outcome as military cause and effect.

Jackson had been wreaking havoc on the confidence of the War Department in Washington. His army's speed and clout, bolstered by the sympathetic civilian population in the Shenandoah Valley, had hamstrung all attempts by Union forces to take control of the region. When Jackson feinted at Harper's Ferry as if to leave the Valley, an alarm went up that he was marching on the capital city. When he marched over the Blue Ridge toward Charlottesville, it was feared that he was on his way to Richmond to blindside George B. McClellan (although the Rebel "Foot Cavalry" promptly returned by railway to Staunton). And since Kernstown, whenever Jackson fought, he tailored the circumstances to give himself the overwhelming force. He wrote:

Always mystify, mislead and surprise the enemy if possible; and when you strike and overcome him, never let up in the pursuit so long as your men have the strength to follow; for an army routed, if hotly pursued, becomes panic-stricken. The other rule is, never fight against heavy odds, if by any possible maneuvering you can hurl your own force on only a part, and that at the weakest part of your enemy and crush it. Such tactics will win every time, and a small army may destroy a large one in detail, and repeated victory will make it invincible.

No one felt the sting of Jackson's successes more than Abraham Lincoln. The president personally ordered his field commanders to try this and try that, stating his goal in the baldest of terms by issuing a directive to finish off Jackson's army once and for all. Still, nothing seemed to work.

The problem stemmed from Lincoln's generals or, more accurately, from his relationship with his generals. The rash of centralized orders coming from the War Department in Washington contrasted sharply with the dissemination of Confederate military directives. Lee was giving Jackson few, if any, specific orders. Jackson marched and fought as he saw fit, while his Union counterparts in the Shenandoah Valley took their cues from telegraph or courier dispatches. The short leash was Lincoln and Secretary of War Edwin M. Stanton's way of keeping the war effort accountable and, they hoped, as brief as possible, but it had the opposite effect.

Then, too, Lincoln made a disastrous choice—not his first—in Frémont. The famous explorer, nicknamed "The Pathfinder of the West," who had been nominated as the Republican Party's first presidential candidate in 1856 (but was defeated by James Buchanan), had a checkered history of military competence. In March 1862, on the heels of Frémont's ignominiously canceled command of the Department of the West in St. Louis, Lincoln appointed him to command the Mountain Department in western Virginia. It was an appointment of political expediency. Lincoln mistrusted Frémont, and the latter made no secret of his distaste for the presidential leadership. The messages passed between Washington and the field illustrate this discord; Lincoln castigated Frémont like a wayward son, while Frémont badgered the president for more supplies, manpower, and authority.

On May 24, 1862, Stanton telegraphed Frémont in Franklin, Western Virginia, telling him of General Nathaniel P. Banks's defeat in an engagement at Front Royal against Jackson and urging him to move his forces to Banks's support in the direction of Strasburg and Winchester. Frémont's reflexive reply was to complain about scant rations and the need for requisitioning 400 more horses.

Upon receiving this reply, the president himself fired off a message:

War Department,
May 24, 1862 — 4 P.M.

Major-General Frémont, Franklin:
You are authorized to purchase 400 horses or take them wherever or however you can get them.

The exposed condition of General Banks makes his immediate relief a point of paramount importance. You are therefore directed by the President to move against Jackson at Harrisonburg, and operate against the enemy in such a way as to relieve Banks. This movement must be made immediately. You will acknowledge the receipt of this order and specify the hour it is received by you.

A. LINCOLN.

Frémont sent word back to "His Excellency Abraham Lincoln" that he would "move as ordered." Lincoln acknowledged the reply in a second, briefer telegram, thanking Frémont and urging him to "Put the utmost speed into it. Do not lose a minute."

But the Pathfinder took his time. He sent scouting parties along the several roads to Harrisonburg, thirty-six miles to the east. They returned to inform him that the most direct route was blocked by trees felled by the Rebels. Meanwhile, Stanton sent Frémont two more messages, both containing bad news: the first announcing that Banks had fallen back from Strasburg to Winchester and was being driven toward Harper's Ferry, and the second, two days later, announcing that the defeated Banks had been forced across the Potomac at Williamsport. Frémont decided to march his army on a road in a wholly different direction, the road along which his supply trains were stationed.

May 27, 1862 — 9:58 P.M.

Major-General Frémont:
I see that you are at Moorefield. You were expressly ordered to march to Harrisonburg. What does this mean?

A. LINCOLN.

The next morning, Frémont replied:

Headquarters in the Field,
May 28, 1862 — 6 A.M.
(Received 10:50 A.M.)

My troops were in no condition to execute your order otherwise
than has been done. They have marched day and night to do it. The
men had had so little to eat that many were weak for want of food,
and were so reported by the chief surgeon. Having for main object,
as stated in your telegram, the relief of General Banks, the line of
march followed was a necessity. In executing any order received I
take it for granted that I am to exercise discretion concerning its literal
execution, according to circumstances. If I am to understand that
literal obedience to orders is required, please say so. I have no desire
to exercise any power which you do not think belongs of necessity
to my position in the field.

J. C. FRÉMONT,
Major-General.

An hour later, Frémont elaborated,

The reasons for my being in Moorefield are, 1st, the point of your
order was to relieve General Banks. At the time it was issued, it was
only known that he had been attacked at Front Royal. When my
march commenced I knew he had retreated from Winchester. 2d. Of
the different roads to Harrisonburg all but one, and that one leading
southward, had been obstructed by the enemy, and if the loss of time
by taking the only open road were no consideration, it was still a simple impossibility to march in that direction. My troops were utterly
out of provisions. There was nothing whatever to be found in the
country except a small quantity of fresh beef, from the effects of
which the troops were already suffering, and, in fact, all my men were
only saved from starvation by taking the road to Petersburg, where
they found five days' rations. With these we are now moving with
the utmost celerity possible in whatever direction the enemy may be
found.

J. C. FRÉMONT,
Major-General.

Since the point was moot, Lincoln and Stanton agreed to keep
Frémont's army in Moorefield for the time being. Reconnaissance units
were sent out to locate the main body of Jackson's force. Due to the
ubiquitous presence of Turner Ashby's Confederate cavalry, it was often
difficult to determine Jackson's whereabouts. Ashby commanded a large,
relatively undisciplined body of horsemen that readily fragmented into

82

squadrons for skirmish fighting wherever they were needed. The net result was a smoke screen, as it were, that masked the concentration of Confederate troops. Earlier in May, three Union generals simultaneously reported Jackson to be in three different places. Irvin McDowell in Kernstown wrote that Jackson was at his front. Robert C. Schenck at Franklin – almost one hundred miles distant – was positive that an attack in his rear by Jackson was imminent. Frémont, then west of the Valley near Petersburg (Western Virginia), was convinced that Jackson was marching toward him.

On May 29, Lincoln telegraphed Frémont to move his force to the vicinity of Strasburg, in order to join General McDowell, who was approaching Front Royal with his 20,000 troops in a concerted effort to surround Jackson. The plan was to have armies from the west and east marching to cut off Jackson's retreat, while from the north, the armies of Banks and Brigadier General Rufus Saxton would press his rear. Jackson himself was headquartered in Winchester, thirty-six miles away from his Stonewall Brigade, which was laying siege to Harper's Ferry and occupying the Loudoun heights. The prospect of 64,000 Federal troops closing in from three directions was staggering.

Frémont sent back a characteristically petulant message from the vicinity of Fabius, Virginia:

> My command is not yet in marching order. It has been necessary to halt today to bring up parts of regiments and to receive stragglers, hundreds of whom from Blenker's division strewed the roads. You can conceive the condition of the command from the fact that the medical director this morning protested against its further advance without allowing one day's rest, the regiments being much reduced, and force diminished accordingly. I could not venture to proceed with it in disorder, and cannot with safety undertake to be at the point you mention earlier than by 5 o'clock on Saturday afternoon.

It was a day of rest and roll calls in the cool mountain air. Scouts returned to camp with hugely inflated estimates of Jackson's troop strength – varying between 30,000 and 60,000 men – which Frémont duly passed on to the War Department. An enraged Lincoln promptly replied:

Washington, May 30, 1862 – 11.30 A.M.

Major-General Frémont,
    Yours of this morning from Moorefield just received. There cannot be more than 20,000, probably not more than 15,000, of the enemy

83

about Winchester. Where is your force? It ought this minute to be near Strasburg. Answer at once.

A. LINCOLN.

On Friday, May 30, Frémont's army left Fabius. A rainstorm turned the road into mud, and the passage was slow. Lincoln forwarded a dispatch the Secretary of War had just received from Saxton, which described a defensive skirmish in the mountains near Harper's Ferry. The president ended the message to Frémont with the prophetic words, "It seems the game is before you."

Although Jackson gave the illusion that he was in no hurry, the reports of his sundry reconnaissance sources made his predicament perfectly clear. On the night of the thirtieth, he ordered his scattered forces to evade the closing circle by withdrawing as quickly as possible to the south toward Strasburg. The march began early Saturday morning, with long columns of Federal prisoners leading the way. Ewell's division brought up the rear. Frémont telegraphed the president:

Headquarters Mountain Department,
Wardensville, May 31, 1862.
(Received 8:30 P.M.)

Main column at this place. Roads heavy and weather terrible. Heavy storm of rain most of yesterday and all last night. Our cavalry and scouts have covered the roads 10 to 15 miles ahead. The enemy's cavalry and ours now in sight of each other on the Strasburg road. Engagement expected today. The army is pushing forward, and I intend to carry out operations proposed.

J. C. FRÉMONT,
Major-General, Commanding.

Frémont's apologia of 1865 recounted the initial clash between pursuer and pursued.

At 7 in the morning of this day, June 1, my advance, under Lieutenant-Colonel Cluseret, first touched Jackson's main body, driving in the advanced pickets of General Ewell's brigade. Pressing forward and encountering and driving stronger bodies of skirmishers the column within a short distance came upon cavalry and a battery in position, which immediately opened fire. The enemy's artillery was engaged by detachments from the Eighth Virginia and Sixtieth Ohio, under Major Oley, supported afterward by a section of artillery under Lieutenant-Colonel Pilsen. The fire of the enemy's musketry now brought into action indicated the presence of two or three regiments. I was entirely ignorant of what had taken place in the valley beyond, and it was now evident that Jackson, in superior force was at or near Strasburg. In anticipation, therefore, of possible demonstrations on his part before some needed rest could be taken, my command as they came up were ordered to position.

About noon the enemy's batteries ceased fire, and my troops were ordered to encamp. Our cavalry, being pushed forward, found the enemy withdrawing and a strong column of infantry just defiling past our front. A reconnaissance by Colonel Cluseret with the Eighth Virginia, pushed to within 2 miles of Strasburg showed the enemy withdrawn, and at night-fall this officer, with his brigade, accompanied by a battalion of cavalry and a section of artillery, was ordered to move forward upon Strasburg and determine the position of the enemy.

The day closed with one of the most violent rain-storms I have ever seen, with really terrific lightning and thunder . . .

At the time, Frémont shared the meteorological news with Lincoln:

> Headquarters Army in Field,
> Strasburg, June 1, via Moorefield, June 2, 1862.

A reconnoitering force just in reports the enemy retreating, but in what direction is not yet known. Our cavalry will occupy Strasburg by midnight. Terrible storm of thunder and hail now passing over. Hail-stones as large as hens' eggs.

> J. C. FRÉMONT,
> Major-General.

Meanwhile, the forces of Brigadier General James Shields, now attached to McDowell's corps, had reached Front Royal, thereby ensuring that Jackson would not slip away to the east and the Luray Valley. It remained for Shields to march twelve miles to the west, to Strasburg, in order to cut off Jackson's escape route up the Valley Turnpike to the south. (Traveling northward in the Shenandoah Valley is down, while traveling southward is up, as the Valley drains to the north.) But Shields's division got a tardy start and marched in the wrong direction, taking the road northwest toward Winchester. When the blunder was discovered, it was already dark. The half-day delay put Shields out of the immediate race, so he was directed instead to march south along the Luray Pike, which paralleled the Valley Turnpike on the far side of the Massanutten Range, in anticipation of a later cutoff. No line of communication had been established between Shields and Frémont owing to the depredations of roaming units of Ashby's cavalry, which controlled the countryside.

To the north, General Banks, nursing his battered army, wired Secretary Stanton:

> Williamsport, June 1, 1862 – 1 P.M.
> (Received 3:40 P.M.)

Have heard nothing of Frémont. The enemy reported in full retreat from Harper's ferry.

> N. P. BANKS.

On the second of June, Banks sent another telegram:

> Williamsport, June 2, 1862 – 10 P.M.
> (Received June 3, 8:45 A.M.)

Our advance troops are near Winchester and several regiments near Martinsburg. It is with great difficulty that they are got ready for marching orders. I hope tomorrow they will all be on the move. Several officers captured at Winchester returned tonight. They represent that the rebels evacuated the town Friday last.

> N. P. BANKS.

The information was helpful, but Banks was staying put. His mission had been to block Jackson's potential escape route to the northeast, toward the nation's capital. Now that Jackson was moving up the Valley, there was little he could do. Again, he telegraphed Stanton:

> Martinsburg, June 4, 1862 – 9 A.M.
> (Received 11 A.M.)

The best information I can get shows that Jackson left Winchester about 11 A.M. Friday, his train in front. He encountered Frémont's advance near Cedar Creek, which he held in check on Saturday until his troops passed up the valley. His rear guard then took a position upon a hill 2 miles beyond Strasburg, which he held Sunday and Monday. The cannonading there is described as terrific by the people. The last heard of him was that he was at New Market. His entire force is represented as near 40,000 by the people of Winchester.

> N. P. BANKS,
> Major-General, Commanding.

As Lincoln had anticipated, the game was before Frémont, whose army had crossed the Alleghenies from Fabius in time to deliver a paralyzing blow to Jackson at Strasburg. The Confederates, minus

Ashby's cavalry and the Stonewall Brigade en route from Harper's Ferry, were strung along the Valley Pike, their flanks unprotected, their wagon trains stretched as far as the eye could see full of plunder and provender from the victory at Winchester.

But instead of swooping down on Jackson with his entire force, Frémont first focused on constructing defenses along the mountainous roads west of Strasburg, just in case Jackson turned, at some future date, in that direction. Belatedly, he sent a meager detachment, mostly cavalry, to the Valley plain where it was met by Ewell's rear guard, which had strict orders from Jackson not to be drawn too far from the pike. Frémont recounted in 1865:

> Disobeying the order to charge, after a scattering fire our cavalry broke in a shameful panic to the rear, passing over and carrying with them the artillery.
>
> To the honor of the Sixtieth Ohio, which at this moment formed the head of the reconnoitering column, not a man of them followed the disgraceful example, but delivered their fire steadily, and checked any movement on the part of the enemy. The officers and men, without exception, of the Sixtieth Ohio and Eighth Virginia [from unseceded western Virginia], which composed this brigade, deserve special mention for the steadiness and bravery which distinguished them during the affairs of this day, when both regiments were for the first time under fire. Having ascertained the position of the enemy, Colonel Cluseret withdrew his men and returned to camp. The reconnaissance showed the enemy in retreat.

But Confederate Brigadier General Richard Taylor (son of former president Zachary Taylor), whose Eighth Brigade of Ewell's division bore the brunt of the charge, commented:

> Sheep would have made as much resistance as we met. Men decamped without firing, or threw down their arms and surrendered, and it was so easy that I began to think of traps. At length we got under fire from our own skirmishers, and suffered some casualties, the only ones received in the movement.

Thus, Frémont passed up a signal opportunity to injure the Rebel army decisively, if not mortally. Ever alert, Jackson took advantage of Frémont's hesitation by halting his withdrawal for several hours to let the Stonewall Brigade and Ashby's cavalry catch up with the main columns. When Jackson's orders to fall back rapidly had reached Harper's Ferry, a hell-bent dash had ensued—a day and a half without food or rest as the

87

men covered the forty-five miles through driving rains and mire. Upon reaching the safety of the main column, the late arrivals dropped in their tracks with fatigue. Jackson was moved to note in a report to Lee that the safe passage before the "contemplated junction" of Union armies was only "through the blessing of an ever-kind Providence."

Frémont watched this heroic flight with a certain smug approval. He telegraphed Stanton:

> Headquarters Army in the Field,
> Camp by Woodstock, Va., June 2, 1862 — 6 P.M.
>
> The enemy was pressed by our advance this morning until about 10 o'clock, when he made a determined stand of an hour. He was attacked by about 1,000 cavalry, under General Bayard, 600 cavalry of my command, under Colonel Zagonyi, and Schirmer's and Buell's batteries, of General Stahel's brigade, under Lieutenant-Colonel Pilsen, aide-de-camp. He repeatedly faced about, and was as often driven from his position during a running fight of four hours. Our force marched 18 miles in five hours. The pursuit was so rapid that it was impossible to get the infantry up before he reached for the night the heights beyond Woodstock.
>
> His retreat was reckless. About 100 prisoners and 200 stand of arms were taken, and there are at least 1,000 stragglers in the woods along the road and country adjoining. Clothing, blankets, muskets, and sabers are strewn also upon the road.
>
> We have a few killed and wounded. Among the hurt is Colonel Pilsen, though not seriously.
>
> At their last stand the enemy lost 6 or 8 killed, and his loss during the day was undoubtedly considerable. With the infantry at hand we should have taken his guns.
>
> At 4:45 P.M. General Stahel's brigade occupied Woodstock.
>
> J. C. FRÉMONT

To Frémont, Jackson's army was like a wounded animal in clumsy, albeit speedy flight. But by turning so readily to fight, and with such ferocity, Jackson kept showing his teeth. The lesson was not lost on Frémont. Throughout the long, rainy Tuesday morning, Union advance guard and Confederate rear guard took swipes at each other, as Frémont later documented in his apologia:

> Although much fatigued by the forced march of the day previous, my command at an early hour of the morning of June 3 were upon the road to resume pursuit. Again the rear guard of the enemy turned to cover his main body, or to gain time for placing obstacles, tearing up

the road, or destroying culverts and bridges. The fire of the opposing batteries was mutually brisk, with at intervals an accompaniment of the dropping shots of small-arms. Strenuous effort was made by the rebels to destroy the bridge over Stony Creek, at Edenburg, about 5 miles out of Woodstock. A portion of the planks were torn up and the timbers so far cut that the structure sank, partially broken, about midway of the current. So prompt, however, were my advance troops that the party left by the enemy was compelled to retreat in haste without further execution of its design. A ford was found at a short distance up the stream, and with some difficulty cavalry and artillery were gotten across. Ultimately my baggage and supply trains passed safely. After some hasty repairs infantry was enabled to cross the bridge. On account of depth of water at the ford ammunition was removed from caissons and wagons and carried over by hands of men.

That afternoon, Jackson gained a distinct advantage by successfully crossing, then setting afire, the bridge across the North Fork of the Shenandoah beyond the town of Mount Jackson. While defending the rear, Ashby narrowly escaped capture by a company of Union cavalry as the bridge burned. Frémont reported the day's events to Stanton in two telegrams:

> Headquarters in the Field,
> Mount Jackson, June 4, 1862.

> The pursuit of the enemy was continued today, and their rear again engaged. The rebels attempted to destroy all the bridges, and succeeded in burning several, the most important of which was that over the Shenandoah at this place. Our loss today is but 1 killed. . . . The late violent rains, which still continue, have raised the rivers so that they are not fordable, but arrangements are being made tonight for crossing, and the pursuit will be continued early in the morning. I hope tomorrow to force the rebels to a stand.

> J.C. FRÉMONT,
> Major-General.

> Headquarters Army in the Field,
> Mountain Department, June 4, 1862.
> (Received June 6, 1:05 P.M.)

It has rained continuously and hard for twenty-four hours, producing one of the two greatest freshets known for many years. The Shenandoah rose 10 feet in four hours, breaking up the temporary bridge just thrown across. The bridge at Edenburg, partially demolished by the enemy, is also now entirely swept away. A regiment of infantry and two companies of cavalry succeeded in crossing the Shenandoah before the bridge was broken, and are now encamped on the other side of the stream. The effort to cross will be renewed tomorrow morning. The prisoners now number 400. We hear nothing yet of General Shields.

J. C. FRÉMONT,
Major-General, Commanding.

With the foresight of a true explorer, Frémont had procured a pontoon train at Pittsburgh (Pennsylvania) some months before, and having kept it well toward the front of his columns, he now supervised its use. It was deployed briefly before the rising water swamped some of the boats, then the ropes had to be cut in order to save the makeshift bridge. During the time in which the flood receded and the pontoon was fixed, Frémont sent couriers to his fellow field commanders, asking to secure reinforcements for his own command now that he alone was in pursuit of Jackson. The delay gave him pause to consider just how far out on a limb he had come. In the apologia, he wrote:

It will be remembered that at the date of my march from Franklin, information was conveyed to me that General McDowell would operate toward the same objects as myself, in capturing or driving out Jackson. Very earnest assurances to this effect were subsequently given me while upon the route both by the President and Secretary of War. Whether in General McDowell's case, as in my own, departmental lines or technicalities of previous orders were temporarily to be lost sight of, was not explained. Arriving, however, within the Shenandoah Valley, I deemed it not extravagant to expect of that officer that he should so far co-operate as, if not himself in advance, to send me troops to secure and hold fast prisoners, as well as to keep intact points of my line in rear. Accordingly, during the delay at Mount Jackson, I dispatched to General McDowell Captain Howard, of my staff, with orders substantially to the above effect.

McDowell brusquely declined, as did Banks, although more cordially. General Franz Sigel said that the sorry condition of his troops would make them more an encumbrance than a help. Frémont continued:

It was not until after I had left Mount Jackson that any of the dispatches embodying the above [request for reinforcements] were received; but the fact stood that at the date of my departure from this town (June 5) the contest with Jackson, so far as concerned the Shenandoah Valley proper, remained upon my hands. Although I

had crossed the mountains on an errand of aid to others, I found myself without conjunction or combination either with the forces
relieved or with a force sent toward the same object as my own from
an opposing direction.

This was not entirely accurate. Across the mountain to the east,
Shields was engaged in his parallel march up the Luray valley. The double threat could have materialized as a pincer if there had been communication between the two armies. Surely, Jackson sensed the danger, for
he was receiving messages from his signal corps (under the direction
of chief topographical engineer Jedediah Hotchkiss, his trusted map-
maker), perched atop the Massanutten headland, overlooking the Valley
at the southern tip of the fifty-mile range. The long Union columns east
and west stretched back as far as the eye could see, creeping forward in
tandem. In 1865, Frémont wrote:

> On the 5th of June, then, crossing safely the bridge of pontoons, my
> column, with scarcely more than half the numbers of the enemy in
> advance, retook the trail and pushed steadily forward. A lapse of
> more than thirty hours since the burning of the main bridge over the
> Shenandoah had given the enemy an advantage he proved not slow
> to use. He was not overtaken upon the 5th, and having made 18
> miles and passing on the way the enemy's fires still burning, my com-
> mand was bivouacked beyond New Market, the enemy's camp being
> but a few miles ahead.
>
> On the 6th I was enabled by an early and rapid march to restore
> the lost contact. Our progress was a little retarded by the burned and
> blazing culverts which had been fired by the enemy along the road,
> but sharp artillery and cavalry skirmishing was renewed during the
> forenoon, and at about 2 o'clock my advance drove his rear guard
> through Harrisonburg. The direction taken by the main force of the
> enemy being uncertain, my troops were ordered into camp around
> the town.

Jackson arrived in Harrisonburg early in the morning of the June 5,
and passed through town, turning easterly in the direction of Port
Republic. His reasons for the turn were threefold. The bridge south of
Harrisonburg in the direction of Staunton had been destroyed, but he
could pick up another road south from Port Republic. Then, too, it was
the only direction to go if he was to prevent the Union armies from com-
bining to amass a force superior to his own. Thanks to Ashby's restless
intelligence and the lookout on the Peak, Jackson had an excellent grasp
of the enemy's whereabouts. By turning to the east, he was also gaining

91

the valuable option of escaping the Valley altogether through Brown's Gap, where a good route crossed over the Blue Ridge toward Charlottesville and, ultimately, to Richmond. Of prime importance to Jackson was the delivery of his windfall of captured supplies to the safe haven of a central supply depot, either in Staunton or Richmond.

But in quitting the macadamized turnpike for the rutted market road, now nearly impassable with deep mud, the army's progress slowed considerably. The wagons laden with the spoils of Banks's debacle mired at once. Barely two miles southeast of Harrisonburg, Jackson halted for the day. Units of Ashby's cavalry guarded the prisoners and trains in front (against incursions by Shields) as well as the rear. The next morning, with Ashby personally in charge of the rear guard, the columns began moving again. Ewell's division was hindmost, as usual, the rear brigade consisting of the 58th and 44th Virginia and 1st Maryland infantry regiments under the command of Brigadier General George H. Steuart. In his report to the Second Corps Headquarters of the Army of Northern Virginia, Jackson stated with characteristic terseness:

> On the 6th General Ashby took position on the road between Harrisonburg and Port Republic, and received a spirited charge from a portion of the enemy's cavalry, which resulted in the repulse of the enemy and the capture of Colonel Wyndham and 63 others. Apprehending that the Federals would make a more serious attack, Ashby called for an infantry support. The brigade of Brig. Gen. George H. Steuart was accordingly ordered forward. In a short time the Fifty-eighth Virginia Regiment became engaged with a Pennsylvania regiment called the Bucktails, when Colonel Johnson, of the First Maryland Regiment, coming up in the hottest period of the fire, charged gallantly into its flank and drove the enemy with heavy loss from the field, capturing Lieutenant-Colonel Kane, commanding.
>
> In this skirmish our infantry loss was 17 killed, 50 wounded, and 3 missing. In this affair General Turner Ashby was killed.

Ashby and his cavalrymen had been dismounted, and their horses grazing, when the 1st New Jersey cavalry, commanded by an Englishman, Sir Percy Wyndham, came charging over the hill. Wyndham, a wealthy soldier of fortune, had boasted explicitly that he would capture Ashby and was about to make good his promise, but Ashby's squadrons mounted with alacrity, meeting the charge with a countercharge that overwhelmed the Federals and caused the "probably spurious pretender to gentle blood"—as the Reverend James B. Avirett, chaplain to Ashby's cavalry, described Wyndham—to fall prisoner instead. Union infantry, comprising the 82nd Ohio and Kane's 27th Pennsylvania, was ordered into the fray, leaving Ashby no choice but to dispatch a courier to Ewell requesting infantry reinforcements to match. A heated contest followed, during which Ashby was in the thick of the action, seemingly everywhere at once, until his horse was shot from under him. On foot and waving his sword, he rushed forward but a few steps when he was shot through the chest, dying almost instantly. Depending on the source, his last words were reported to have been either "Forward, my brave men!" or "Charge, men! For God's sake, charge!"

It was late in the afternoon when Ashby fell. His body was borne on horseback to Port Republic, where it was placed in the parlor of a merchant's house and posted with a guard of honor. Today, that house is still standing, its singular fame stemming from the night it sheltered the body of the dead folk hero. Ashby's death stunned Virginians; no other military leader with a larger-than-life reputation had been killed in the state. His troopers were inconsolate over the loss. But while the dashing cavalier had made inroads into the hearts of the men who served under him, as well as the hearts of the populace who took courage from his exploits, Ashby had been the antithesis of Jackson as a disciplinarian. Abhorring drills of any kind, Ashby was more of a tribal chieftain than a commanding general; he developed a web of personal accountability among his cavalrymen in lieu of an orderly chain of command. In Jackson's eyes, it was a willy-nilly, unregimented fealty that passed for leadership.

In his irritation, Jackson had tried to sack Ashby on several occasions, but had been politically unable to carry it through. Ashby was indispensable to the war effort. Having been promoted to the rank of brigadier general (over Jackson's objections) just two weeks prior to his death, the cavalry commander had become the embodiment of his own legend: a leader that bullets couldn't hit. Surely, "Old Jack" could recognize the mystique. As the solitary Jackson viewed the body late that night in Port Republic, he must have been formulating the phrases with which he described Ashby in his report to Lee: "His daring was proverbial; his powers of endurance almost incredible; his tone of character heroic, and his sagacity almost intuitive in divining the purposes and movements of the enemy."

It was a précis of Jackson's own strengths. He stood on the threshold of his definitive strategic ploy—fleeing from, and defeating at the same time, not one but two armies.

THIRTEEN

ONE HUNDRED AND TWENTY-SEVEN years later, the commandant of the Marine Corps organized an educational expedition to acquaint general officers with the finale of the Valley Campaign—a classic study in small war mobility. The otherwise chairbound officers got a tour of the battlefields at Cross Keys and Port Republic, as well as the opportunity to examine and evaluate tactical perspectives still current in the textbooks of military science.

They came from Quantico in four helicopters, black CH-46's referred to as "slicks" (in other words, uncamouflaged) from the HMX-1 squadron. This is the squadron that flies the president and other top government officials. HMX-1 pilots are required to maintain the highest level of proficiency, and the aircraft have to be test-flown routinely for safety checks, so the expedition benefited the squadron as well.

The officers, about fifty of them including the commandant, embarked from the Marine Corps Air Facility at 0700 hours on a morning in late March. Forty minutes later, there was audible notice of their approach, and within a minute or two, the helicopters were sighted through the tops of the budding trees. Advancing in pairs, the CH-46's beat the sky into a rippled sheet of sound. For once, it was a pollution I welcomed. Having granted them advance permission, I had hoped they could land right in the hayfields, but government regulations stipulated the flights be terminated in the presence of runway firefighting equipment. After banking low with an ear-splitting thunder, the copters flew on to the regional airport at Weyers Cave. The overflight charged the quiet spring morning with an almost unbearable excitement. In the studio, my concentration was shot.

The final leg of the expedition, from airport to battlefield, was conducted in minibuses furnished by the Virginia Military Institute. It was heartening to note that the Corps left little or nothing to chance. Weeks earlier, when the tour coordinator, who happened to be the curator of the Marine Corps Museum at the Washington Navy Yard, had come by for a visit, he had expressed concern as to how the officers would get over the barbed wire fence between the hayfields and the Lee-Jackson property. I showed him where my family and I crossed at the base of the largest and oldest oak on the property, which interrupted the fence-line in such a way that if we hugged its trunk and placed our feet in gnarled footholds just right, we could step over the barbed wire with ease. There was a bit of history in the old tree, too, I added. Undoubt-edly, it had been a sapling back in 1862.

The curator must have been unimpressed, for a few days later while I was eating lunch and staring absentmindedly out the window, I no-ticed in the woods what looked like a glorified step ladder. I went out-side for a closer look and discovered a well-constructed wooden stile, strictly government issue, straddling the rusty fence so that no officer, however agile, would have to hug a tree, even if it was one of Civil War vintage. Around the same time, a V.M.I. minibus, outfitted with a video camera behind its windshield, had been driven down our lane for a test run. The curator had also been concerned about the muddy ruts and the width of the turnaround in front of our house. (Luckily, mud season was over by the day of the tour and the radius of the turnaround proved more than adequate.)

It couldn't have been a prettier, balmier March morning. Becky's cro-cuses dotted our front lawn and walkway. The hayfields were greening, air quality was excellent, the pond was algae-free. As soon as I thought I heard the buses discharging passengers at Port Republic Road, I drove over in the pickup to join in the proceedings, but my hearing had not been acute enough. By the time I reached the highway, I was too late. Already, the tour had been divided into two groups: a Confederate group which had gone eastward to retrace the opening line of battle on the Lee-Jackson property, and a Union group which was in the process of concluding its field tour from the direction of the Keezletown Road. Lecturing beside the United Daughters of the Confederacy marker, a ci-vilian staff member of the Army War College glared at me for my tardy intrusion.

In jeans and flannel shirt, I cut a crude figure beside the starched spit-and-polish of the officers. I felt awkward, out of place, and being late only made things worse. Extricating myself, I made a U-turn and drove back down the lane. There was still a chance I could catch up with the Confederate tour. Evidently, the group hadn't crossed over the stile yet, which meant that the officers were somewhere in the thicket, heading in my direction. If I hustled, I could intercept them. Jamming down the accelerator, I bounced over the hayfield to the edge of the woods, where I leaped out of the truck and took off through the trees, hurdling a low spot in the barbed wire.

Like the flight of helicopters, the Confederate group was heard before it was seen. My first glimpse of the officers threading single-file through the honeysuckle and cedars stopped me cold. These were men and women on active duty, treading the unspoiled ground of history. To walk through a battle was not to fight it, but this was as close to the real thing as I would ever see. These were genuine military personnel in garrison caps, fatigues, and combat boots. It didn't matter if they carried no weapons and wore twentieth-century uniforms. It didn't matter that they were led by a historian with a bullhorn instead of a ranting general on a horse. These were soldiers who had come to study, not to fight. They were the modern equivalent of that original militia entrusted with the sacred duty of defending the Constitution. For the moment, the battlefield belonged to them.

Breathlessly, I slipped into their ranks, and they seemed glad to have me along. One by one, we clambered over the stile. A good idea, I thought to myself. If we had more stiles, there'd be fewer torn clothes. I was basking in an unaccustomed deference. "So this is your property?" the commandant inquired. "How does it feel to own a battlefield?"

I forget the exact wording of my precipitate reply, but it was something to the effect that my ownership was accidental, and I felt wonderment more than anything else. My wits were too uncollected to express myself coherently, having run so hard to catch up.

The curator finished his remarks and switched off the bullhorn. A question-and-answer period ensued. The what-ifs were brought up, theorizations of radically changed conclusions from slightly altered circumstances—the stuff of war college dissertations. As in any battle, the outcome here had teetered on the tightrope between good and bad decisions. The decision makers themselves had been in a state of flux—having a good day or a bad one, acting with competence or its opposite. The cast of personalities in the leadership of both sides had been interesting—downright quirky, in fact—certainly no two were alike.

It was a lively discussion, but the curator kept glancing at his watch. They were on a "fast march," as a retired colonel pointed out to me. The tour was already twenty minutes behind schedule. Where the hell were the buses? With the parameters of battle talk dissolving, the tour was turning into a peripatetic social call. Having gotten my second wind, I contributed significantly, but the group of us had trekked no further than the cross-fence when the buses reappeared. Camaraderie was cut short with handshakes and good-byes and promises to keep in touch.

An hour later, I was lying on my back at the foot of the barn bridge, changing the oil in the tractor, mulling over the excitement of the morning and its contrast to my usual self-employed solitude. Again, the air turned leaden with chopping waves of pressure. The four CH-46's thundered above the battlefield, even lower now, as if proffering a final salute. The tour would make an overflight of the entire Valley, including a stop at V.M.I. in Lexington for lunch and critique, before the beeline back to Quantico. I stood and waved to them with an oily wrench.

I could give a tour of my own, I thought. The stile was still in the woods. The curator's learned patter was lodged in my memory. All I needed was an audience, and as it turned out, an audience wasn't hard to find.

An end-of-semester blowout was being held in the neighborhood, the kind of afternoon party that centered around a keg, a volleyball game, and later, the singing of golden oldies before a bonfire. Recognizing my opportunity, I set about notifying my fellow revelers: "Don't know if y'all are interested, but if any of y'all wanna come along with me, I'll show you where the-Battle-of-Cross-Keys took place." The response was overwhelming. Nobody knew beans about the battle, but everyone was in a mood to learn. I had found my audience—a mélange of partygoers who could hardly wait to put themselves under the spell of my alleged expertise.

I planned an easy hike into the Lee-Jackson acreage, then back over the stile and across the hayfields. Although my understanding of the battle was still incomplete, I was, by now, well acquainted with the basics, and I only had to fudge them a little to keep continuity in my narrative. Of course, there were adjustments to be made for leading so merry a group over hill and dale. I needed pithy remarks and good laughs. The story of the battle had to be presented in a way that caused no intellectual stress. As we crashed along, sleeves and pantlegs would snag on barbed wire, feet would trip over logs, and faces would be lashed by bending brush. It would be a journey through unexpected physical frictions, but mentally it would go as smoothly as silk.

And so we toured. We ducked under the fence along the Lee-Jackson border and climbed the long, flat-topped hill, where we walked along the concealed position of the brigade that foiled the Union advance. "No kidding, right here?" "Honey, look out for those briars." "Hey, gimme a swig!" Ahead on the path, a rabbit poised, quivering, mesmerized by the rowdiness. I told them that the German immigrants had come straight toward the Confederate line, which had held its fire until the last possible moment. I quoted the words of Confederate Brigadier General Trimble:

> As the enemy appeared above the crest of the hill a deadly fire was delivered along our whole front, beginning on the right, dropping the deluded victims of Northern fanaticism and misrule by the score.

With peals of laughter and fists thrust in the air, my audience yammered with delight. "Give 'em hell, General!" "Tell it, dude!" "The South *will* rise again!" The reaction pricked my scholarly conscience. All this time, I had been overlooking an important fact: every battle had a hero. Why would the Battle of Cross Keys be an exception? But so far, in the accounts I had read, no hero had been singled out. It wasn't Jackson, because Jackson hadn't been on the field. Neither Ewell nor Frémont were likely candidates. This Trimble, he may have been the one. I resolved to find out.

By this time, to all appearances, I was bursting at the seams with keg-induced bravado. My embellishments soared with theatricality. I ranged the emotional scale, from deadpan to shrill. In whispers and screeches, I purveyed my flimflam account, and the more I breathed fire and ice, the more my listeners loved it. I led them over the countryside, scrambling under boughs and briars, dodging between cedars, all the while narrating the battle until I was blue in the face. As we crossed over the stile, I reached my apogee in extemporaneous rap:

> The Rebels were hiding,
> Their time they were biding.
> The immigrant brigade
> Thought they had it made.
> But the bullet hail was hot,
> *"Ich töte. Ach mein Gott!"*
> Then the bugle was bleating
> And the Yankees were retreating.

Suddenly, my well of invention went dry. Like an old windbag, I ran out of air. "Any questions?" I lamely concluded, but my audience was caught up in the momentum. "That was it?" someone asked in disbelief. "What happened next?"

I looked him in the eye and shrugged my shoulders. I had no more energy to expend, and I told him so. Port Republic was not on the menu. Inwardly, I thrashed myself for cooling the loquacity so abruptly. Better I should have ended with a dénouement, a trailing of statistics or a tapering quotation.

In silence, we trudged along the lane, a bedraggled exodus of party-goers thirsty for beer and starved for munchies. Only as we approached the festivities, much expanded now from recent arrivals, did spirits tangibly lift. Greeted with the usual, "Where y'all been?" and proffered foaming cups from the keg, we veered onto the crowded lawn, melting into the merriment.

Yes, the tour was a resounding success, but I felt a little stupid. For entertainment's sake and the cheap thrill of approval, I had turned the Battle of Cross Keys into a carnival ride. I had spiced it up and watered it down, all because I had wanted it to zing with a prime-time sensibility. But the battle did not come alive in sound bites; it did not come alive in anecdotal blather that homogenized fact and fantasy. To be a good soldier in the war against progress, I needed to edge closer to the truth, and be forthright about it. My future audiences would respond just as positively.

I vowed to continue my research and improve my lecturing ability. For better or worse, the tipsy tour was a thing of the past.

FOURTEEN

Saturday, June 7, 1862 was comparatively quiet. Taking advantage of the lull — and, more to the point, recovering from the fighting of the previous day — Frémont telegraphed Stanton:

> Hdqrs. Mountain Dept., Army in the Field,
> Harrisonburg, June 7, 1862.
> (Received June 9, 9 a.m.)

> The army reached this place at 2 o'clock yesterday afternoon, drawing out the enemy's rear guard from the town. Severe skirmishing continued from that time until dark, the enemy's rear being closely pressed by our advance. At 4 o'clock the First New Jersey Cavalry, after driving the enemy through the village, fell into an ambuscade in the woods to the southeast of the town, in which Colonel Wyndham, of that regiment, was captured and considerable loss sustained. Colonel Cluseret with his brigade subsequently engaged the enemy in the timber, driving him from his position and taking his camp. At about 8 a battalion of Colonel Kane's (Pennsylvania) regiment entered the woods under the direction of Brigadier-General Bayard, and maintained for half an hour a vigorous attack, in which both sides suffered severely, driving the enemy. The enemy attempted to shell our troops, but a few shots from one of our batteries soon silenced his guns. After dark the enemy continued his retreat. Full particulars will be forwarded by mail. The condition of the force is extremely bad, for want of supplies. We have been obliged to leave our single pontoon train at one of the bridges behind, in order to get our supplies over, and are now without any.

> J. C. FRÉMONT,
> Major-General.

The Pathfinder could be counted on to be preoccupied with his supply line to the rear. When he had been an explorer, the trail behind served

as his umbilical cord to civilization. Regular depots, caches, and rearward communication had been the keys to his successes on the western
frontier. Leaving the pontoon train behind on this march, however, was
an outright mistake. Experience should have taught him that Jackson
was a burner of bridges.

Frémont followed his first message with a second:

> Headquarters Army in the Field,
> Harrisonburg, June 7, 1862—9 P.M.
> (Received June 9, 7:40 A.M.)

The attacks upon the enemy's rear of yesterday precipitated his retreat. Their loss in killed and wounded was very severe, and many
of both were left on the field. Their retreat was by an almost impassable road, along which many wagons were left in the woods, and
wagon loads of blankets, clothing, and other equipments are piled up
in all directions. During the evening many of the rebels were killed
by shells from a battery of General Stahel's brigade. General Ashby,
who covered the retreat with his whole cavalry force and the three
regiments of infantry and who exhibited admirable skill and audacity,
was among the killed. General Milroy made a reconnaissance today
about 7 miles on the Port Republic road, and discovered a portion
of the enemy's forces encamped in the timber.

> J. C. FRÉMONT,
> Major-General, Commanding.

Ashby's body was carried in a wagon to Waynesboro, where it was
taken by rail across the Blue Ridge to Charlottesville and buried. Receiving fresh intelligence of the speed of James A. Shields's approach, Jackson knew his army could not be in two places at once. He decided to
divide his army near the hamlet of Cross Keys, leaving the majority of
Ewell's Third Division to check Frémont's progress, while continuing
with the rest of the army to Port Republic, where he expected to con-
front Shields. Jackson wrote:

The main body of my command had now reached the vicinity of Port
Republic. This village is situated in the angle formed by the junction
of the North and South Rivers, tributaries of the South Fork of the
Shenandoah. Over the larger and deeper of those two streams, the
North river, there was a wooden bridge connecting the town with
the road leading to Harrisonburg. Over the South River there was
a passable ford. The troops were immediately under my own eye;
were encamped on the high ground north of the village, about a mile
from the river. General Ewell was some 4 miles distant, near the road

leading from Harrisonburg to Port Republic. General Frémont had arrived with his forces in the vicinity of Harrisonburg, and General Shields was moving up the east side of the South Fork of the Shenandoah, and was then at Conrad's Store, some 15 miles below Port Republic, my position being about equal distance from both hostile armies. To prevent a junction of the two Federal armies I had caused the bridge over the South Fork of the Shenandoah at Conrad's Store to be destroyed . . .

The next morning Captain Myers' company came rushing back in disgraceful disorder, announcing that the Federal forces were in close pursuit. Captain Chipley and his company of cavalry, which was in town, also shamefully fled. The brigades of Generals Taliaferro and Winder were soon under arms and ordered to occupy positions immediately north of the bridge. By this time the Federal cavalry, accompanied by artillery, were in sight, and after directing a few shots toward the bridge they crossed South River, and dashing into the village they planted one of their pieces at the southern entrance of the bridge.

The spirited Union raid, known as Carroll's incursion, was a premature forward action without sufficient backup, and hence doomed from the start. Nevertheless, it gave Jackson a close call. He and a group of his aides who were in the village had to make an ungentlemanly dash across the bridge to save their skins. There is an anecdote (of undetermined authenticity) about how Jackson, having gained the far side, tried to con the Federal artillerists into withdrawing the cannon by pretending to be an irate Union officer. (Jackson habitually wore his old blue field jacket.) He was unsuccessful. It took an infantry charge across the bridge to capture the field piece, occupy the town, and chase the Yankees out.

Historians have excoriated Jackson for this inexplicable lapse of security. Why hadn't he positioned a substantial picket force beyond the bridge and over the ford along the road to Conrad's Store, the known path of the enemy's approach? Captain A. S. "Sandie" Pendleton of Jackson's staff may have had the answer when he reported that "Old Stonewall [was] completely broken down from exhaustion." The harrowing march from Winchester, the loss of Ashby, the dividing of his fatigued army, and the unforeseen variables of the pending action were taking their toll.

Meanwhile, not far to the north, Shields sent a message to Irvin McDowell's chief of staff, Colonel Schriver, to bring his departmental command up to date on the events as he saw them:

Hdqrs. First Div., Dept. of the Rappahannock,
Columbia Bridge, June 8, 1862 – 7 P.M.
(Received June 9, 4:30 A.M.)

Colonel: A dispatch has this moment arrived from Colonel Carroll, commanding the advance of this division, stating that he moved forward today with some cavalry, infantry, and two pieces of artillery on Port Republic, drove a small force of the enemy from the bridge, and crossed the bridge in pursuit of this force. Three brigades of Jackson's army, covering at least three batteries, assailed them at once on both flanks. The cavalry fled the first fire; his two guns were captured, and he, with the residue of the brigade, is in full retreat on Conrad's Store, where he (Carroll) sent me the dispatch, no time being mentioned. It must have been this morning.

There is another brigade advancing to his support; and a third brigade moving forward at this time from this place to support them. The Fourth Brigade is still at Luray, awaiting the arrival of forces from Front Royal. I have sent information of this to General Frémont, who seems to be lying at Harrisonburg, urging him to attack them with all his force in their rear at once, while I am hurrying forward the others to maintain our position, and try to repulse the enemy. The general commanding will see at once the necessity of immediate action to recover this loss.

Very respectfully, &c.,

JAS. SHIELDS,
Commanding Division.

A day earlier, Saturday morning, Frémont was indeed lying at Harrisonburg, trying to figure out what direction of pursuit he should follow after the skirmish with Ashby's cavalry. His natural instinct was to take a day of catching up, as he had done at Fabius, a notion quite foreign to the relentless Jackson. In 1865, Frémont wrote:

On the 7th a reconnaissance in force was sent under General Milroy in the direction of Port Republic, and reconnaissances pushed toward Keezletown and McGaheysville and on the Staunton turnpike to the Middle River, where the bridges were found destroyed. These reconnaissances showed that Jackson, abandoning the turnpike, had struck by a difficult and troublesome road toward Port Republic, and that he was about to turn in force to dispute our farther advance. Accordingly a movement in the new direction taken by him was determined on for the 8th, and early upon the morning of this day the march was resumed, the command taking the road leading directly through the woods from Harrisonburg to Cross Keys.

Frémont's force consisted of seven brigades of infantry, four companies of cavalry, and eleven artillery batteries.* Roll call at Fabius had counted over 11,000 able-bodied soldiers. Since then, the rigors of the march had reduced that number by a few hundred, but there were still approximately 10,500 on hand. Three and a half years later, Frémont persisted in tabulating Jackson's force (of early June, 1862) at 18,000, a figure inflated by nearly a third; moreover, the dividing of the Confederate army near Cross Keys still didn't seem to have occurred to him. The truth of the matter was that on the morning of June 8, he faced an enemy not quite 5,000 strong. Frémont's inability to admit the error stemmed from an impuissance that characterized his professional life as a soldier. He was too timid to be bearing down on the likes of Jackson. The fixed idea that Jackson was leading a numerically superior army hamstrung his every offensive option.

The Confederate Major General Richard "Dick" Ewell, on the other hand, was spoiling for a fight. Along the retreat from Strasburg, his division had borne the brunt of the Union thrusts and parries, and now Ewell openly scoffed at Frémont's threat. Left under Ewell's command early Sunday morning after the departure of Brigadier General Richard B. Taylor's brigade (on Jackson's orders) were three brigades of infantry with four attached batteries of artillery.**

Major General Ewell was an 1840 West Point graduate who had fought in the Mexican War, then served fifteen years as a cavalry captain on the western frontier. His equitation skills were on a par with Ashby's, but unlike the folk hero, Ewell cut a determinedly undashing figure. In Brigadier General Richard Taylor's memoirs of the war, published in 1879, the following thumbnail sketch of Ewell appeared:

> Bright, prominent eyes, a bomb-shaped, bald head, and a nose like that of Francis of Valois, gave him a striking resemblance to a woodcock; and this was increased by a bird-like habit of putting his head on one side to utter quaint speeches. He fancied that he had some mysterious internal malady, and would eat nothing but frumenty, a preparation of wheat; and his plaintive way of talking of his disease, as if he were some one else, was droll in the extreme. His nervousness prevented him from taking regular sleep, and he passed nights curled around a camp-stool, in positions to dislocate an ordinary person's joints and drive the "caoutchouc man" to despair. On such occasions,

*See Appendix B for a complete list of forces.

**See Appendix C for a complete list of forces.

after long silence, he would suddenly direct his eyes and nose toward me with "General Taylor! What do you suppose President Davis made me a major-general for?"—beginning with a sharp accent and ending with a gentle lisp. Superbly mounted, he was the boldest of horsemen. . . . With a fine tactical eye on the battle field, he was never content with his own plan until he had secured the approval of another's judgement, and chafed under the restraint of command, [preferring] to fight with the skirmish line. On two occasions in the Valley, during the temporary absence of Jackson from the front, Ewell summoned me to his side, and immediately rushed forward among the skirmishers, where some sharp work was going on. Having refreshed himself, he returned with the hope that "old Jackson would not catch him at it."

A Virginian by birth, Ewell had resigned from the U.S. Army at the start of the rebellion; upon receiving his new commission, he rose with bewildering speed to the rank of division commander, a trajectory that justifiably baffled the modest cavalry captain himself. Lee had sent Ewell's division to reinforce Jackson not two months earlier, more than doubling the size of the Valley army after its singular loss at Kernstown. In the following weeks of marching and fighting, "Old Bald Head," as he became known behind his back, quickly earned Jackson's trust as a dependable subordinate.

On Saturday night, Ewell's command bivouacked where the army had divided. Today, that stretch of road just south of Cross Keys and half a mile to the west of our forty acres, snakes through the countryside much as it did back then, except now it is paved. Sunday morning, confirmed reports of Frémont's departure from Harrisonburg along the Port Republic road led Ewell to order his remaining three brigades and four artillery batteries into defensive positions. At Brigadier General Arnold Elzey's suggestion, the Confederate line was placed perpendicularly to the road along the aforementioned ridge with a splendid view back toward Harrisonburg. Steuart's brigade was on the left, the batteries were in the center with Elzey's brigade at their rear, and Trimble's brigade, minus one regiment sent forward on picket duty, was on the right.

When Frémont brought his six active brigades of infantry and ten active batteries of artillery into position opposite the Confederate line, he placed the brigades of Stahel (or Stahl—his name was spelled both ways) and Bohlen on the Union left. Milroy's, Schenck's, and Cluseret's brigades were on the right. In the center were massed the main batteries, with additional guns somewhat in advance on hills to either side.

FIFTEEN

AN IDEA CAME TO ME as I sat on the front porch one evening, watching the sun go down beyond the rise in our hayfields where the leftmost Union battery had been positioned. The hill commanded a view for miles in every direction. Why not build a monument there? The site had become a landing strip for the radio-controlled model airplanes Van was building. With the lawnmower, he had scalped a long, skinny rectangle in the field, but I knew the time would come when he'd tire of his hobby, and runway grooming would be one chore he'd be happy to strike off the list.

The monument I had in mind was quite simple: two tall flagpoles of uneven height tilted toward each other like prongs of a bent U-magnet. The continuous loop of pole would be anchored to a cast concrete pedestal of asymmetrical volume. The Stars and Stripes would wave from the taller pole, the Stars and Bars from the shorter. Old Glory alone wouldn't be enough. The Confederate battle flag stood for a nation, a way of life, and, above all, an object lesson in the evolution of a democracy. All three were worth remembering.

Symbols of remembrance still pervade the South, from the marble Confederate soldiers that direct traffic in the old town squares to contemporary iconography of Asian manufacture, flogged by convenience stores from Manassas to Mobile. Reminders adorn all manner of merchandise – belt buckles, T-shirts, hats, hankies, scarves, cigarette lighters, mugs, towels, and toiletries. Automotive accessories celebrate the Confederacy on mudflaps, bug guards, aerial pennants, window appliqués, license brackets, bumper stickers. The battle flag waves and shimmers, gleams and glows. It remains an emblem of pride, tainted with connotations of white supremacy in certain sectors, but nevertheless an overt signal of individuality and defiance.

Although the local battle was an ostensible victory for the South, Old

Glory ascendant would remind onlookers that the Union won the war. My monument would not monkey around with the stern truth. Four grueling years and 618,000 lives lost were absolute proof that the Southern Cause could not and would not prevail—despite popular song. Like other Confederate victories, the Battle of Cross Keys had been a reprieve in the gradual obliteration of the rebellion. For the Cause, it had been a lucky day.

The proposed monument would not be without its drawbacks. Frankly, it would stick out in the hayfield like a sore thumb. But if its pedestal were positioned equidistantly from the field edges, it might be useful during haymaking as a reference by which to gauge the number of remaining passes. I warmed to the idea of a utilitarian monument; the nation needs more of them. Emblematic sculptures tend to lose relevance with the passage of time. I have seen too many bronzed black holes, plaques that nobody reads, pigeon perches.

But was I planning ahead? Was I prepared for an onslaught of visitors? A monument, however utilitarian, would surely draw attention to itself—that's what monuments are for, isn't it? At the very least, by erecting two slanted flagpoles in the middle of our property, I would pique the instant curiosity of our neighbors. "Whatcha got there, Pete? Wind knock yer flagpoles out of whack?" In their eyes, only a dimwit would take the trouble to build a monument to drive a tractor around.

Thinking about the future, I became positively clairvoyant. Yes, rubberneckers would arrive. They'd drive down the lane single file. My children and I kidded around on this topic. Hope had already volunteered to run the concession stand. Van had a hankering to build a working replica of a cannon. We could wear period clothing, trading blue and gray kepis as the occasion demanded. Through concealed speakers, there'd be a continuous serenade of martial music—"Dixie," "The Battle Hymn of the Republic." Two dollars for parking. Special group rates.

But ten years down the line? Twenty years? Visitors would tire of stumbling through the tick-infested hayfields. If tourism were to flourish, it would have to be accommodated, pampered, cajoled. A monumented battlefield beckoned picture-takers of every description, including the handicapped. A ribbon of concrete would have to lead up to the monument. Maybe two or even three such ribbons, each radiating from a parking area ringed by young trees. And restrooms. And trash barrels, plenty of 'em, emblazoned with an upbeat logo, a simplification of the skyward prongs and banners.

The battle could be merchandised as a saga, and the saga transformed into a seasonal passion play. We needed a gripping title—how 'bout Victory Valley? I could script it in a week or two, no problem. The area's high schools and colleges would be fecund pools of thespian talent. The next step would be the incorporation of a nonprofit foundation. Once the money was rolling in, we could invest in colored lights, smoke generators, television commercials. And the barn could become a haymaking museum, a touristic dividend. The battle and the farm rolled into one— two for one money! And the elderly artist-farmer, in baseball cap and ear protectors, his face greasy with sunscreen, could putt-putt around the barnyard. "Check out that antique tractor! Wonder if the old geezer'll stop a minute, so I can pose the wife 'n' kids."

Quite possibly, the imagined monument needed to remain in my imagination a little longer. That way, it would attract no visitors. Meanwhile, before old age hit, Becky and I could plot a graceful retreat to the south of France. Van and Hope would inherit the monument.

I was aware of my swings of mood. Cracks of levity in a facade of high seriousness had long been a trademark of my behavior, and they seemed to be exacerbated under the accumulating weight of tragic knowledge. To the world, of course, I was showing a serious demeanor, perhaps a more serious one than usual because of my enlarging empathy with the battlefield. My friends assumed that I had become a Civil War buff. But was I one? An honest answer required further definition of the term. If a buff was a person who donned an ersatz uniform and shouldered a replica of a muzzle-loader, I did not qualify. If a buff devoted at least eight feet of bookshelf to volumes pertaining to the war, I wasn't one. If a buff collected military memorabilia and pored over maps of bygone campaigns, I still didn't fit the description. But if a buff was someone who analyzed the Civil War from a compassionate point of view, who had done a little dredging in history and a lot of thinking as a result, then I filled the bill.

My research was beginning to flesh out. At best, it uncovered facts and bridged gaps that led me toward a plateau of understanding, from which I could truthfully say, "I see, now, how it must have been." At worst, it bared conflicting evidence and untrustworthy remembrance, the footnoted path occasionally skirting the abyss of contradiction.

Initially, my delving into the story of the Battle of Cross Keys resulted in more questions than answers. Detailed descriptions of the battle were hard to find. Early on, I discovered that school of prominent Civil War historians who occupied themselves with larger themes, broad sweeps of scholarship that quantified the war in dates and events, like pinheads on the big map. In multivolume tomes that encompassed the whole she-bang, from Fort Sumter to Appomattox, the Battle of Cross Keys usually weighed in as a one-liner, or, at most, a dependent clause buried in a convoluted sentence.

In treatises that dealt specifically with the Valley Campaign, the battle merited a page or two, a streamlined version of the day that segued quickly into the Battle of Port Republic. By skipping over the penulti-mate battle in order to focus on the ultimate one, authors conserved their energy for a grand summing up, but by no stretch of the imagina-tion could both battles be condensed into one, nor could one battle be considered more noteworthy than the other. Both battles figured equally in the successful conclusion of Jackson's campaign.

Then there was the question of whether or not the Battle of Cross Keys had been a battle at all. One historian described it as a "rambling skirmish." The line of battle had stretched for more than a mile across the countryside, and, barring the fierce cannonade, the infantry action along most of the line had been sporadic and localized. The only decisive action occurred on the Confederate right, or Union left, ground that en-compassed our forty acres and its immediate surround. The skirmish-versus-battle disagreement originated on the day it was fought, due to differing descriptions by observers along the front. (Thus a new twist was given to the old parable about blind men seeing the elephant.) Ap-parently, members of Jackson's staff got into a heated argument over the issue until Stonewall himself intervened to pronounce it a battle.

When I sought out local people who were knowledgeable about the Civil War, I was often astounded by their partisanship and the eagerness with which they browbeat minutiae into the minds of those, like myself, whose introduction to the war had begun along more generalized lines. In many ways, the personalities of the military principals interested them more than the events. About the Battle of Cross Keys their facts were hazy; about Jackson their facts were razor sharp. The way he sucked le-mons all day long, the way he meted out harsh discipline to his subor-dinates—this was what mattered to them. I had the feeling that they didn't quite know what to make of me—an abstract painter with a bot-tomless interest in one particular battle—but we became friends anyway. I was even invited to a meeting of the Shenandoah Valley Civil War round table, one among many American Civil War round tables across the nation and around the world. The topic for the evening's discussion was a recently aired TV documentary about the war.

About twenty-five people were convened at the Harrisonburg Electric Commission's home demonstration auditorium, a leftover from the days when utility companies promoted all-electric kitchens by giving cooking lessons. The proscenium opened onto a 1960s-era kitchen, replete with wraparound maple cabinets and avocado-green appliances. As a backdrop, the kitchen lent a century's remove to the proceedings; a more felicitous juxtaposition could not have been dreamed up by a Hollywood set designer.

The documentary, composed of photographs and narrative from the war interspersed with insightful commentary, had been a hugely popular piece of programming. I had sat through all twelve hours of it. Although its treatment of the Valley Campaign had been minimal (Cross Keys was mentioned but once), its overview of the war had appealed to me, and to millions of other viewers, because of the hard evidence with which it evoked the 1860s. Unlike the more common dramatizations that tend to simplify and romanticize the war, this program adhered to the guidelines of reality.

But five regional experts, sitting as a panel, took it upon themselves to tear the documentary apart. The first panelist, a professor of communication with a carapace of published credentials, pointed out a quick half-dozen discrepancies that placed the documentary, in his estimation, somewhere between hearsay and slander. The next panelist, a factory worker who had absorbed an encyclopedic knowledge of Civil War lore, expanded on the prevalence of wrongful facts and mistaken conclusions. The third panelist, a docent at the local historical society, made no spectacular claim for himself other than liking the sound of his own voice. His principle objection was what he perceived to be a pro-Yankee bias. The fourth panelist, a professor of Far Eastern history at a small college and a pacifist, thought the documentary glorified war. The fifth and final panelist was a diminutive, bearded pedagogue whose chief reason for being present was a willingness to pontificate on any subject whatsoever, to any length. Basically, he thought the documentary was a piece of crap and unworthy of his attention, but before he dismissed the subject entirely, he managed to work in a ten-minute harangue on academic freedom, and a lecture on the need to peruse the bibliography *before* the text in an historical opus.

In the audience were one or two war experts of equal stature, who chimed in with references and opinions that corroborated the general trend. Seated on the hard kitchen chairs, the panelists shifted their posteriors in discomfort, nodding sagaciously. A question-and-answer period sputtered. The documentary had been so thoroughly raked over the coals that few dared to contradict or even comment upon the authoritative dicta. I sat there, fully at loggerheads with the tenor of the proceedings, but saying nothing. If someone had let slip an asinine remark about Cross Keys, I might have had an excuse to deliver my own peroration. Alas, my growing expertise wasn't called upon. Anyway, there were altogether too many crusaders present. The meeting was brought to a close with unctuous words of gratitude, followed by announcements of upcoming events.

Half angry, half blitzed with contempt and frustration, I walked out of the room. In vivid neon, phrases blinked in my head: "Newly Revised and Updated" . . . "Definitive History" . . . "The Real Civil War." Would America's most personal, most comprehensively dissected crisis be forever scrutinized? The war had become a vast treasure trove in which facts were jewels, stupendous facts were crown jewels, and the seekers, from whose midst I had emerged, were driven by an insatiable intellectual greed. Their appetite for anything or anyone that touched upon the war unsettled me. Upon reflection, perhaps I wasn't a buff at all, but just a landowner trying to puff his few square acres of planetary surface into a marketable commodity. I was becoming an expert on a single battle only—and what kind of provincial, picayune creature was that? The axe I had to grind was every bit as didactic as that of the panelists because I was literally defending my own home.

Later, I learned that the Round Table had sponsored a three-day reenactment on the Cross Keys battlefield in June 1976. Most of the present-day members had no recollection of the event, which was probably a good thing, because it did not seem to have been an especially noteworthy reenactment. What information I was able to glean came from a slender, photocopied publication sequestered on a restricted shelf at the James Madison University library. Tracking it down had taken no small amount of sleuthing, and for my trouble I had expected to be rewarded with a detailed explication of the battle. Instead, I got a half-assed reminiscence of a weekend game. Typos were plentiful. The layout reeked of disorganization. Murky photographs, said to have been taken with a nineteenth-century-style camera, primarily illustrated the fledgling cedars as they began taking over the Lee-Jackson fields.

The people in the photographs were busy with sundry diversions. A scraggly line of fifteen alter-ego soldiers represented a regiment. One hefty fellow, his made-in-Taiwan kepi rakishly perched, sat on a camp

111

stool and cleaned a reproduction rifle. Women cooked over pit fires and modeled for the Ladies Dress Competition, in which snaps, zippers, and Velcro were not permitted. Parked in the distance, pickups and vans formed an encirclement that threatened to break the slight spell the reenactors were trying to cast. I could almost hear the idling engines and blaring radios as they drowned out the nineteenth century.

Reenactments of this sort are well-intentioned, educational to a degree, and undoubtedly fun, but I'm not sure I would ever want one again on the Cross Keys battlefield. There are other ways to absorb the endgame of the Valley Campaign besides putting on a brass buttoned uniform and firing blanks. For starters, a person can read about the battle, and walk the battleground (walking in solitude, that is, without the pressure of peer distraction). Quiet reflection seems to be the key to figuring out what happened here; only at such moments do the woods and fields truly echo for me.

But there had been more amiss during those three days of pretend. Judging by the crude graphics included in the text, I could see that the reenactors mistook several key positions. Ignorant error had compounded error, and the general mis-orientation, once established, had put the whole reenactment awry. I knew, because my quest for truth had led me over and over the ground. I was beginning to see that certain experts weren't really experts at all, but just authority figures whose mistakes went unnoticed. In some instances, it was the careless inking of a battle line on a map; in others, it was the misreading of an official report.

I was pleased to note on the final page of the pamphlet, however, a mention of gratitude to the Lee-Jackson Foundation and the farmer who sold us the land. At the very least, permission had been sought – and granted – for the weekend of mimicry. But could the reenactors have sought permission from the dead? In a way, that seemed to be the relevant issue, perhaps more relevant than permission from the living.

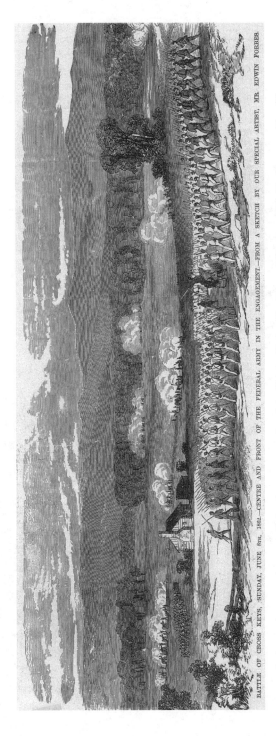

BATTLE OF CROSS KEYS, SUNDAY, JUNE 8TH, 1862.—CENTRE AND FRONT OF THE FEDERAL ARMY IN THE ENGAGEMENT.—FROM A SKETCH BY OUR SPECIAL ARTIST, MR. EDWIN FORBES.

Lithographic reproduction of a battle panorama sketch by Edwin Forbes for *Harper's Illustrated Weekly*. Courtesy Tom Thomas.

Union Major-General John C. Fremont ineptly pursued "Stonewall" Jackson up the Shenandoah Valley.

Lieutenant-General Thomas J. "Stonewall" Jackson wasn't actually present at the Battle of Cross Keys, preparing to fight the next day's battle at Port Republic.

Confederate Major-General Isaac R. Trimble, whose superb control of his brigade carried the day at Cross Keys, was ready to continue the battle into the night.

Cutting hay in the heat of the afternoon, with mirage-like Massanutten headland in the background.

Square bales of hay await pickup in the field (looking toward the ridge where Trimble's Confederate line was hidden).

Colonel Albert Tracy (US), General Fremont's Assistant Adjutant General, who found a stolen viand cooked in camp to be "toothsome in the extreme."

Lieutenant-General Richard "Dick" S. Ewell, CSA, a veteran of the Mexican War affectionately known as Old Bald-Head, restrained General Trimble from routing the Union forces at Cross Keys.

Van cutting hay with the Kubota. Bank barn, built in 1921, stored hay every season since then.

The newly completed house flanked by the two art studios.

Walking back from ice skating on the farm pond.

SIXTEEN

DEEP IN THE CARD CATALOGUE of the Virginia Historical Society in Richmond, I came across a morsel of research that brought the battle home to me as no other item had done. More than information it was a glimpse through a window that opened onto a frightened individual's soul. On Sunday morning, June 8, 1862, twenty-five-year-old Joseph H. Chenoweth, a major in the 31st Virginia Regiment, C.S.A., sat on his horse in a field to the south of our forty acres and wrote in his diary.

The feat itself was thought-provoking. How could someone be writing in a diary—on horseback, no less—in the midst of a raging battle? Yet he had been doing exactly that, sitting there and scribbling away, introspective, brimming with sublimity, fully aware of his surroundings but somehow detached. And then I saw myself sitting in my own battlefield—the one that had to do with progress and my own trials as an artist in a society that does not place much value on art, especially the kind that takes a leap of courage to readily understand—and the image of Chenoweth did not seem so farfetched.

By volunteering for duty, he had taken leave of a promising career as a mathematics teacher at Maryland Agricultural Institute. Like Jackson, his commanding general and former professor, Chenoweth affected an academic demeanor. He had graduated second in his class from Virginia Military Institute. His diary, as well as his letter writing, attested to a finely wrought patriotism and sense of religion. He had acquired the habit of interrupting his observations from time to time with heartfelt, written prayers, and in doing so he may have been nursing a premonition of his own death.

His first entry for the morning gave his location as "Near Harrisonburg on the road to Port Republic, June 8th. 9 o'clock A.M." "Cannon have been heard to the left of us near Port Republic. Gen. Jackson I

113

doubt not understands his position, but I think we will have a hard battle soon."

By ten o'clock the Confederates' long defensive line was at the ready and, with the emplacement of the Union batteries, the "galling" (a nineteenth-century adjective used by many soldiers to describe heavy fire) artillery exchange began. Chenoweth's regiment was in a reserve position to the rear of center.

> Later 12 o'clock A.M. Heavy cannonade is being kept up on the side of us next to Harrisonburg. Some of our men I think have been wounded – I saw on going to the road. The 31st is supporting the battery which is engaged. I do not like our position, though it is a commanding one. We may possibly have our flank turned but Jackson is here if Frémont is with the enemy. Our movements yesterday and today are incomprehensible to me.

Jackson wasn't "here" per se; he was four miles to the southeast at Port Republic. What Chenoweth meant was that Jackson would be there to lead the army out of danger if the battle took a turn for the worse. It was a statement of faith. Old Jack was a hero and an inspiration. War duty had turned the former agnostic into a devoutly religious leader, whose example inspired many of his soldiers, including Chenoweth, to see, as he did, a moral imperative in the Southern Cause. God was on their side, the side of the just, although He alone was privy to Jackson's decision making, a fact that led to consternation among his aides and incomprehension among the troops.

The ferocity of the barrage distressed the young major. He sat on his horse toward the rear of the center of the Confederate line and considered the fragility of his life and that of his fellow soldiers.

> Later – there is a lull in the firing – I know not why. My fervent prayer is that our Heavenly Father may lead our beloved country through the labyrinth of troubles which envelop her – and give peace to her persecuted and much-tried people. We seek not, O God, for conquest . . .

The prayer rambled on, as if the act of writing it were a shield of sorts, and as Chenoweth wrote, the tide of the battle turned. News of the Confederate infantry brigade's advance on the right cheered him and the rest of his comrades in the center. The flank was holding. Chenoweth mustered more courage after this to the point where he could acknowledge a grim beauty to the fight.

Later, 2:30 P.M. This is decidedly the warmest battle with which I have ever had anything to do. The artillery fire is superb — and the musketry is not so slow. We are in reserve, but the shells fly around us thick and fast. We will soon be into it.

Now that the Confederates seemed to be gaining the upper hand, the bolder officers and men of the 31st Virginia were vexed by their lack of participation. Their inaction was ended with the repositioning of Elzey's brigade (of which the 31st was a part) in response to a renewed Union offensive. Chenoweth was getting a stronger taste of battle.

Later, 4 P.M. We have been firing in the fighting and poor Lt. Whitly has been killed, shot thro' the head. A cannon has been planted on our left, and several of our poor men have been wounded. I pity them from the bottom of my heart. We will be at it again soon I think. And, Oh God, I renew my earnest prayer for the forgiveness of my many sins and for strength. In the name of Thy Son, grant me mercy. Amen.

With casualties nearby, the shadow of disaster cast a pall over the good news received earlier. Half an hour later, the artillery duel was still going strong, but Chenoweth steeled his nerves and reported what he saw: "Later, 4:30 P.M. The cannonading has recommenced and is very severe on the part of the enemy."

Not quite two hours afterward, the firing ceased. Chenoweth had weathered the worst of it and now he recorded a gentler scene: his regiment in repose. This brings to mind his former professor's prescription for the Foot Cavalry. During marches of thirty miles or more in a day, Jackson recommended periodic, fully prostrated rest, for "when a man lies down, he rests all over."

Later, 6:13 P.M. All is now quiet. Our regiment (31st) is lying down on line of battle, in full view of the enemy's battery, which only one hour ago was pouring grape into the regiment's noble soldiers! It tortures me to see them wounded. How many of them now, as they rest, looking quietly and dreamily up into the beautiful sky, are thinking of the dear ones at home, whom they have not, many of them, seen for twelve months. This is a hard life for us refugees who fight and suffer on without a smile from those we love dearest to cheer us up.

There followed another prayerful entreaty about the "fires of patriotism" and the power of dreams in which loved ones' faces appeared. "Sometimes I fear, but always put aside the thought, that these very

115

homes of which I have written will never be as happy, as peaceful as they were before the war commenced."

Then, in a philosophical digression, Chenoweth wondered if the invading Yankees would need to be forcibly removed from the continent in order to reunite the divided nation.

> Can the convictive feelings of hatred which burn in the breasts of our Union neighbors be obliterated by a treaty of peace? Or will they be compelled to expatriate themselves—or be exiled deservedly—exiled from a land to which they have all proven themselves traitors in thought if not in deed?

It was a protest against unjust persecution, and a solution that came straight from the bowers of make-believe. It showcased the young major's ivory-tower innocence. He had no more understanding of hate than he had of his commanding general's tactics. He didn't belong in the middle of a war. Honor and duty had put him there, but he was totally confused. As Chenoweth lay contemplating the sunset, he was moved to write a brief, concluding entry for the day: "Later. The firing has recommenced. Musketry brisk and ceased as soon."

The flare-up, a demonstration from the Confederate center, was answered (and silenced) by the Union guns, after which, to all appearances, calm reigned along the front. The smoke from the cooking fires supplanted the gun smoke, and the sun went down without the initiation of further hostilities.

During the night, the 31st Virginia was marched to Port Republic to rejoin the main body of Jackson's army. Monday morning found the major committing to his diary the brisk beginnings of a new battle, but this time his regiment was in the thick of it. Although the nearby figure of Jackson exerted a calming influence, Chenoweth's literary style shifted to nervous metaphor.

> Port Republic, June 9th, 1862—8 o'clock A.M. The ball is open again and we are from what I see and hear to have another hot day. It is [in] sheets this time. I may not see the result, but I think we will gain a victory though.

The crossfire, in which he wrote, intensified. There was not even a moment for prayer. His diary stumbled to a halt with two disjointed sentences. "I do not think our men have had enough to eat. I can't write on horseback."

Chenoweth was killed shortly after he dismounted. Why did he leave the saddle? Did he feel too exposed? Did he decide to finish the paragraph on solid ground? In a memoir by his friend and fellow soldier Joseph H. Harding, the following account was given of his death:

> We had scarcely joined our position when the dense columns of the enemy were thrown forward and we were subject to a most deadly and destructive front and enfilading fire, so murderous indeed that of the 226 men in our regiment who went into action, 116 were killed and wounded in that fatal wheat field . . . As the battle progressed, he was . . . advancing up the line encouraging the men and calling upon them to advance and follow where he led when he was shot, the ball entering just behind his left ear and passing entirely through the head. He fell without a groan with his sword still in his grasp pointed toward the enemy, nobly discharging his duty.

Harding lapsed into mellifluous sentiment at this point, his words intended no doubt to assuage the bereaved Chenoweth family. Yet his description of the young major's last moment hints at a disquieting thought: Chenoweth may have been killed by his own men. The forward-brandished sword and the rearward entry of the musket ball are disconcerting evidence. Then again, this may be a false trail of flowery prose composed for the sad occasion. It just seems possible that Harding was describing another, euphuistic sword—Chenoweth's pen.

SEVENTEEN

In the farming community of Cross Keys during the 1860s, the virgin forests were not regarded as inviolable and irreplaceable. Although firewood was collected and logs were hauled to the local sawmill for lumber, and fence rails were hewn out of the towering chestnut trees, whole areas of woods were simply burned to the ground to get rid of them. The woods were everywhere the cropland wasn't. Today, of course, with the proportions the other way around, a single tree is a valuable commodity. The stories I hear about how old-timers used to walk for miles across the neighborhood without leaving the woods contrast sharply with my own experience. Whenever I walk in woods, I can always see through them to civilization.

New as our house was, we heated it during the unpredictable Shenandoah Valley winters with a central woodstove. All year long, my children and I kept an eye out for dead or dying hardwoods of respectable size. We tagged the trees with orange ribbon while the forest was still in leaf; later, when the weather cooled, we went out with a chainsaw to harvest them, leaving the cordwood in piles to be hauled to the front porch as needed.

Among the trees in the ravine behind our house and just inside the Lee-Jackson line, age, disease, and lightning had been taking a steady toll. We were the scavengers, the cleanup crew that removed the moribund growth so that the living crowns could compete for sunlight. A neighbor on the far side of the Lee-Jackson property, who leased the land for his cattle, had a proprietary interest in the standing dead timber, too. In a year when I cut one or two trees from across the fence, he cut five or six, but it was a matter of honor between us to leave the living trees undisturbed.

An ecology-minded friend lashed out at me when I told her about this.

Didn't I realize that dead trees hosted innumerable insect parasites which, in turn, fed birds? Didn't I understand that certain other creatures lived exclusively in dead trees? And couldn't I see the importance of letting dead trees rot to the ground in order to enrich the molds and fungi in the soil, thus keeping nature's cycle of renewal in balance?

Yes, yes, I knew all that. Still, I needed the wood to keep my house warm in winter, and so did my neighbor. The living trees—the vast majority of the woodlot—remained undisturbed in our simple forest management scheme. It was the best we could do, since both of us would have been hard-pressed to pay conventional heating bills. As I told her this, I braced myself for her next utterance. At such a juncture in an argument of this sort, I could expect to be parried with the old ad hominem feint: get a job.

But as I saw it, the problem wasn't one of money, or lack of it, but rather one of guilt. Because I had the good fortune to have firewood at my disposal—and it was hard work to acquire; it warmed a person twice, as the old-timers said—I was supposed to bear a burden of guilt for burning it. Were I to heat with electricity, oil, or bottled gas, I could defer my guilt to a collective body and rationalize my consumption. When the burden is shared, it becomes impersonal and diluted, more of a national dilemma than an individual one.

A two-cycle chainsaw is an obvious example of the good-evil equation that guilt conspires to erect in our consciences. The chainsaw facilitates the destruction of the wilderness, but it is unarguably one of the most useful inventions of the century, ranking at the very top of the list with the airplane and controlled fission. A sharp chainsaw that starts with one or two pulls of the recoil cord is like a friend, and to befriend a machine is no small accomplishment. Few relationships between a laborsaving device and a laborer were so agreeable. Whenever I cut firewood, I ruminated upon the old days. I had been a child when the chainsaw's predecessor, the crosscut saw, was in common use. Then, the problem had been finding the manpower and the time. Now, the problem was finding the wood.

I busted up the bigger logs with a nine-pound splitting maul, often with the aid of a sledgehammer and steel wedges. Log- and rail-splitting had the aura of a legendary occupation, reputed to build character and align the internal organs, but I found it extremely taxing on my middle-aged frame. Whenever I got the hankering to split wood, I lived with the debilitating results for days—cramped shoulder muscles, strained forearms, creaky knees. True efficiency with a maul required a ferocity that a person of my physicality could muster only in short bursts.

At the conclusion of an unusually cold winter, when I realized I was getting too old to compete with folk heroes, I decided to build a hydraulic log splitter from scratch. It was a challenge not unlike building a house in a hayfield; if I could convince myself that I needed something badly enough, I could make it materialize. All winter, I had been struggling with several rock-hard hickory trunks, trying to split them into logs small enough to fit in the woodstove. Because of their size, the logs hadn't seasoned properly, and when it came time to burn them, their combustion added a thick coating of creosote to the chimney.

A hydraulic splitter is a work-saver that operates on the simplest of principles. A small, valve-controlled hydraulic pump activates a ram cylinder that pushes a block toward a stationary wedge. Under several thousand pounds of pressure, the log placed in between divides along the grain. I needed a splitter that fitted a farm tractor's three-point hitch and ran off the tractor's hydraulic system.

My first task was to locate the raw materials, beginning with the I-beam on which the assembly would sit. I spent an afternoon poking through a scrapyard for odds and ends that might be of use. I paid a few dollars for my retrievings: an I-beam of perfect length and pieces of angle-iron, steel tubing, and flat plate, including an assortment of nuts and bolts. The aesthetic experience cost nothing.

Then I went to another scrapyard, one specializing in heavy equipment, to locate a large, long-stroked hydraulic cylinder. I found one on the boom of a gutted road maintenance machine, a Gradall. Climbing to it and emerging above the petroleum-scented clutter, my eyes lingered on the weathered yellows of high-visibility paint—citrons and saffrons and deep cadmium golds. As the yard mechanic and I wrestled with the cylinder, prying loose its rusted clips and retaining pins, an authentic junkyard dog, a doberman with yellow eyes that burned with hate, strained at the end of a fifty-foot chain.

I took my collection of scrap to Rick's machine shop, where he commenced the cutting, drilling, and welding necessary to reincarnate the diverse pieces. I added the finishing touch by giving the final assembly a coat of paint. The chosen color for rebirth: John Deere industrial yellow.

There was no log the finished product couldn't cleave, even long ones that had to be positioned vertically between wedge and block. Van and

Hope and I cheerfully fought over who did what. One of us manipulated the valve, one positioned the logs, and one stacked the split wood. We worked so rapidly it hardly seemed like work anymore. The stove burned hotter, the firewood supply lasted longer, and, best of all, the rigors of maul-swinging were banished forever.

EIGHTEEN

OFFICIALLY, THE CASUALTIES resulting from the Battle of Cross Keys were as follows: 288 Confederates—41 killed, 232 wounded, 15 missing; 684 Federals—114 killed, 443 wounded, 127 missing. (Those killed were killed outright. The official casualty figures did not take into account soldiers who died later from their wounds.) These figures alone demonstrate that the battle was lopsided, the larger force absorbing more than twice the loss, and even though the fighting lasted over an entire day, strategically the battle was over as soon as it began. From the Union point of view, it resulted in a consolidation of Frémont's army in order to renew the fight the following morning. From the Confederate point of view, it checked Frémont in an unanticipated but successful manner. Whichever way, it was universally acknowledged that Jackson had scripted the drama. The pivotal player, however, came from an unexpected quarter—the Confederate right—in the person of Brigadier General Isaac Ridgeway Trimble.

Sixty years of age in 1862, "Old Trimble" was the only sexagenarian commander on the field. He was born May 15, 1802 in Culpeper County, Virginia. His family moved to Fort Sterling, Kentucky, in 1805, where he passed his childhood. In 1818, he was the sole cadet appointed from Kentucky to the United States Military Academy at West Point, from which he graduated in 1822.

He served in the U.S. Army for ten years, chiefly on ordnance, garrison, and topography duties. His first assignment was to survey a military road from Washington to the Ohio River. He was commanding the Artillery School for Practice at the garrison at Fort Monroe, Virginia, when he resigned his commission on May 31, 1832. Trimble then put his civil engineering skills to use with the rapidly expanding railroad systems as they interlaced the young nation. From 1832 to 1835 he worked for the Boston and Providence Railroad. From 1835 to 1838 he was chief engineer of the Baltimore and Susquehanna Railroad, while he also served concurrently as chief engineer on the York and Wrightsville Railroad. From 1842 to 1853 he held the position of general superintendent on the Philadelphia, Wilmington, and Baltimore Railroad. He was general superintendent on the Philadelphia and Baltimore Central Railroad from 1854 to 1859, then general superintendent on the Baltimore and Potomac Railroad from 1859 to 1861, when war broke out.

Trimble unabashedly supported the secessionist movement. At the outbreak of hostilities in the spring of 1861, he hastened from Cuba, where he had been hired as a consultant for a pioneering railroad venture, to his home in Baltimore, a city seething with secessionist fervor. In April, he committed a very public act of defiance by commandeering a train from Baltimore to Washington for the purpose of burning railroad bridges to delay Federal troops in transit to the nation's capital. By May, he had applied for and received a commission as colonel in the newly established Confederate Engineering Corps, and General Lee sent him to supervise the construction of the defenses around Norfolk. Trimble's single-minded devotion to this duty resulted in his promotion to the rank of brigadier general, after which he was tapped for field command in Jackson's army. He was the second-oldest commissioned officer from Maryland (his adopted home state), and by the end of the war the most decorated.

In 1861 there were ten graduates of the West Point class of 1822 in civilian life. Two went South, while eight remained loyal to the North—a proportion that nearly coincided with the loyalties of all the graduates who remained on active duty. (By 1861 there were 820 West Point graduates who were career soldiers, and more than three-quarters of them remained faithful to the Union.) Like Trimble, most of the West Pointers who were civilians at the start of the war were civil engineers—a testimony to one of the more prestigious engineering degrees available on the North American continent. The other popular occupations were, in descending order, officers of state militias, attorneys and counselors at law, then planters or farmers. Way at the bottom of the list, next to last, were artists. In last place were bishops.

If his civilian resume read like a continuation of his military career, one tour of duty followed by another in rising increments of authority, it was because Trimble was an exceedingly energetic individual. In the

Confederate army, he acquired a reputation for strong opinions, but his more considered words, and surely his deeds, proved him to have been above all a practical leader. A photograph of him in dress uniform shows a ramrod-stiff, balding, silver-haired gentleman with a stern visage peering from behind enormous black eyebrows and mustache.

The age difference between Trimble and Jackson's other field commanders—not to mention Jackson himself—set Trimble apart. As the old man of the corps, a warrior of the old school, he became the butt of jovial innuendo. Although his military bearing was imposing, few thought he would acquit himself with any particular distinction during the campaign. He was greatly underrated. Henry Kyd Douglas, of Jackson's staff, remembered overhearing a conversation between Trimble and Jackson in July, 1862, in which the former declared, "General, before this war is over, I intend to be a Major General or a corpse."

Trimble knew how to place soldiers and guns. He was not one to agonize over a thorny situation. Given the opportunity, he didn't hesitate to act instinctively. Nearly thirty years of experience as a decision maker for the railroads had given him confidence in his authority. At Cross Keys, he chose a better position in line of battle than that to which he was assigned. Then he improvised a flanking maneuver, a combination of three charges, that brought Fremont's entire initiative to a halt. Following that, he stood at the ready to press for further gains, even to the point of making a night attack.

Trimble was a dutiful subordinate to Ewell, his junior by almost fifteen years, but it rankled him when Ewell showed a predilection for indecision. The profane, hyperactive Ewell preferred to be fighting, not directing, and displayed limited ingenuity on the battlefield. Trimble had been around long enough to know the type: an officer who moved up the career ladder by a can-do attitude in implementing the directives of his superiors. As long as Jackson was in charge, Dick Ewell functioned ably enough. After Jackson's death at Chancellorsville in 1863, Lee was forced to retire Ewell from corps command to the relative backwater of the defense works of Richmond. Describing Ewell's faltering leadership at Gettysburg, Lee said, simply, "Jackson was not there."

There were times when Trimble thought it best to sidestep, if not ignore, Ewell's leadership, and oddly enough, Ewell did not object. The original, unedited report that Trimble submitted to Ewell—technically, to Ewell's chief administrative officer (Assistant Adjutant General), Major James Barbour—three days after the battle here told the whole story.

Head quarters 7th Brigade,
Brown's Gap, June 11, 1862.

Major J. Barbour, A. A. Gl.

In compliance with the orders of Maj. Gen'l Ewell I send a statement of the operations of my Brigade on the 8th and 9th inst. in the battle of Cross Keys:

At his request I rode forward with you on the morning of the 8th at about 10 o'clock to examine the ground most desirable for defense. It was decided to post my artillery (Courtney's Battery) on the hill to the South of the small stream, and immediately on the left of the road from Union Church to Port Republic. You directed my Brigade to take the right of our line of defense, and occupy the pine hill to the East of the road and the Battery, but somewhat retired from the front, in escholon [sic] position.

In 1972, the hill chosen for Courtney's battery was cut in half to accommodate a straightened Port Republic Road (Route 659). The new route, superimposed over a gravel lane that had given access to several farms as well as a four-room schoolhouse, bypasses the old road to Port Republic (Route 679) for about a mile and a half before rejoining it just behind the hill. At the time of the regrading, no historical impact study was undertaken, nor was a search for artifacts conducted. Today, a student of the battle can stand by the stop sign at the intersection of Routes 659 and 679 and visualize the former hill with an imaginary filling-in of the road cut. The cannon would have been an improbable eighteen to twenty feet above the ground.

The pine hill to the east, rising above a stream identified on property deeds as Black Anchor Creek, remains as it was in 1862, although the pines are slowly dying from a blight, and the empty spaces are being taken over by second- and third-growth hardwoods. The hill had been part of the Moffet H. Craun farm, which is now the southern tip of the Lee-Jackson property. In all probability, its defensive potential had been recommended by Brigadier General Arnold Elzey, with the instant approval of Ewell, who passed the order to Trimble. Trimble, however, did not approve.

Previous to assigning my Brigade its position in line of battle I rode forward in front and to the right about half a mile, and examined a wooded hill running nearly parallel to our line of battle. Finding this position advantageous, with its left in view and protected by my Artillery, and its right by a ravine and densely-wooded hill, I at once occupied this position with two Regiments (the 16th Miss. and 21st

125

Georgia) about 10 and ½ o'clock, leaving the 21st North Carolina with the Battery to protect it.

The hill of Trimble's choice was a long, flat-topped rise, squarely facing the rolling terrain to the northeast. It declined gradually toward the right and the ravine. By standing in the hayfields and looking back at the hill (now denuded of its woods), a viewer can assume the perspective of the advancing Union troops. Curiously, the hill resembles a railway embankment as it spans the contours of the surrounding fields.

Since the day of the battle, the hill has been unofficially known as Victory Hill. It comprises the portion of the Lee-Jackson tract that was the Grover M. Hooke farm, running parallel to and just across the border from our forty acres. At the western end of the hill, the four-room schoolhouse, built in 1903, served to remind farm children of the heritage that lay beneath their feet. Victory Hill School was closed in 1935, with the centralization of the county school system, but to the present day, its structure is in good repair, having remained the capacious residence of the lady who bought it at auction on the courthouse steps in 1938.

Trimble's report continued:

> Col. Cantey, of the 15th Alabama, by Gen'l Ewell's orders, had been left on picket at Union Church, one mile in advance. This Regiment was the first engaged, resisting the enemy's advance by a destructive fire from the Church, the Graveyard, and the woods. Their force was checked and they did not pursue the Regiment which soon after retired, finding itself outflanked on right and left, and narrowly escaped being cut off, from the *failure of cavalry pickets to do their duty*. Colonel Cantey's own pickets, thrown out as a precaution, though told the cavalry was on that duty, alone saved his Regiment. In retreating in good order, he passed the enemy's Flanking forces on the right and left within long gun shot range, and succeeded in reaching my position with trifling loss.
>
> Colonel Cantey was placed on the right of the two regiments before named.

In the late 1950s, Union Church, empty and without a congregation, was refurbished and enlarged for secular purposes, becoming the Cross Keys–Mill Creek Ruritan Hall as well as the polling place for the local precinct. The building still manifests a somewhat ecclesiastical exterior, thanks to its Gothic arched windows, but the interior has been brought

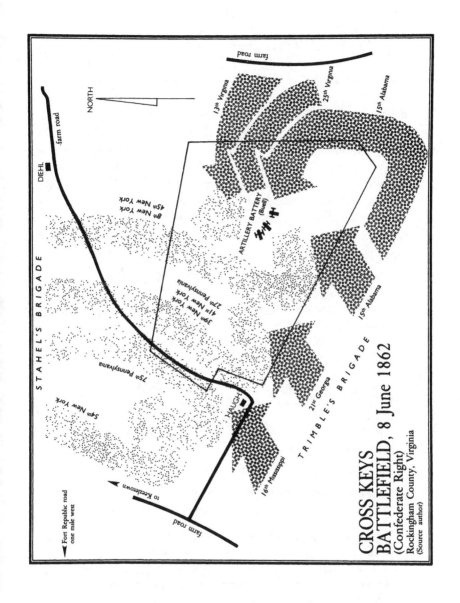

CROSS KEYS
BATTLEFIELD, 8 June 1862
(Confederate Right)
Rockingham County, Virginia
(Source author)

up to date with a dropped acoustical ceiling, a linoleum floor, and folding chairs instead of pews.

Old Port Republic Road, turning southeast from the Keezletown Road, runs between the former church and its graveyard, which is delineated by a silver-painted, turn-of-the-century iron fence. Many of the slender limestone markers date from the early 1800s. Some show pocking and breakage, whether by that historic crossfire or more recent vandalism. Thick, contemporary headstones of polished granite interrupt the grid of the graves like supertankers between sailing vessels.

It was here that the battle began, a little after 9 o'clock in the morning. There was an hour of desultory small arms fire while the Union forces advanced to the left and right. Frémont's chief of artillery, Lieutenant-Colonel John Pilsen, wrote in June 1863:

> The attack was prepared before the enemy was discovered in position, from a point where the road leading to Port Republic divided into two branches. Without having either county maps, or guides, or knowledge of the ground, knowing only the vicinity, and supposing the probable position of the enemy, the whole command, without hesitation or delay, was formed into two nearly equally strong columns, which entered upon the two branches. So we followed rather our own impression, and the supposition proved itself correct. When the enemy soon after was discovered, we had the advantage of being able to deploy both columns at once, and had in a very admirably short time a well combined line of battle in the whole extent of the enemy's position.

As Frémont's army came into view, the twenty-four cannon at Ewell's disposal opened fire, and soon thereafter, the Union batteries were unlimbered, countering with a heavy barrage. Pilsen remembered:

> We had ten batteries, of which eight and a half, in the short time of less than thirty minutes, were brought into favorable positions in the immediate face of the enemy, although he was posted in the woods greatly to our disadvantage, and we were compelled to go in search of his precise position, often coming upon him in very close quarters.

The artillery exchange lasted for five hours until the Confederates ran low on ammunition. Along both lines, firepower was employed to the maximum, and the thunder reverberated across the Valley, from the Blue Ridge to the Alleghenies. Confederate Major Jedediah Hotchkiss, recently down from the Peak and not feeling well, reported in his diary that he saw the gun smoke through field glasses from Weyer's Cafe, four miles distant on a bluff overlooking the South River.

Because of the furious shelling from the Confederate center and left of center, which faced open ground and was deemed too hazardous an area to advance troops in formation, Frémont decided to send an infantry probe to his left, against the enemy's right flank. It was a tentative plan, a test of the Confederate line where he thought his soldiers would meet the least resistance. The Pathfinder was unwilling to venture a larger offensive, facing, as he believed, Jackson's overestimated and undivided army. Frémont wrote in 1865:

> To give this effort any chance of success it would have been necessary to lose valuable time in reconnoitering the ground, during which he [the enemy] could have withdrawn his troops, crossed and destroyed the bridge at Port Republic, and possibly, too, the command of General Shields.
>
> I was without reliable maps or guides, but from what could be seen of the roads, and from the understood position of the bridge at Port Republic, I judged that the enemy's right was his strategic flank. I decided, therefore to press him from this side, with the object to seize, if possible, his line of retreat, and accordingly gave all the strength practicable to my left.

"Practicable" was a key word. Although Frémont waited nearly an hour to implement his decision amid the din of the artillery, he acted too soon with too few. On his left, the majority of the infantry column had not arrived at the front. The forward regiments of Stahel's brigade were ordered to advance against the Confederate right, which they proceeded to do in the face of minor resistance. Wisely, Colonel Cantey had withdrawn his 15th Alabama cross-country from Union Church toward his fellow brigade members. The Rebel regiment was melting into the trees on the flat-topped hill a mile distant; to Union eyes, the regiment was headed toward the pine hill beyond, the one Ewell (with Elzey's help) had originally chosen for Trimble. But the 15th Alabama went no further than the nearer hill, where they took the rightmost position. Concealed in the trees left to right, the infantry line of the 16th Mississippi, the 21st Georgia, and the 15th Alabama had formidable stopping power. Each regiment numbered four hundred men or more; in this instance, Trimble had in excess of thirteen hundred soldiers just inside the border of woods. Trimble's report continued:

Half an hour later the enemy were seen to advance with Gen'l Blenker's old Brigade (among the Regiments, as prisoners informed us, the 8th New York and Buck Tail Rifles, from Pennsylvania) driving in our pickets before a heavy fire. I ordered the three Regiments to rest quietly in the edge of an open wood until the enemy, who were advancing in regular order across the field and hollow, should come within fifty steps of our line, the order was mainly observed, and as the enemy appeared above the crest of the hill a deadly fire was delivered along our whole front, beginning on the right. The repulse of the enemy was complete, followed by an advance, ordered by me, in pursuit. As the enemy's rear Regiments had halted in the wood on the other side of the Valley, I deemed it prudent, after the field in our front had been cleared, to resume our position on the hill and await their further advance.

It was the most lethal moment of the battle – if not an ambush, then a propitious lying-in-wait maintained by a superhuman restraint, a united holding of the breath. As the hapless Union troops drew near, Trimble's mettle proved to be extraordinary, and the discipline of his men was equally sure.

When Frémont ordered Brigadier General Stahel's 1st brigade, forward on the left, a backup brigade, Brigadier General Bohlen's, was not close enough to offer prompt support. Bohlen's backup, Von Steinwehr's brigade, commanded by Colonel John C. Koltes, was still marching on the road. Neither had Brigadier General Schenck's brigade come into position on the right. The order of march had placed Stahel's German-speaking neophytes before more experienced troops in reserve. This may have been the result of an unofficial segregation, a xenophobic isolation of a brigade because its troops couldn't communicate in English. Then, too, the veteran brigades may have rated a few extra winks of sleep in the early morning.

The immigrants of the 8th and 45th New York regiments were the first to advance into the wheat field that rose to the flat-topped hill. Slightly to the right and behind them were the 41st New York and 27th Pennsylvania, the famed DeKalb and Bucktail Regiments. In 1865, Frémont described his initiative as follows:

> Continuous firing had been kept up during the time occupied in getting my forces into position, and with the full establishment of my lines the battle became general. Urging vigorously forward his brigade, General Stahel encountered in the first belt of woods a strong line of skirmishers [the 15th Alabama], which with hard fighting was

driven out of the timber and pushed by the Eighth and Forty-fifth New York over the open ground beyond the edge of the woods, where these regiments suddenly came upon the right of the enemy's main line, held by the troops of General Trimble . . . Two of General Stahel's best regiments, the Twenty-seventh Pennsylvania and Forty-first New York, had been diverted to the right in the timber, and the shock of the entire force here was sustained by the Eighth and Forty-fifth New York, principally by the Eighth . . . This regiment behaved with great gallantry, charging with impetuosity into the enemy's ranks, and for a time holding its own, but yielding at length to the great superiority of numbers was driven, together with the Forty-fifth, back over the open ground and through the woods upon Bohlen's brigade, which had in the mean time advanced to Stahel's support and joined in the action, supported by our batteries.

The Eighth Regiment of Infantry, First German Rifles, of Blenker's Rifles, had been organized by Brigadier General Louis Blenker for two years' active duty on April 23, 1861. Three-hundred young men — with names like Johann, Heinrich, Christian, Wilhelm, Georg, and Friederich — were recruited from Manhattan and Brooklyn, many just off the boat. As soldiers, they ascribed to an old-world morality that did not rule out personal access to the spoils of war. The regiment left New York on May 28, 1861. When it was honorably discharged and mustered out at Brooks' Station, Virginia on April 23, 1863, sixty-four of its soldiers had been killed in action. Another 29 had died of wounds, 33 were missing, and 40 had died of disease and other causes (of the sick, 107 recovered).

Statistics of New York State volunteers, compiled after the war, noted that 1.86 percent of the men were killed outright in battle, 15.12 percent were wounded in action, and 11.14 percent died from disease and other causes. Of the wounded, 42.10 percent died. Of the 380,000 Union soldiers who died, one in seven was a New Yorker.

Two hundred twenty of the 8th's casualties occurred at Cross Keys: 43 dead, 134 wounded, and 43 captured or missing. To compensate for its harsh luck, the regiment was held in reserve at six later battles, including Gettysburg, although it saw limited action at Groveton and Second Bull Run.

To the detriment of truth, some secondary-source battle raconteurs — authors from the present and past who slipped into print with sloppy research — have added imaginary detail to help their readers visualize what happened on the flat-topped hill. They speak of a split-rail fence,

131

behind which the Confederates hid. When Trimble gave the command to fire, his troops stood up and . . . but it is pure fantasy. If Trimble had hidden his brigade behind a fence, he would have said so. Thirteen hundred men were more successfully concealed just inside a leafy woods, with the morning sun at their backs. No primary source mentions anything about a fence.

And what of Trimble's conduct? Did he nervously pace among his troops? Did he cry "Fire!" in a high-pitched voice? These and other flourishes grace the prose of the history embellishers. There are also doctored descriptions of the surprise volley. Some writers claim the Confederates fired three volleys, others claim two, still others claim but one. The distinctions are altogether irrelevant. Although soldiers from both sides were drilled to reload and fire three times a minute, standards of drill were meaningless under actual battle conditions. It is safest to say that Trimble had excellent command of his troops. Having assessed the effect of its surprise fire, his hidden brigade pressed the advantage. They fired and fired again, however many times, until the Union troops were repulsed and reeling. Then the Confederates charged out of the woods and down the slope, brilliantly and brutally effective. Within minutes their work was done and they trudged back to the sanctuary of the trees. Trimble was satisfied that his troops had inflicted mortal damage, and now he awaited the enemy's next move.

> Remaining in our position some fifteen minutes and finding the enemy not disposed to renew the contest, and observing from its fire a Battery on the enemy's left half a mile in advance of us, I promptly decided to make a move from our right flank and try to capture the Battery—as I reported at the time to Gen'l Ewell who, at this stage of the action sent to know success and to ask if I wanted reinforcements, to which I replied I had driven back the enemy, wanted no aid, but thought I could take their Battery, and was moving for that purpose.

Trimble's target was Captain Frank Buell's battery, a cannon position at the far left of Frémont's semicircular line of artillery, on the hill to which my twentieth-century sensibilities had been unaccountably drawn, viz. the champagne toast, the miniature airstrip, and the proposed monument. To the Confederate brigade, it was the closest Union gun position, sitting just beyond the valley of wheat and overlooking the massed troops in blue. Trimble could sense the Federals' disarray. The timing and topography were right for a stealthy attack.

I accordingly in person moved the 15th Alabama to the right along a ravine and, unperceived, got upon the enemy's left flank and in his rear, marching up in fine order, as on drill. I had, on leaving with this Regiment, ordered the other two to advance rapidly in front as soon as they heard I was hotly engaged with the enemy. These Regiments, before the order was executed, stood calmly under a heavy fire of the enemy's Artillery, directed at the woods. The 15th Alabama completely surprised the force in their front (the enemy's left flank), and drove them by a heavy fire hotly returned from behind logs and trees along the wood to the westward.

In a letter to William Allan (formerly Lieutenant-Colonel, C.S.A., and Jackson's chief ordnance officer), written in February 1880 when Trimble was an undimmed seventy-seven years of age, he recounted, in third person, his participation in the battle.

The enemy had crossed the valley and were advancing gallantly up the slope toward Gen. Trimble's position, thus receiving the full fire of the two right regiments at about sixty paces distant. They wavered, and then fell back in disorder . . . Then a charge was ordered, but before the men advanced over the crest of the ridge Gen. Trimble arrested it, as he saw the enemy reforming with supports on the opposite ridge. He waited twenty minutes for another attack, but as the enemy did not move, though formed to do so, he went to the right regiment, Col. Canty's [sic], and marched it by the right flank to the right, as if moving from the field. When concealed by the woods the regiment was marched to the left, and gained, unobserved, the ridge occupied by the enemy at a point not over fifty paces from his left flank in the woods. Before making this flank movement Gen. Trimble had ordered the two regiments left on the ridge to charge across the valley as soon as they heard a brisk fire opened by Col. Canty.

There are two discrepancies between the letter and Trimble's report to Ewell: sixty versus fifty paces (the distance at which the brigade fired) and twenty versus fifteen minutes (the period of rest). Ten paces and five minutes! In the intervening seventeen years, Trimble's memory had remained fresh.

The flank assault followed by the frontal attack began as planned. Word must have reached Frémont about the repulse of Stahel's brigade, for the Union artillerists commenced a violent shelling of the woods over the flat-topped hill, but now the woods were empty. The 21st Georgia and 16th Mississippi had already advanced. Trimble's report continued:

Meantime the 21st Georgia and 16th Mississippi moved across the field and fell in with the remainder of the enemy's Brigade which had reformed in the woods to our left and delivered a galling fire upon the 16th Mississippi which omitted to throw out skirmishers [and] turned up the woods to its left after the main body of the enemy, thus exposing its men to an enfilading fire. Colonel Mercer of the 21st Georgia came to their timely rescue and both soon gallantly drove the enemy out of the woods, killing and wounding large numbers.

The letter to Allan corroborates the action:

As soon as Col. Canty got into position he was ordered to charge. A sharp conflict of a few minutes ensued. The Twenty-first Georgia charged across the valley, followed by Col. Posey, with the Sixteenth Mississippi, when the enemy was driven back in front of our whole line. It was here that Col. Posey, in advancing, did not look to his left and was attacked on his flank by a force which was stationed in the woods, throwing his regiment into some disorder. Col. Mercer, with much presence of mind and judgment, came to his aid with the Twenty-first Georgia, and by a charge, drove off the enemy.

Extricating the 16th Mississippi from the flanking fire in which six were killed and twenty-eight wounded led to a harrowing few minutes that the elderly Trimble could not forget. Bohlen's brigade, having made its way to the front, reinforced the remnants of Stahel's brigade with the 58th New York and 74th Pennsylvania. It was the 54th New York, holding Bohlen's right, that crossed a bog and struck the 16th Mississippi in the flank—a brief, bad taste of the Confederates' own medicine.

The report to Ewell continued:

On marching to the right flank with the 15th Alabama I found parts of the 13th and 25th Va. Rifle under command of Col. James A. Walker, of Gen'l Elzey's Brigade, had been ordered to my support by Gen'l Ewell. I ordered Col. Walker to move to my right through the woods and advance on the enemy's line of battle perpendicularly to *his* line, and in rear of the Battery. Unluckily, as the woods trended to his right he marched directly on, fell in with my Regiment 15th Ala. and lost time by having to move by the flank to regain his position. In doing this he was exposed to the view of the battery which turned its fire on him with galling effect, compelling a resort to the woods.

And compelling a resort to the woodshed, in Trimble's estimation of Ewell, for scotching the almost flawless execution of his attack. Despite the message in which Trimble pointedly refused help, Ewell had sent the 13th and 25th Virginia anyway. What did these unsolicited troops accomplish? They marched in the wrong direction, entangling themselves in the 15th Alabama and blowing their cover, so to speak, in the maneuver to capture the Union battery, which now began cannonading them at close range.

> At this time the right wing of the 15th Ala. had advanced unperceived, under my direction, to within 300 yards of the Battery, then playing rapidly over their heads on the 13th and 25th Va. Perceiving the 16th Miss. and 21st Geo. had advanced, I gave orders to charge the Battery. Upon reaching the top of the hill I found it had limbered up and rapidly retired, having lost several horses by our fire. Five minutes gain in time would have captured the guns. This was lost by the Miss. Reg't in misconstruing my orders.

In the letter of February 1880, Trimble had this to say:

> Gen. Trimble then gave orders to charge a battery on a high plain, but by the time the Fifteenth Alabama reached the top of the hill the battery was moving off with precipitation. A few minutes before this Col. J. A. Walker, with the Thirteenth and Twenty-fifth Virginia regiments, had been sent over by Gen. Ewell, and was directed by Gen. Trimble to advance on the right of the Fifteenth Alabama. Col. Walker, passing too far to the right, was observed by [the] battery, and for a few moments was under a warm fire; but his troops gallantly advanced, and as the battery drove off rapidly we saw the infantry force in full retreat towards the Keezletown road. Thus the enemy's force in front of our right was driven by three successive charges from the field to a mile in rear of their first position . . .

Reading between the lines of the report, Ewell must have realized the needlessness of the gift of Walker's regiments, for Walker, too, contributed to the delay. Trimble was politic enough not to dwell on the incident. The empty-handed result of the Confederate charge could be construed as a cautionary experience—the pursuit of a goal that vanishes just as it comes within reach. Trimble simply chalked it up to the vicissitudes of war. Calling the flank movement to the right a "handsome success," he went on to say,

> Although we failed to take their Battery, it was not attributable to unskillful maneuvering, but to one of those accidents which often decide the results of battles and partial engagements.

Writing in 1865, Frémont saw the event in a different light:

The enemy now brought up additional artillery into the open ground on my extreme left, and General Taylor's reserve brigade entering the woods, the fighting continued with great severity continuously along the timber in front of our position. A Mississippi regiment, charging with yells upon Buell's battery, was gallantly met with a bayonet charge by the Twenty-seventh Pennsylvania, under cover of which the battery was withdrawn.

Frémont's imprecision notwithstanding, the tide of the battle was turning decidedly in the Confederates' favor. Worried that his left flank was about to become engulfed, the Pathfinder ordered a final, skewed countercharge. Trimble reported:

Another Brigade of the enemy supporting the Battery, 200 yards to its left, our right, advanced into the open ground and at the time the Ala. and the 13th and 25th Va. reached their positions, this force was driven back by them (insert—wasted action) and retired with the Battery. After some minutes brisk fire by the enemy's sharp shooters their entire left wing retreated to their first position near Union Church on the Keiseltown [sic] road.

Frémont remembered:

Every attempt of the enemy to emerge from the cover of the woods was repulsed by artillery and counter-attacks of infantry, and his loss at this portion of the field, inflicted especially by artillery, was very great. On our part the loss was heavy, the Eighth New York alone losing 46 killed and 134 wounded. One of my aides-de-camp, Capt. Nicolai Dunka, a capable and brave officer, was killed by a musket-ball while carrying an order to this part of the field. Colonel Gilsa, of the Forty-first New York, Captain Miser, and Lieutenant Brandenstein, of General Blenker's staff, were severely wounded.

The enemy's movement in the bringing up of artillery and fresh troops threatening entirely to envelop my left, a new position was taken at the edge of the timber on the line B [Frémont's map is no longer extant], and the enemy reoccupied the belt of woods lost to them at the beginning. Up to this point the musketry and artillery fire had been incessant and the fighting throughout the field generally severe.

The cannon duel continued into the afternoon. Behind the Confederate line, both Elzey and Steuart were to retire with wounds. Earlier, Frémont had ordered Brigadier General Milroy to begin an attack on Ewell's center, which only succeeded in pushing back skirmishers.

Around one o'clock, as soon as Brigadier General Schenck's brigade arrived on the field, Frémont ordered an attack on Steuart at the Confederate left. The Federals made gains against the 44th Virginia until they were stopped by two reserve regiments, the 12th Georgia and the 31st Virginia. Then Schenck swept the 32nd and 73rd Ohio around to the right, pivoting his line like the hand of a clock, driving the Rebel pickets deeper into the pine wood. At the same time, he advanced his other infantry regiments toward the concealed Confederate position.

Schenck desperately sought to pursue the offensive at this point, as he was on the verge of making real progress, but he was denied permission. Instead, Frémont ordered him to withdraw to the left in support of Stahel. The incredulous Schenck sent the message back for confirmation, but it was relayed a second time. In Frémont's words:

> Farther to the right our artillery, under the immediate direction of Colonel Pilsen, had been hotly engaged with the batteries of the enemy's center. Milroy and Cluseret were opposed to Generals Elzey and Early, commanding the enemy's right and center. Our own center, under Cluseret, after an ineffectual attempt upon the enemy's batteries, had held obstinately every foot of its advanced ground, repelling with steadiness and gallantry repeated assaults of the enemy. General Milroy had been warmly engaged driving in a strong line of the enemy's skirmishers, attacking their main body at close quarters, and suffering severely in an attempt to plant a battery upon the heights. Upon the extreme right General Schenck, in support of Milroy, had advanced his line, extending it into contact with the enemy, occupying them with skirmishers, shelling the woods, and checking their advance in flank.
>
> Notwithstanding the fair promise held out to an effort on the right, I judged it best at this point to re-establish my whole line in conformity to the change on the left preparatory to a renewal of the battle. Accordingly the brigades of the right were withdrawn for a space, and, except from a portion of Cluseret's strong position at the center and occasional exchanges of artillery shots, the firing subsided, the enemy meantime remaining in his position and our pickets occupying securely the points temporarily relinquished by the main line.

But as soon as Schenck began withdrawing his brigade (under the protective fire of its battery), Frémont sent a third communication, which gave Schenck permission to hold the ground, if he chose to do so. Incensed and disappointed, Schenck knew it was too late. Milroy, with Colonel Cluseret's advance brigade in reserve, was already in the process of withdrawing to the rear. To prevent his own regiments from becoming dangerously isolated, Schenck had no choice but to follow suit.

What prompted Frémont to cancel his offensive just as it was ripening with "fair promise"? He wrote:

> Pending these preparations I received from the hands of one of my scouts the following letter from General Shields:

Luray, June 8 – 9:30 A.M.

Major-General Frémont,
Commanding Pursuing Forces:

I write by your scout. I think by this time there will be twelve pieces of artillery opposite Jackson's train at Port Republic, if he has taken that route. Some cavalry and artillery have pushed on to Waynesborough to burn the bridge. I hope to have two brigades at Port Republic today. I follow myself with two other brigades today from this place. If the enemy changes direction you will please keep me advised. If he attempts to force a passage, as my force is not large there yet, I hope you will thunder down on his rear. Please send back information from time to time. I think Jackson is caught this time.

Yours, sincerely,

JAS. SHIELDS
Major-General*, Commanding Division.

This was most welcome intelligence. Hitherto I had received no direct information from General Shields, and beyond the fact that he was somewhere near Luray I had no positive knowledge of his whereabouts or intentions. As the moment approached when it became of critical importance that we should act together, I had the day before pushed my scouts into the Luray Valley. Several of them were taken by the enemy, but one succeeded in reaching me with this letter. With the certainty now that General Shields was already holding the bridge in force I at once decided to defer until morning a renewal of the battle. My men had been marching and fighting since early in the morning. They were fatigued and hungry and needed rest, and I knew they required every advantage I could give. I therefore directed the command to bivouac and operations for the day to be brought to a close. My force was established for the night upon the line B B, Colonel Cluseret's brigade being withdrawn into the woods near Un-

---

*As a conceit, Brigadier General Shields often used his old brevet rank of Major General (United States Volunteers), which he had been awarded at Cerro Gordo, Mexico, in 1847.

ion Church, and our pickets remaining, as stated, in occupation of other points of the battleground.

Earlier in the afternoon, the persistent roar of artillery – predominantly Union now, since the Confederate batteries had nearly exhausted their ammunition, and the resupply wagons never arrived – convinced Jackson in Port Republic that Ewell was having a rough time of it. The brigades of Colonel Patton and Brigadier General Taylor were marched back to Cross Keys. Ewell promptly sent Taylor to reinforce Trimble on the right. It was Ewell's second unsolicited gift of manpower, this time an entire brigade. Trimble stated in his report:

> At this time Gen'l Taylor with his Brigade joined me. He had previously been ordered to my support. I called Gen'l Taylor to an interview on an eminence in view of the enemy, then a mile distant, where a Battery with an infantry force, of what strength we could not discern, was in sight. I proposed to move forward and renew the fight. Gen'l Taylor's reply was that "we could soon wipe out that force if it would do any good," but proposed to return his Brigade to camp, as he had, that morning, marched rapidly to Port Republic and returned and his men needed rest and food. I replied that we had better attack the enemy, but as he did not agree with me, and as I at that time understood that he was sent to aid me in the contest which was then ended, I did not insist on his remaining. He left me about 4 P.M. I then disposed the three Regiments in the woods in regular order, about one-half mile distant from the enemy, with skirmishers in front and on the flanks, sending word to Gen'l Ewell that the enemy had been repulsed on our right and that I awaited orders.

Ringed by his skirmishers, Trimble consolidated his astonishingly forward position. The shade of the trees afforded a welcome refuge from the heat of the afternoon. Although Taylor had come and gone (and with him, a strong offensive capability that was to see action the following day), Trimble fully expected to renew the attack – on his own, if necessary.

> About half an hour after Gen'l Taylor left, Maj. Barbour came to me with orders from Gen'l Ewell to move to the front and that a force would be sent forward on the enemy's right to make a combined attack before night. It was too late to recall Gen'l Taylor. I moved through the woods and halted in line, 500 yds. from the enemy's front (disposed along the Keiseltown road) prepared to attack him as soon as I could hear from their fire that our force on his flank was engaged.

139

I waited half an hour, without any intimation of this attack and sent a courier to Gen'l Ewell to say I awaited the movement on our left. Half an hour afterwards, I sent another courier with the same message and soon after Lieut. Lee, of my staff, to say that if the attack was made on their flank to divert their attention from my movement, I thought I could overpower the enemy in front, but that it would be injudicious to do so alone, as I could plainly see three Batteries of the enemy, all able to bear on our force as we advanced across the open fields, and what I estimated as Five Brigades of infantry.

But no word came from Ewell. Apparently, his promise of an attack was a theoretical possibility, not a concrete plan of action, and yet Trimble waited, repeating his messages. Ewell stated in his report to Jackson that the absence of his cavalry, combined with the threat of a Union offensive on his left, kept him from committing troop support to Trimble. These were flimsy excuses; the infantry was doing fine without the cavalry, and as for the threat on his left, it was plainly defused with the withdrawal of Schenck and Milroy.

Ewell sat astride his horse at his headquarters to the rear of the Confederate center, pondering the current state of affairs and fretting over the safety of a junior lieutenant on his staff who happened to be the son of the widow he hoped to wed. Wounded, Steuart and Elzey were out of commission. Steuart's batteries had been withdrawn for lack of ammunition and loss of horses, leaving Courtney's (Latimer's) battery, Trimble's own, to return fire singlehandedly to at least four Union gun positions. The ammunition train sent from Port Republic seemed to have lost its way. Taylor's brigade, the belated gift of fighting power from Jackson himself, was headed back to Port Republic.

But what surmounted all reasons and excuses was Ewell's unwavering adherence to Jackson's master plan. He dared not expand upon or modify in any way his original orders, which had been to check Frémont—not rout him. When Ewell saw with his own eyes that the Union forces were retreating to a static position north of the Keezletown Road, he knew that his mission was fulfilled. Jackson would be proud of him. So Ewell denied his brigadier's impatient request in a classic manner—he stalled for time. Trimble recounted:

I waited in suspense until after dark, saw the enemy go into camp, light their fires, draw rations and otherwise dispose themselves for the night, evidently not expecting any further attack. I then sought Gen'l Ewell to recommend a night attack and found he had gone to report to Gen'l Jackson. Before leaving I was strongly tempted to make the advance alone at night and should have done so had I not felt it a duty to secure complete success by waiting for the combined attack before alluded to; and having some scruples in regard to possible failure if acting alone, which might have thwarted the plans of the Commanding General whose success the day after would be seriously jeopardized by even a partial reverse, after the fortunate results of the day.

Trimble ended the paragraph with a sentence that surely contained one erased or otherwise deleted syllable, which needs to be restored. The syllable was *out*:

I regretted that I had not detained Gen'l Taylor until Maj. Barbour reached me, as with his Brigade and my own, the result would have been reasonably certain, with[out] consulting G. Ewell.

It wouldn't be fair to say that Ewell was unmoved by Trimble's pleas. Mindful of the opportunity for a real victory, one that would avenge the death of Turner Ashby and heap laurels on his own command, Ewell felt obliged to lay the matter before Jackson. In doing so, Ewell resorted to the second classic ploy of deferred decision making—he asked his superior to recommend a course of action.

Major R. L. Dabney, Assistant Adjutant General and preacher to the Stonewall Brigade, claimed that Jackson rode back to Cross Keys for the conference, a claim unsubstantiated by any other source. Dabney wrote this in 1865, while he was still grieving for Jackson, who had been mistaken for a Yankee and mortally wounded by his own troops two years earlier. In matters pertaining to Jackson, Dabney had a reputation for stretching the truth; it was he who promulgated Jackson's apotheosis as the most brilliant, the most pious, the kindest, the bravest, etc. According to Dabney, the late commanding general had been everywhere at once, too. But given the battle preparations at Port Republic, not to mention the shock of Carroll's incursion, Jackson had his hands full. While the commanding general was keenly interested, of course, in his Third Division's success at Cross Keys, more than likely it was Ewell who made the four-mile ride to Port Republic.

Jackson counseled his visitor, in modern parlance, to hang tough. He was more concerned with laying the groundwork for his own defensive stand at Port Republic. But Jackson's plans had changed slightly: now Ewell was to evacuate his position at Cross Keys before dawn and march his troops, with the exception of Trimble's infantry, to Port. With Frémont's attention undoubtedly focused on the Confederate right, the withdrawal would be unhampered and largely unnoticed if Trimble's force remained as a foil. Once Shields was defeated, the whole army would return to Cross Keys to reengage Frémont.

Meanwhile, as twilight suffused the battlefield, the Seventh Brigade maintained its vigilance. Night attacks were unusual in the Civil War, an attack on a sabbath night being even more of a rarity, but Trimble had too strong a soldier's instinct to ignore the idea. The stumbling block—Jackson's master plan, as interpreted by his obtuse compatriots—had to be dealt with first. It behooved Trimble to take leave of his troops in order to intercede personally at division headquarters. He wrote:

> Fully convinced that we could make a successful night attack and dispersion, capture Gen'l Frémont's entire force; certainly all his artillery—I awaited Gen'l Ewell's return and strongly urged more than once this attack and urged him to go with me and see how easy it was.

Aware of the legitimacy of Trimble's heated petition, Ewell resorted to a third, equally classic ploy for deferring a decision. He passed the buck.

> He said he could not take the responsibility & if it was to be done I would have to see Gen'l Jackson—I accordingly rode four miles to see him, obtained his consent to have Col. Patton's battalion to cooperate with me & his directions to consult Gen'l Ewell "be guided by him"—on returning to Gen'l Ewell with this permission he declined taking the responsibility, which he said rested on him—& continued with Gen'l Taylor to oppose it, against my urgent entreation to be permitted to make the attack alone with my brigade—He only replied "You have done well enough for one day" & even a partial success would interfere with Gen'l Jackson's plans for the next day.

Ewell's fourth and final ploy—getting a yes man to back him up—added little to his argument. Echoing Ewell, Taylor amplified the drawbacks, so irritating Trimble that the narrative of his report rose to a telegraphic fury. Taylor was the last person in the world to see any advantage in continuing the fight. Trimble's patience was at the breaking point. He had ridden all the way to Port Republic for nothing. Try as he might, there was no way he could entice Ewell into redefining the master plan. In frustration, Trimble quitted division headquarters with a final warning:

I replied that we should have this army of Frémont's preceding us tomorrow, if not driven off, and that we had better fight one army at a time—I ended the matter—

My Regiments remained under arms all night and I moved to camp at daybreak with reluctance.

As it turned out, Trimble's worst fears were groundless, given Frémont's indisposition to stir his army to renewed activity. The day ended in a standoff, with the smaller force by half inflicting more than twice the casualties, and in this statistic alone, the Battle of Cross Keys was unique. Trimble's repulse on the right, followed by his thrust which advanced the Confederate line by more than a mile, served to deepen Frémont's loss of nerve. The gain in ground at Cross Keys was especially meaningful as a gain in time. By keeping Frémont and Shields apart, the Confederates won the edge that tilted the odds in their favor at Port Republic.

NINETEEN

THE DISRUPTIONS OF WAR notwithstanding, the Haugh farm in the 1860s must have been a placid place. As I thought about the prospect of haymaking on my own, I did my best to visualize how the hay was harvested back then.

An invention of supreme importance to agriculture, the reciprocating scissors cutter was patented in various forms in the early nineteenth century. The reciprocating cutter made the scythe and sickle obsolete because the cutting action of scissors multiplied along the length of a bar (like a hedge trimmer or hair clipper) mowed easily through standing vegetation. It was no longer necessary to swing hard at the crop with a long sharp blade. By the 1860s, most of the hay in the United States was cut with a two-horse mower. Cutting either a five- or six-foot swath, the implement's mechanical action was powered by the traction of its ground wheels. With reins in hand, the driver sat in a scooped pan on a flat spring to the rear, stabilizing his or her feet on iron footpegs.

A few days later, when the hay was dry, a horse-drawn dump rake was pulled over the field. The rake consisted of a long row of crescent-shaped spring tines between two tall wheels. Hay was collected until the tines were full, whereupon the operator (also in a pan seat at the rear) tripped a lever that lifted the tines and dumped the hay. By continuing to rake and dump across the length of a field, long field-wide windrows were created.

The next step was to prepare the hay for storage. Few farms had barns large enough to hold a hay crop. The most prevalent procedure was to build haystacks in the field. Poles were arranged crosswise on the ground to serve as elevated foundations, or ricks, at various windswept, well-drained locations. The windrowed hay was consolidated by hand pitching into sizable, though movable stacks called shocks. Two field hands on horseback looped a long rope around the bases of these shocks, then attached the rope ends to their saddles. With careful synchronization, the shocks were dragged to the ricks, where they were pitched, forkful after forkful, in a way that left the hay stems radiating around a central point (sometimes, a vertical pole was set in place). An experienced stack builder stood right in each haystack as it rose, making sure it was packed properly and tapered slightly as it grew in height, and peaked in the center to repel water.

The sight of huge haystacks in these fields — some fifteen feet and taller, as high as hay could be pitched with a long-handled fork — is a memory only to the oldest residents of the area. When I think of haystacks I think of Van Gogh and Monet. Haystacks were monolithic light-collectors and light-reflectors, synonymous with earth-friendly, nonpolluting enterprise. A well-put-together haystack could last for two years with very little spoilage. When it came time to use the hay, a farmer took a hay knife like a long, serrated scimitar and chopped out a section.

When Becky and I first bought the land, the farmer and I agreed that he would continue making the hay on a year-to-year basis, and keep all of it. In doing so, he would pay a nominal price for two out of every five bales, an arrangement known as making hay for shares. It took me three years to make the transition to full stewardship of the forty acres. My most pressing priorities were to finish the house and resume my interrupted career as a painter. Once these accomplishments were behind me, I turned my attention to the making of hay — twentieth-century style.

Nearly sixty-five tons of mixed hay were harvested annually from our fields, which in the past had also provided fall and winter grazing for approximately forty head of cattle. During his last months of ownership, the farmer had squeezed the last ounce of forage value from the fields by grazing twice as many cattle. When Becky and I took possession, the ground was as close-cropped as a putting green, liberally dotted with cow-pie hazards. In places, the thatch was eaten right down to the dirt.

From a farming standpoint, there wasn't much we could do right away except to let the fields regenerate themselves. It was a matter of limited money and machinery, the former being funneled into house construction, and the latter being my Kubota tractor, an orange, twenty-one-horsepower workhorse I had owned since 1973. As for implements, I had no tillage or haymaking equipment, just some rudimentary tools for the upkeep of a small farm — a scraper blade, a finishing mower, a drag rake, and a two-wheeled cart.

With respect to agriculture, nonfarmers like myself cling to sentimental, misleading notions. Barns are picturesque, silos are statuesque, and a fenceline is the rural equivalent of a picture frame. Crops in the field are wind-rippled shags of green, and farm animals are big pets with cute personalities (trite generalizations about barnyard smells factor here). Lastly, farm machines are complicated toys for grownups in coveralls.

Ever since I was a child, I had been guilty of this perspective. One of my favorite playthings had been a farm set which consisted of a stamped metal barn (with polychrome detail inside and out) and plastic animals that grazed on small plots of plastic earth. By assiduously cultivating my weekly allowance of ten or fifteen cents, I was able to expand my farming operation with a tractor or two, a hay wagon, and some fence sections that kept out the reality of the hardwood floor and the legs of nearby furniture. I collected grass clippings to press into haystacks and mat into bedding for the animals. To complete the illusion, I encircled the outermost fenceline with my electric train tracks. In my busy imagination, the friendly engineer waved to the friendly farmer in the field.

Now, almost four decades later, I lived amid the genuine articles: a real barn, real fences, real fields . . . and, yes, when the wind was right, real hoots from the airhorn of a Norfolk & Western freight as it approached grade crossings on a spur three miles away. But the farmer who sold the property said, "A feller can't farm forty acres anymore because it ain't enough land to generate a decent income, no matter what a feller does." The property was good for two things: grazing cattle and making hay, neither of which would amount to much, in his opinion.

When we bought the property, the opportunity to work myself silly as a back-to-the-lander was farthest from my mind. After twenty-five years of hacking out a living, or semblance thereof, by my so-called creative wits, I was too firmly embarked upon the quest for the big-time-that-never-materialized to deviate from my course. My career required occasional promotional trips, which meant that I could not be counted on to fulfill the daily requirements of animal husbandry. Restricting my farming efforts to the making of hay, however, would allow sufficient leeway in my schedule. Farming interested me. A limited amount of it would challenge my learning skills and generate additional income. And for all my trouble, there would be the grace of privacy and room to roam around in.

Reduced to its essentials, modern haymaking sounded easy: mow the fields, rake them, bale the hay, and put the bales in the barn. I was not deceived. Haying on forty acres would be an engrossing and time-consuming operation. Acquiring and maintaining the equipment would be a job in itself. Toiling in the field, and later, selling the hay out of the barn, would add long hours to my already full days. I would be embarking on a concurrent career. As I contemplated the prospect, I did my best to plan ahead. I resolved to start looking for used, but not totally worn out equipment. I promised Becky I would not go over my head in debt. I would keep the fields in mixed hay for the time being, until they needed renovation. Lastly, I would square bale because there seemed to be a strong local demand for hay among animal owners who didn't have the capacity for round bales.

Coincidentally, I happened to notice a square baler, a New Holland #65, in the back lot of an implement dealership in Harrisonburg. The baler beckoned me. Its red and yellow paint had faded to pink and cream, and rust was beginning to form along the sheet metal edges and on flat surfaces where rainwater pooled. Made in the sixties—the era of the Corvair and the Falcon—it had been New Holland's "compact" baler, and it looked just the right size for the Kubota.

A square baler is a contraption par excellence. No better term exists to describe one. Its forerunner was the stationary baler, or hay press, a turn-of-the-century invention that was moved from farm to farm at haying time and hooked up by belt to a power source (often a wood-burning steam engine). Loaded haywagons were drawn up alongside the press so that farmhands could pitch forkfuls of hay into the path of its plunger. Between every fifteen or twenty plunger strokes, wooden dividers were inserted by hand along the chuteful of compressed hay. Two additional workers standing on opposite sides of the chute fitted pre-cut lengths of wire between the dividers, tying off bales.

With the advancement of agricultural engineering, tractor-drawn balers performed all these functions mechanically, and the only person left in the link was the tractor driver. By the 1940s, New Holland proudly called its baler, "The Automaton." It collected the hay from a windrow, chopped it to uniform length, compressed it, tied off bales with two strands of rodent-proof sisal twine, and chuted the bales out the back. Farmers had the option of towing a flatbed wagon behind the baler, so that bales could be collected before they fell to the ground. More recently, kickers had been developed, ejection systems that flung the bales into tall-sided wagons, also towed behind.

The #65 was owned by a mechanic at the dealership, a sympathetic fellow who didn't mind my revisits and questions. He had baled with it for more than ten years, he said, "and she never missed a lick." Originally, the baler had been equipped with a gas-engined kicker, which he had removed because it tended to pitch bales erratically, sometimes right over the wagon. He said the kicker could be fixed, but it would cost extra. I decided to buy the baler as is. We did some perfunctory haggling, and the sum of $1,400 changed hands. A day later the implement was delivered to the main floor of the barn, where I proceeded to acquaint myself more thoroughly with its intricacies.

At the front of the baler was a long tongue that hitched to the tractor, and a telescoping driveshaft, universally jointed at either end, that attached to a tractor's power take-off shaft, or P.T.O. The hindmost joint was bolted to a slip clutch on the face of a large flywheel, and the flywheel connected directly to a gearbox, which powered every function. A drive belt turned a pickup reel with stubby spring tines that lifted the windrowed hay to a feeder chamber. A chain yanked a feeder carriage back and forth, pushing the hay at right angles into the path of the plunger. Attached to one side of the plunger was a knife that sliced through the hay, separating that which the plunger was about to compress. Another chain ran the knotter assembly, a complex device that pushed two twine-threaded steel arms, or needles, up through the chuteful of compressed hay at timed intervals, tied the knots, cut the twine, and advanced the bale counter by one.

As I studied the baler, I began, quite unconsciously, to clean it. Wiping here, scraping there, my attentions became methodical, ultimately comprehensive, as I ventured deeper into the machine. I could not stop myself. My family thought I had taken leave of my senses to be spending such long hours in the barn; over the course of three weeks, the baler occupied every minute of my spare time and I returned to the house filthy with grime. The more I scraped and sanded, removing deposits of dried lubricants, caked dirt, and hay, the more I realized how vast a surface area I was committed to. Channels, flanges, and ledges awaited my attention. It was impossible to start at one end and wind up at the other. The baler's dimensions seemed to fly in all directions. Having reached bare metal at one place, I immediately applied elbow grease somewhere else, keeping at it until I was satisfied with the cleanliness of every nook and cranny.

I returned to the dealership to purchase a quart apiece of New Holland Red and New Holland Yellow paint. I wanted original equipment enamel. No cheap substitute would do. My goal was a total refinishing; my standards were exacting. With the barn doors opened wide, I began the paint job with my best china bristle brush. Since I wanted to preserve every decal—the logotypes as well as the numerous warnings and maintenance reminders—it took several rolls of masking tape and some artful brushwork. I resorted to spray cans of matching enamel to get in the tight places. The underside was painted just as conscientiously. One evening, when I was nearly finished, Becky walked over to see how things were going. She thought that, much to her surprise, I had traded the faded baler for a new one. I had really *Svensonized* it, she said.

I burst out laughing and, for the first time, stepped outside of my chambered nautilus of single-mindedness. It could have been the paint fumes. Cosmetically removing twenty-five years of service from a farm implement *was* a crazy thing to do. Farmers didn't give a damn about the shine on their balers. I was still the worst kind of neophyte—an adult with a child's eye for perfection. Even though I fully intended to return the old contraption to the field, I wanted it to gleam in the sun like a big toy.

TWENTY

————

BEING MOTIVATED TO DISCOVER any account by a primary source that could shed additional light on the battle, I came upon two pieces of writing, both by Union officers, that brought June 8, 1862 into sharper focus. The underlying events were pretty much ensconced in my mind, but I needed some fleshing out of the story from a Union perspective. The running commentary penned as a personal memoir by Colonel Albert Tracy, Frémont's Assistant Adjutant General, did exactly that.

> June 8th [Sunday.] Our force, present and effective, of all arms, numbered by my returns upon the special roll call at Fabius, in the mountains, May 29th, something over eleven thousand total. Deducting now the drain for garrisons, guards, working parties, and the rest, at rear, together with killed, wounded, sick, and stragglers, and if there [sic] were in their places, in the ranks at this date ten thousand five hundred men, it was as much as the most sanguine ought to look for. The force of Jackson has never been estimated lower than sixteen thousand—many insisting upon eighteen.
>
> With the earliest practicable moment of the morning, then, and with every available man and corps, we are in motion upon the high road [from Harrisonburg to Port Republic]. Cluseret, with his light troops, has the advance, the main body following in a stated and regular order . . . the way was hilly and at points miry, and in other respects difficult to overcome.
>
> At about eight, however, [in actuality, closer to nine] the crack of rifles at our front indicated an engagement with the enemy's pickets, while soon the receding of the fire informed us that these were undoubtedly driven in.

Tracy was hearing the gunfire at Union Church as Colonel Cantey's 15th Alabama, which wasn't to taste defeat until the battle for Little

Round Top at Gettysburg more than a year later, withdrew toward the flat-topped hill.

> Then came a muffled detonation above the hills, and through the brush and forest interspersed at our right and left, the sound of heavier guns, and the main body of the enemy's force had been struck, and could not be far off. As usual, there was a tightening of belts, and a readjustment of knapsacks, blankets and the like on the part of the men, for a more rapid advance. With the General the Staff drove in their spurs and galloped in the direction of the firing at the front. Ambulances, ammunition wagons, guns, caissons, and all, we dashed past, splashing with entire recklessness the pools at this side or that, till arriving behind the point or shoulder of a projecting hill at the right, a halt was had, with the view to a more careful reconnaissance and study of the ground, and the prompt placing in position of troops, as they should arrive.

To the men in columns, slogging through the mud, the staff's passage must have charged the atmosphere. After the protracted march up the Valley, the hour of reckoning was at hand.

> Just now a shell came hurtling from the right, over the point of the hill, passing barely above the heads of some infantry, moving by a flank, and plunging—with an emphatic scattering of the mud, just in front of Colonel Tracy's horse . . . Matters were, beyond question, becoming both exciting and absorbing . . .
>
> The ground, as occupied by the enemy, and as we saw on rising the point of hill in question, by a turn somewhat to right—was in the nature, mainly, of an elevation upon the opposite side of a hollow considerably broken, and, in parts, wooded, lying between ourselves and them. At the right, from our position and upon a somewhat precipitous ridge, beyond a stream, with a marshy flat at the hither side, they had massed, with strong supports, the bulk of their artillery. It was from this point, as well, that they covered the road of main approach. To the left, with, at intervals, lesser batteries, and marked by inequalities of the ground, or by brush, or fence, or fringe of the taller forest, extended in chief their line of battle. In this direction, also, and at what was to them their right, they had established, of course, still other guns in support, with the cavalry in body, at the rear. The flanks of the rebels, curving somewhat, inclined toward us.

Perhaps Tracy mistook Ewell's mounted staff for cavalry; at any rate, he conveyed a graphic description of the disposition of Ewell's front. His words seemed to imply that he did not overlook Trimble's forward position on the Confederate right, but this side of the battle line did not look nearly as formidable as the other. To avoid the concentration of firepower aimed at the open ground in the vicinity of the main road, Frémont would be considering an alternate route of attack.

> Along the crests of a species of intermediate minor elevations, and covered at points with brush or timber, in like manner with the enemy, Pilsen had established, within the space of half an hour, his series of batteries, concentrating liberally upon the enemy by the farther ridge, and pounding away with vigor. To the right of Cluseret, and partially within a patch of woods in which there was a church—called Union Church—went promptly into position Milroy's brigade. To the left of Cluseret, and past woods from which he drove out additional skirmishers of the enemy, the brigade of Stahl. Schenck was in echelon to the right and rear of Milroy. Bohlen took ground in support and opposite to the interval between Stahl and Cluseret. Off upon our left and right, cavalry with a sufficient of reserve guns at points as required. The plan of operation as proposed in the main, was to turn the rebels at their right or strategic flank. Extend as we might, however, so far as our lines stood concerned, the enemy was so far superior in numbers as to overlap us—whether at the right or left.

The breadth of Ewell's defensive position, impressive as it was, led Frémont to believe he should concentrate his attack at one place. In this respect, the movement of the 15th Alabama may have served as a lure. Frémont's exploratory intuition told him to follow the withdrawing pickets. If he had waited to advance simultaneously at other points along the front, the Confederate line might have crumpled, particularly at its center, but he had no insight into this possibility.

> In the meantime, and during the conduct to position of our people, the low and sullen roar of the enemy's guns, as heard at first above the hills, and through the forests by the way, had risen to positive thunder—in which our own batteries now joined with a vim of detonation not surpassed. The dropping patter of the skirmishers had swollen to the crash of volleys by battalions, as our lines closed yet nearer in, till, with the whole, the rattling and din upon all sides seemed positively devilish.

Thus, Tracy witnessed the ardor of the exchange, including the coordinated rifle volleys on the left as Stahel's immigrants walked headlong into Trimble's brigade.

The rebels were too many for us. Penetrating the open, to a belt of woods beyond that from which he had expelled the enemy's pickets, Stahl was met by a fire so murderous as well-nigh to cut to pieces two of his regiments — the 8th New York alone losing killed forty-six, and wounding one hundred and thirty-five. In return, he repulsed both by battery and bayonet, a charge of Mississippi and [Georgia] regiments, with an almost annihilation of one of the latter. In the midst of the bloody work, however, he was nevertheless pushed back, even to the hither side of the first patch of woods.

Tracy was describing the 16th Mississippi's reckless advance, before neutralizing the ground to either side with skirmishers. The crossfire could have destroyed the regiment if Colonel Mercer of the 21st Georgia had not remedied the danger with timely support.

Milroy, at the right, after a hot bout with a strong line of the enemy's advance people, drove them in; but assailing at close range their main body, and endeavoring in the meantime to get planted a battery upon some higher ground, was punished with great vigor, and even put to it at last to hold his own as far back as the point of original establishment of his line. Cluseret, at the centre, charged in upon the guns of the enemy, but was repulsed, and charged in turn. He, however, maintained himself with skill and perseverance — keeping practically intact his position. Schenck, swinging forward his right, brushed with emphasis the rebels, and shelling also the woods, held them from any counter-demonstration in flank. Thus, although our right lost less, and even gained somewhat in point of ground, our left, more rudely handled, fell back well upon the points occupied by the reserves.

In this contingency, and with the getting to the front of fresher men, and the ordering up and distribution both to the batteries and the infantry, of an additional supply of ammunition, we proceeded with vigor to the re-establishment of our line, the basis, as taken, being that of the point of retirement by Stahl.

In a nutshell: retreat. The Union left had been pushed so far back that Frémont thought it prudent to return his entire army to that "point of retirement," the far side of the Keezletown Road.

While, then, thus engaged, and with everything bent toward our immediate renewal of that fight — the firing of which had now to a considerable extent dropped away — there dashes up to me, upon a little rise overlooking the ground by headquarters a Scout — splashed and travel-worn, in the uniform of our Cavalry — and inquires for General Frémont. To present him was the work of a moment, when the soldier drew from the breast of his jacket, and handed to the General a dispatch – evoking from the latter, with the reading, a smile not only of satisfaction, but almost of relief. The dispatch was from General Shields . . .

It was Shields's announcement that he would have arrived at Port Republic with twelve pieces of artillery and two brigades of infantry by the time Frémont got the message.

Frémont was smiling at the thought of Jackson's predicament. The wily enemy was good as bagged! It didn't occur to him that Jackson might have divided his forces the day before and already reached Port Republic with a formidable, though nearly halved army. Had Frémont known he was only fighting part of Ewell's Third Division, he might have found the courage to breach its line and truly "thunder down" on Jackson's rear. Instead, he imagined the entire Confederate force to be stalled of its own accord; hence, he deemed it quitting time on the battle-field. (More than anyone else, Frémont was responsible for limiting the fight to business hours.)

Tracy summed up a veritable catalogue of reasons that enabled the Union staff to justify the cessation of hostilities.

> For many days our people have been marching; for a portion of them they have been starving; through the whole they have been suffering from general wear and exhaustion, and they are here today, in their broken and dilapidated condition, only because of the chances of a contest, following upon which, they may realize the at least temporary relief, they so much need. The battle, as it now stands, is not in our favor; but with the recuperation of a night's rest, the concentration at our front of a force to prevent the escape of the enemy, with the encouragement and strength to be infused by the whole – we will be better able to renew the fight with the morning, than continue it now.
>
> Such was the conclusion at once and intuitively reached by all; and accordingly, with the best thorough disposition to maintain intact our force at large; as well as to assail, with the earliest practicable moment of the dawn, Jackson, as now enclosed; it was determined that further demonstration upon our part, as of a hostile or aggressive nature, should, for the day, be brought to a close.

He then described the retrograde movement of the Union line to conform with Stahel's position. The regrouping was accompanied by a "gradual cessation of the heavier firing," and finally with the emplacement of pickets "thrown out athwart the general front." Ever liberal with his commas, Tracy continued:

> In the meantime the rebels, remaining at large in position, but confused, perhaps, as to what we purposed to do, or—what is possible— with a view to cover the commencement of an immediate movement on their part towards Port Republic—had run up by a road in the woods, a battery to a point directly across the hollow, or interval, from headquarters. Presently, too, from the timber, a flash, a gush of thick white smoke, and the ring of the report was upon us. With the report, as well, the rush of a round shot through the air, and then, a yard or two behind Dr. Sukely, who had just turned to go to the right, a heavy "sumph," and the burial of the missile full two feet in the ground.
>
> The Doctor, with a curiosity, possibly pardonable to one of his temperament, halted a moment to poke his scabbard into the hole made, when with another crack, came the rush of a projectile, drawing our attention nearer home. For this second shot—one other shell as it proved—hurtling above the heads of those more in front, fell with a crash, by the edge of a pile of rails upon which Colonel Tracy sat just then, munching a piece of hard-tack. Fortunately there was no explosion, or the Colonel might have appeared in a sadder list.
>
> In the meantime, however, another, and yet others of those non-exploders in rapid succession: a portion polishing themselves in some ploughed ground through which we had deigned to move, to cover of some guns in positions on a little elevation just at our left; while one in particular struck in front of, and partly between the General and Milroy as they stood talking "ammunition"—dashing upon both, with liberality, the soil. Yet farther: a shell sent apparently after my orderly—mounted—whom I had directed to proceed wholly over the hill with "Charlie" [Tracy's horse], struck, in its course, a tree, bursting with a roar which accelerated in no light degree, the speed of both man and animal. Report, since made, informs me that although fragments were heard to whizz at all points, no damage was suffered, save by the tree, which was nearly torn to pieces. Lastly, as among our headquarters folk, a second round shot struck in the flank of the horse of little Boggs, just as he was in the act to mount. Stepping back for a moment from his stirrup, and noting the animal as he settled to his last upon his haunches, Boggs with the coolness of none but the practiced plainsman he was, undid the surcingles, removed the saddle, and taking a pistol from his holster, placed it mercifully to the horse's ear and fired—the beast, of course, falling dead.

Having identified the coordinates of Frémont's headquarters, an isolated Confederate cannon crew could not resist a final act of defiance with the dregs of its ammunition. The shelling garnered a quick reaction:

> In the meantime, what demonstration else went forward upon our side! With a vim and a rapidity rare to note, our batteries, at the right and by our left, got into play; and ejecting from their brazen throats projectiles of like deadly intent and capabilities, the guns roared again, as it were, in joy with the conflict. In a shorter space, as well, than I have ever seen before in the course of my experience, these lions of the fight disposed of the case of their adversary; and within twenty minutes after the firing of his first shot, the rebel was glad to limber up, with horses and men lost, and one of his pieces disabled, and withdraw as he might. He had, in a spirit of inquiry, for whatever purpose, projected himself somewhat into the air, and having, doubtless, found us sufficiently alive and upon the lookout, his mission appeared to close.

Despite the braggadocio, Tracy's lapse into first person suggested that the quirky cannonade unnerved him, if only momentarily. He went on to describe the scene behind the Union lines as the sun went down.

> Our losses during the day were—as has been intimated—neither light nor trivial; and the groaning and misery of the crowds brought in by our parties of fatigue, and deposited by the banks of the road, or in the church spoken of, or other of the few buildings about—converted suddenly to hospitals—attested full sadly the destruction wrought both of limb and body . . . With the decadence, however, of the later sound of the batteries, and the exception, perhaps, of a shot at some remoter point, within or without our lines, the firing now had fairly ceased; while with the now growing twilight the forces of Cluseret [located somewhat in advance] lit up their more cheering campfires, and went, with comparative quiet, into bivouac.

His narrative told of the comforts of camp, as experienced by a staff officer. Not only did he have an orderly at his beck and call, he also had a serving-man.

> By the foot of a noble trunk, upon the hither edge of a patch of woods to the left of the road by which we had entered upon the ground of battle, and upon a pile of straw, abstracted from a stack in the yard of a small farm-house in the hollow, this side of the rise, Colonel Tracy had also spread out his blanket for the night. The General, upon a similar heap, with members of the Staff, were within easy distance, while "Charlie," returned from his adventure above the

hill, stood ready saddled, and made fast to a sapling hard by, in case he were needed.

A captain on the staff had stolen a lamb, butchered it, and presented Colonel Tracy one of the hindquarters. Martin, his serving-man, barbecued it over the campfire and Tracy found it "toothsome to the extreme."

> At any rate we all of us made terrific inroads upon the juicy quarter; and this portion of the feast, sustained by hard-tack, and tea, both hot and strong, restored us in no light degree from the fasting, and as might be said, anxiety of the day. Supper, then, done, we were not long with our prayers—though, I trust, not forgetful of the same—and, together, after a few moments converse, recumbent upon the straw, were lost in slumber.

By contrast, it should be noted that Ewell's army did not draw rations that evening—there was no food available other than that which the Rebels carried in their haversacks. Nor did they sleep but briefly, since Jackson wanted the bulk of Ewell's forces decamped that night and arrived at Port Republic by first light.

Then, Tracy recorded the events of Monday morning as Frémont's army stirred to life. The march began:

> June 9th. Through the forests, above the ridges and generally over the ground but recently in occupation by the enemy, our command in battle order, and with its supporting lines, batteries, and cavalry, moved upon the morning of this date. The rebels, availing themselves of the advantage of the darkness, had fled, utterly—leaving us but their unburied dead, and the groaning masses of the torn and mangled of the fight—crowded into every available shelter—barn, shed, or house, wherever found.

By Wednesday, June 11, according to former Confederate William Jordan in his letter of 1912, only Union dead were left on the battlefield. On Saturday, three days later, Jackson's topographer Jedediah Hotchkiss's diary entry stated:

> Lt. J. K. Boswell, Mr. J. Davis Craig and myself rode over to see the battle field of Cross Keys. We had a very interesting time; saw the miserable Dutch of Fremont's army that he had left, wounded, behind him. The enemy did a great amount of damage; plundered the houses of the people near the battle field and burned up one house in which it is supposed he had put his dead. One citizen dug up and

reburied 100 or more Yankees which had been buried too near his house.

Neither army had taken the time to properly bury its dead; both were racing to consummate the next day's fighting at Port Republic. Tracy described the acceleration of momentum:

It was yet but 8 o'clock, and, with the limited time for so large a body [Jackson's overestimated army], with its trains and stores, they might yet be within our reach. With the closing in of our lines, and the formation in compact columns, the order was spread to push forward at the maximum of the march. In this, order, as well, we had made but the matter of a mile or so, emerging fully into the more open area beyond the [Dunker] Church and the woods, when, for the second time appeared in our pathway the sign of wrath and destruction, and a dense and dingy cloud of smoke rose slowly upward toward the heaven. It was the bridge at Port Republic.

Seeing the smoke, Colonel Tracy wondered which army had set fire to the covered bridge. Could Shields have either pushed or maneuvered past Jackson to this side of the river, then burned the bridge to protect the Union rear? The column in which Tracy rode was ordered to march double-time. Momentarily, Frémont's soldiers were held in suspense.

And still the roar of guns redoubled upon our ears, mingled as we drew nearer with the rattle and crash of small arms, and still above the whole, went up the great black mass of smoke—diffusing at last at its top its volumes abroad in the air, as it were in a sort of somber path.

With a vigor and determination of effort, putting every nerve to the strain, we have compassed the distance, and gained upon the crest of a high rolling ridge upon the hither side of the Shenandoah, a glance above the scene beyond. At our right, Port Republic, with the charred and shattered remains of a bridge leading thereunto; at our left, where the battle has now ceased, a lengthened line of men in their uniforms of blue, guarded, and about to be put in march under conduct of the force in gray, with the added strength of a battery of field guns—as likely to have been our own as any. The distance from us of the whole, as across the river, and at a space beyond the banks, was perhaps half a mile.

As a helpless observer on the wrong side of the river, Tracy bore witness to the aftermath of Shields's defeat. The Battle of Port Republic had been a more characteristically Jacksonian victory, determined ultimately by his preponderance of force, but it had been a hard fight over ground that was repeatedly won and lost. Union casualties numbered more than 800; Confederate casualties were close to 1,000. The Confederates captured 450 soldiers of Shields's advance force and most of his cannon. With the Yankee prisoners in plain view, Frémont ordered his artillery to begin shelling across the river. His apologia of 1865 stated:

> A parting salvo of carefully aimed rifled guns, duly charged with shell, hastened the departure of the rebels, with their unlucky though most gallant convoy, and the whole were speedily out of sight.

The salvo endangered Jackson's ambulances as they were collecting the wounded from both sides. Benumbed Union prisoners watched helplessly while the friendly force, supposedly come to their aid, now fired at them from across the water.

The second account that brought the Union side of the Battle of Cross Keys to life for me was Brigadier General Robert H. Milroy's lengthy letter to his wife (printed here with Milroy's spellings and punctuation unaltered).

Mount Jackson June 15th/ 62

My dear Mary,

It has been several weeks since I wrote to you and did I not know that the news papers would keep you fully posted about our movements since we joined Fremont, I would feel that I had been culpably negligent in not writing to you more frequently, but the truth is I have not had time to write a line since we left Franklin, having been all the time so intensely occupied, marching night and day, mostly through constant rain and mud, skirmishing fighting etc. We left Franklin on the 26th ult and though I have frequently been in the rain from morning till night and from night till morning, wet to the skin, my boots full of water, yet my health has been universally good. The distance from Franklin to Petersburg is 30 miles about half the road is the worst I ever saw, and we were so detained by the dutch brigades [Blenker's Germans] who were ahead of us with their long trains of baggage waggons which they had no skill in getting through the terrible roads. At noon on the 26th we had got but 6 miles from Franklin, I then recd. an order from Fremont to push ahead with my Regiments and batteries and pass all baggage waggons which I did, marched my poor tired boys all night and got to Petersburg at 8 A.M. the next morning 27th ult. We encamped on the south Branch of the Potomic and were ordered to leave all our tents and baggage except a few cooking utensils for each company. This has proved a great hardship to both officers and men who have been compelled to lay out exposed to all kinds of weather day and night ever since without a change of clothes. I do not have time or space now to describe our march from Petersburg—the splendid scenery, over mountains and through deep defiles—our skirmishing with the reble army we encountered at Strasburg under the reble Genl. Jackson who had made a bulge at me at McDowell. From Strasburg our pursuit was closed for 75 miles up the splendid valley of Virginia and along the splendid stone turnpike. I have never seen a better or more beautiful country in my life than this valley of Virginia—The rebles burnt the splendid bridge at this place across the Shanandoah river and it rained so furiously and raised the river so high that we did not get our pontoon bridge across the river for two days. We then dashed on and our advanced guard overtook the reble rear guard on the evening of the 6th inst. About 5 miles beyond Harrisonburg 30 miles from here shortly after my Brigade arrived at that place and getting into an ambuscade was pretty roughly handled. The Pa. Bucktales under Gen. Byard, advanced to their support but after fighting despartly for an hour were compelled to fall back leaving their dead and wounded on the battle field. I cannot account for Fremont not ordering up other Bgds. to their assistance—we were all anxious to go but got no orders. The next morning My Bgd. was ordered to proceed over the battle grounds to collect the dead and wounded and proceed a few miles beyond to see where the enemy were. This splendid pike turns on up the valley to Staunton which is beyond Harrisonburg 25 miles—but the bridge across the river 6 miles beyond Harrisonburg had been burned by the rebles when Banks was pursuing them about 2 months ago so they could not cross there but had to turn off the pike a mile beyond Harrisonburg to go to another bridge at Port Republic 15 miles below the Pike. A large portion of the road from where it leaves the Pike to Port Republic (12 miles) is very bad. I passed over the battle grounds of our cavelry and infantry of the day previous—had my men collect the dead and wounded and sent them back in ambulances and going on a few Miles my advanced guard commenced skirmishing with the rebles; I found that they were encamped a short distance ahead about 20,000 strong—but being positively prohibited by Fremont from bringing on a battle and ordered by him to return. I done so reluctantly. The next morning (Sunday the 8th Inst) Fremont started early with all his force about 12,000 to attack rebles. They were found the same place I left them I dashed on ahead of my Bgd. as soon as I heard the thunder of battle ahead—was shown the place where I was to form—I had hurried on my artillery (3 batteries) which arrived a little ahead of the infantry—I immediately threw them into position but the enemys batteries opened on mine about a mile off before we could get ready for firing and threw the shot and shell over so rapidly—but my batteries silenced theirs in 15 minutes after they commenced. Schencks Brigade was formed on my right and 3 German Brigades on my left—our line of battle was over a mile long. Seeing no enemy in sight I asked permission to advance which was granted and I advanced my four Regiments by heads of Regts. about half a mile when I found a fine position for my artillery in full view of 3 reble batteries—I threw my Regts. into a ravine under shelter from their batteries which had again opened on us and sent back by aids for my batteries. They soon come. I had them again thrown into position and they commenced preaching to the rebles in a most eloquent and striking manner. As soon as they got to work in fine style, I road forward myself to examine the ground and discover the best way of getting my Regiments up where they could use their Minnie Enfield rifles. After a few hundred yards I discovered a ravine, which could be reached without exposire, which led up into another ravine—that run along the foot of the hill on which the reble batteries were situated. I determined to bring my brigade up and deploy at the foot of the hill, silence the batteries with my rifles and take them at the point of the bayonet. I brought them up caustiously along the ravine leading up to the 2nd but as soon as the head of my columns got within 60 or 70 yards of the 2nd ravine we discovered it was full of rebles laying behind a fence in the tall grass almost wholly concealed from view but they mowed down the head of my column by a deadly fire almost as fast as they appeared, and we could not return their fire with any effect as we could not see them—One of the best captains of the 25th Ohio fell mortally wounded here. I tried to dislodge or raise them by skirmishes but without effect. I then determined to throw my Bgd. across into a forest which I observed over the hill to my right. I sent skirmishes forward to feel the way—as soon as they rose the hill in the tall heavy wheat (we were in an open wheat field) they recd. a perfect storm of bullets from the woods which appeared to be full of rebles, but the folage was so thick we could not see them. I brought up my Regiments and opened a tremendous fire into the woods but a deadly fire come out of it and my boys were droped by it so rapidly—my noble horse Jasper recd. two shots in quick succession—the first across the hind leg the second in the left breast which ranged across and lodged in his right shoulder and totally disabled him. He rared and plunged and nearly fell with me—I sprung off and saw the blood spurting out of his breast and gave him up for dead. I ordered my Regts. to push on and turn more to the right in order to turn to the left flank of the rebles. They did so and the 25th Ohio which was leading got half into the forest when one of Gen. Fremonts aids dashed up to me with an order for me to fall back with my whole Bgd. a mile to the position first occupied by me in the morning. I was never so astonished or thunderstruck in my life. I could not believe what the dutchman said and made him repeat it three times, the balls were whizzing around him like bees and he was dodging his head down behind the horse like a duck dodging thunder while he was repeating the order and as soon as he got through he dashed off at break neck speed. I was standing close behind the center of my Bgd. but felt ashamed to order them to cease firing and file to the rear. I called my aids to me and told them to order the Regts. to do so being careful to carry back all their dead and wounded—seeing them all fairly under way I turned my attention to Jasper and found he could hobble along on three legs his right fore shoulder being disabled. I led him slowly along bringing up the rear—I had ordered my Regts. to halt and form line in rear of two of my batteries which they did with as much coolness as on a parade in peace, all mad and cursing the order to retreat. I directed the batteries to fire rapidly with shell and canestor into the woods on the other side of the field where the rebles were—which they did with such good effect that the rebles were soon driven out. I was very greatly surprised upon coming to these batteries upon observing a short distance to the right of the batteries in the woods the left of Gen. Schencks Bgd. standing perfectly idle as spectators of the battle—thus 5 splendid Regiments consisting the finest Bgd. in our army had taken no portion in the battle—Had this Bgd. been thrown forward on my right to have cleared the rebles out of the forest, which they could have done with perfect ease—we could have swept the battle field like a tempest and captured the whole of Jacksons army—with his artillary and baggage. I have lost confidence in Fremont tremendously and so has his whole army here. After giving my batteries time to peg the rebles well I sent over an aid back to Fremont still ½ mile further in the rear to ask whether he still desired me to fall back and recd. for answer that I must send back my artillery and come on after it with my infantry. I slowly and reluctantly obeyed and as soon as I got to him I told him I was very sorry to have to fall back as I could have held my position where I was a month. He expressed surprise and said he was sorry he did not know it. He had a whole cloud of aids and it was his duty to know everything that was going on in his army when in battle at least. He and his staff were on the ground setting around on their horses just in the rear of where my batteries had drawn up. About ten minutes after

I got to where he was the rebles commenced pitching cannon balls among us from the same position they had commenced firing on us in the morning. The first shot fell or rather struck among the horses and men without hurting any one but threw the dirt over many—the 2nd shot struck the horse of one of Fremonts aids behind the saddle and he fell dead without hurting the man. I was talking to Fremont at the time and was amused to see what a hurry he and his staff were in getting back to the rear out of reach of the rebles—Our batteries again opened on the rebles and silenced their battery in a few minutes. Our forces drew up on the ground when we commenced the battle bivouacked for the night. We went into the fight about 10 oclock A.M. and come out about 6 P.M. The reason why we were ordered to fall back was that the German Brigades on the left had been partially rebuked and thrown back by the rebles and Fremont fearing for the safety of the right wing ordered us to fall back also, but had he ordered the advance of his whole right wing we could have swept around and captured everything for at that time our forces under Gen. Shields or rather a part of his forces (a Bgd. under col. Carroll) was holding the bridge across the river at Port Republic, but this force was defeated and driven away the next morning and Jacksons army with all his baggage crossed the bridge and set it on fire before we got down to the river. (6 miles) We got there in time to find the bridge in flames and to see the long lines of reble baggage wagons and their cavelry filing away for miles in the distance on the other side. Our batteries were thrown into position and dispersed their cavelry and stoped a few of their wagons by knocking their teams to pieces. We encamped on the banks of the river for the night and commenced building a bridge, but for some reason Fremont ordered us early the next morning to start back the way we come. We had some time to look at our battle field of the day before as we passed over it. Our artillery had evidently been very destructive to the rebles and their horses. There were large numbers of horses laying around where the reble batteries had been and their Cavelry companies had occasionally appeared. The rebles dead had mostly been collected in heaps—I did not count them but a number of our officers who counted them—made the numbers as high as 600 a portion of the Germans had evidently fought well before they gave way was evidenced by the number of dead rebles in front of their position—but a large number of them had been mown down by our artillery, the deadly fire of which had checked their advance after the Germans gave way. The loss among the Germans was fearful in killed and wounded. I lost and killed in my Bgd. 16—in wounded 95—missing 4—the total 115. The whole loss in killed, wounded, and missing on our side is about

700. The dutch brigades are composed of the most infernal robbers, plunders and thieves, I have ever seen, our army is disgraced by them. They straggle off from their companies and Regts. for miles on each side of the road as we march along and enter every house—smokehouse – milkhouse – chickenhouse – kitchen – barn – corncrib and stable and clean out everything—frequently open drawers, trunks, bureaus etc for plunder—leaving women and children crying behind them—but no tears or entreaties stop or affect them, the only answer they Make is "Nix forstay" [*nichts versteben*, "I don't understand"]. The officers of these soldiers are to blame for the demoralized character of their soldiers—as they encourage and share the plunder with them —such conduct has injured our cause very much and the name of the Blenkers dutch will be as celebrated in history as the vandals—the army of Peter the Hermit and the Hessians of the American Revolution. Gen. Fremont has not used the energy he might in trying to stop this disgraceful conduct—He has issued an order now—of day before yesterday of sufficient stringency to stop it—making it a death penalty for any soldier to take anything from any citizen or enter any house unless by command of an officer. The plundering has been indused to some extent by the great scarcity of provisions—our men being most of the time on very short allowance—Since before we left Franklin till after we got back to Harrisonburg—sometimes being a day or two without anything. The whole country is in the greatest terror of the dutch. I have been implored hundreds of times for the protection and guards. Carl Schurtz Brig. Genl. joined us two days ago. He called at my quarters to see me today—I am much pleased to see him and think he will have a good influence with the dutch. We have fallen back here to rest and recruit our worn out soldiers a while and may be here for ten days yet. I recd. your letter of the 8th inst. today and was greatly pleased and relieved to learn that our dear little Brucy is getting better and that you had recd. that package of money I sent you—I will send you $300. more in a few days. I still have my wounded horse Jasper with me and will try to send him home when he gets better. Now Mary this is a private letter for yourself but you may show it to any of your friends you wish. If there is anything in it that any of them may desire to have published—have them be careful to omit such portions as would not be prudent to publish. Give my love to our dear children—and my warmest respects to our good Neighbors—you and Ella write often— Remember me to Ben.

Truly your Husband
R. H. Milroy

TWENTY-ONE

THE SPANKING NEW farming implements in rows along the road frontage of the dealerships were unattainable. Whenever I wandered wishfully among their ranks, salespeople emerged from their offices to troll the bait with enticing facts and figures and convenient time-payment plans, but I was out of reach. I was just looking. Once cognizant of my limitations, the salespeople shunted me to the back lots where the trade-ins were on display. The used equipment bore the stigmata of a prim farm ethic. There was scant reference to the sorcery of consumerism — no pizazz, no get-up-and-go, no sexiness. Only hard work and long hours echoed in the configurations of weathered metal, a rebuke to the purlieus closer to the highway.

I was looking for a tractor-drawn field mower, also called a sickle mower or cutter-bar. Successor to the two-horse mower, it was an implement that had already been replaced on most farms by a machine called a mower-conditioner. Mower-conditioners crushed, or conditioned as they cut, so that crops dried faster. But I figured that to get started in the haymaking business, I didn't need the very latest in equipment. Neither my line of credit nor my tractor could handle the size and expense.

There were plenty of used field mowers around, although few remained functional. The old trade-ins stuck out from the weeds like coarse combs aimed heavenward, relics of bygone family farms, long since relinquished as farmers updated their equipment fleets, or retired, or went broke. The accumulation of human tedium that emanated from the rusty projections was as real as the rust itself. These mowers had been in use row after row, season after season, decade after decade. I parted the weeds and carefully examined each candidate; surely, one or two would retain a semblance of a service life. I made it my business to invade the privacy of bearing races. I studied shims and tolerances. I ran my fingers along worn surfaces to assess the viability of moving parts.

In a sense, a cutter-bar is one big moving part. A flat rod seven feet long, to which twenty-seven triangular, serrated knives are riveted, slides side to side within a framework of twenty-eight extended teeth (called guards) bolted to a long, tapering bar. A ball joint links the knife assembly to a pitman arm, often made of hardwood, which is driven by a small flywheel stepped down by belt from the power take-off driveshaft. The implement is usually mounted on the tractor's three-point hitch, although some models are outfitted with wheels for towing. Whichever way, the cutter-bar itself is drawn over the ground on two slightly raised skids, or feet, at either end and counter-sprung from its transport frame so that it can follow the unevenness of the terrain without undue drag. Upon hard contact with an obstacle, the entire assembly swings backward on a breakaway hinge to minimize damage to the guards and knives. When the mowing is done, the bar is manually elevated to a vertical, or traveling position.

Likewise, the bar is manually lowered to the working position. The heavy bar requires some exertion to lift and lower, and many a straining farmer has lost fingers doing this, for whenever the bar is moved, the knife assembly has a tendency to drop suddenly, like a guillotine with twenty-seven tiers.

I singled out an Oliver 356 mower that appeared to be reasonably close to working condition. The salesman congratulated me on my choice, adding that he'd reduce the price, as is, with no guarantee, if I paid cash. We struck a deal ($190), and he helped me winch the heavy implement onto the pickup. Later, unloading it by myself on the barn floor, I was mindful of finger placement. With every jerk and heave, the knife sections slipped dangerous inches.

I soon realized that the old Oliver was more or less a basket case. Like every other mower I had looked at, it would need a major rebuilding to operate dependably. I proceeded to tear it down, part by part, and correct its deficiencies. My investment grew to twice, then three times the initial amount. In the process of rebuilding, I had no choice but to scrape away the crusts of grease and dirt, much in the manner of my travail on the baler. By the time the mower was in working condition, there was no good reason not to paint it, so another ten dollars went toward a quart of Meadow Green, the trademark color of the Oliver line, slightly darker and bluer than the John Deere hue. The paint job fooled one local farmer. "Where on earth did you find that thing?" he asked. He knew that Oliver had gone out of business twenty years earlier.

A hay wagon was a hay wagon, I thought. How could they have changed much through the centuries? Horse-drawn or tractor drawn, the four-wheeled wagon had a flat bed and a steerable front axle attached to a tongue. Pneumatic tires had replaced iron-rimmed spoke wheels, but what else was new?

My education in the niceties of a hay wagon began when I noticed the following ad in the classifieds: "Flatbed wagon, 18 ft., must see to appreciate, $350 firm. Call anytime."

The price seemed steep, but a good, used hay wagon was a necessity. The square bales I planned to make would be transported directly to the barn. I had already looked over a couple of wagons without wanting one badly enough to buy it. Either the boards of the bed were rotten, or the tires were flat, or some other defect kept me from committing my checkbook, although I knew that time was running out and I'd have to settle for something.

With more curiosity than expectation, I dialed the number. In a Valley twang, the farmer described his wagon as a "real special old rig," reiterating the firmness of his price. Five people had called him already. If I was interested, I should come right over.

Oh, I knew the old telephone sales pitch. The whole world was beating a path to his farm, begging to buy his old wagon. Still, I jotted down directions. It turned out that he lived just over the second hill to the east of the Lee-Jackson property.

A blacktop drive, bordered by a whitewashed board fence, opened onto the farmstead. Charolais cattle were grazing on plush pasture. To one side, soybeans carpeted about ten acres, and to the other side, a newly planted cornfield stretched to the horizon. The farm looked perfect—a cover photograph. I spotted the haywagon just inside a spacious, three-sided utility building, a veritable showroom of farm machinery. Every implement and tractor looked immaculate, field-ready. I knew instinctively that oils had been changed, greasing and pressure-washing had been done on schedule. Here was a guy who took pride in upkeep and appearance. The wagon bed had been recently creosoted.

"See how low she sits?" In crisp denim, the farmer emerged from behind a manure spreader. He was a trim sixty-year-old with a full head of hair. Farming had not worn him out. "That's the first thing you look for in a hay wagon."

Right off, I knew he had sized me up as a novice, but his tone was friendly and direct. I regarded the wagon as requested. The long, wide bed loomed just above the four tires. Less than an inch of clearance showed between the tire treads and the underside of the oak planking. It was low, all right, and a slight swayback in the center of the bed exaggerated my perception of its lowness.

"You be makin' the hay yourself?" he inquired. I told him I would be. "No kicker?" he asked. No kicker, I replied. He had me pegged to a tee: a brash beginner who would insist on doing things the hard way.

"In that case, you be needin' a wagon as long and low as you can get."

I understood his point. The bigger the wagon, the fewer loadings and unloadings, and the lower the wagon, the shorter the lift. A matter of inches would factor mightily when hefting bales by the hundreds.

"She's the wagon you need," he announced.

He proceeded to enumerate the wagon's features. Its running gear was a composite of front and rear automobile axles extended by a length of well casing, and its steel tongue was amply stout. I was invited to note the hay racks fore and aft, which were removable. The rear one displayed a reflective triangular warning sign, or fanny flag. There was also a set of removable side rails for hauling dirt or poultry litter.

"See this lever?" he asked, directing my attention to a bar just above where the tongue joined the front axle. "That's your brake."

I had looked at plenty of hay wagons, but I had never seen one outfitted with brakes. When controlling a heavy load with a lightweight tractor, brakes would be handy. In the days when draft horses pulled wagons, rear-wheel brakes had been standard equipment.

"You need this wagon," he repeated, hypnotically.

Then he showed me the spare tire, another novel feature, but surely a most useful novelty. At this point, I began to be impressed. My hat was off to the anonymous wainwright, a person who had planned for all eventualities. The farmer was reading my mind. "She was built thirty-five years ago by a feller who lived down the road, long since passed on."

Then, out of the blue, I was asked if I liked old Fords. I replied in the affirmative.

"Then look at these," he commanded, pointing to the wheel rims. "Thirty-eight Ford. Hard to find. Hot-rod fellers pay big money for these."

It was true. The classic sixteen-inch "holey" rims, including the spare, were much sought after by automotive devotees. It so happened that the two-wheeled cart I built for the Kubota years ago boasted the identical

168

rims. These five plus my other two . . . hm, I would be rim-rich. The prospect tickled. But I was just noticing an even bigger bonus, one I had missed earlier in the shadow of the flatbed overhang: each wheel had an original, chromed hubcap with the Ford "V-8" incised in red. My discov-- ery verged on the sublime—a hay wagon with hubcaps! My resistance slipped entirely. The farmer had played me like an old fiddle.

"I need this wagon!" I exclaimed, awestruck to realize I was thinking out loud.

"You can have her for two-hunnert'n-fifty," he said, "and I'll run her over to your place."

I had connected with a man who appreciated my appreciation.

The one thing left to acquire was a hayrake. The dump-rakes of yore, the one or two extant examples I saw, had been transformed into yard ornaments stuck in the middle of flower beds. I needed a modern rake, one that was worked concentrically around the field and left long, baler-ready windrows.

On a page of auction notices in a Saturday morning's newspaper, an unusual listing caught my eye. It bore the typical preface: "Due to age and ill health, the following items will be sold . . . " In other words, a gentleman was moving to a retirement home. There followed an itemi-zation of his household: his beds, his chairs, his tables, his sofa, his chests of drawers, and so forth, and at the very end, as if in afterthought, his wheel rake.

On such an auction-filled Saturday, when at least half a dozen of them were going on within a ten-mile radius of Harrisonburg, the bargain-seeking public tended to come out in droves. But this auction was taking place a good fifteen miles out of town. There was a chance, an outside chance, it would draw only a modest crowd. As I followed the treasure map of unfamiliar route numbers across the county, another positive fac-tor materialized. The sky was clouding over. If it rained, there would be lower attendance still. Then I saw the ragged row of parked vehicles. My luck was holding. Despite my tardy arrival, I was only the thirty-seventh person to sign for a bidding card.

A stationary parade of wood-grained furniture old and new rimmed the front lawn and wound along the perimeter of the house. Dispersed, each piece would be exhibited again on far-flung lawns a few years down the line, and again and again as it was auctioned off into eternity. But there was no wheel rake in sight. Had the ad contained a misprint? I did see a spinning wheel, fake, that purported to be some kind of floor lamp.

Then I spotted the hoops of radiating steel behind a bedroom suite, like multiple sunbursts peeking over a city skyline. The rake was an import from Italy, a Sitrex, with not too many seasons behind it. Although its frame had faded to Neapolitan pink and its four rake wheels glowed a slightly rusty Tuscan tan, it seemed to be in excellent shape. Why and how it came to be included in this impromptu exhibition of bad veneer, I could only guess. It was exactly what I was looking for.

A wheel rake is an inexpensive alternative to the more popular side delivery rake. The side delivery mechanism, either P.T.O. or ground-driven, utilizes a series of angled, horizontally rotating bars with spring tines that scratch the hay to one side, thus forming a continuous windrow. A wheel rake, on the other hand, consists of four moving parts – its four, tined wheels. Overlapping slightly in a semirigid frame, the five-foot-diameter wheels are drawn at an angle along the ground so that each rakes the hay to the left in succession. As the hindmost wheel passes, the hay has been consolidated into the windrow.

A wheel rake is mounted on a tractor's three-point hitch, which means that it is raised and lowered hydraulically. A modern side delivery rake is towed. Because mounted implements tend to bounce and pitch with the tractor, a towed rake does a better job over uneven ground. Our hayfields were reasonably smooth, though, and a wheel rake's relative lightness suited a small tractor. But what cinched my preference for a wheel rake was its inherent low maintenance. Four slowly rotating hubs – each surrounded by forty easily replaceable bolt-on tines – was simplicity itself. Between the baler and the cutter-bar, I anticipated plenty of breakdowns; implements of their complexity would give limited service between repairs.

The auctioneer's microphone jarred me from my musings. The rake was on the block, the bedroom suite having just been dispatched to a new boudoir. There was a chill in the air. Clouds had scumbled into a wadding vaporous with the beginning of a drizzle. I had a fleeting memory of an old black-and-white whodunit, one I had seen aboard ship during my hitch in the Navy. The movie featured a wheel rake that doubled as a murder weapon. In a misty setting like this, the rake had been deliberately parked behind a stone wall, a horse jump. As the equestrian victim approached, his mount spooked and stopped short, pitching him headlong over the wall and onto the rake. Impalement by implement, an image hardly conducive to the bidding war in which I was now engaged.

A grizzled fellow in coveralls wanted the rake as much as I did. I had overestimated the irrelevance of the sunbursts behind the dressers. Higher and higher our bids entwined. It was unusual for me to hang on like this, to persevere just beyond the envelope of my opponent's determination. He stayed with me, the son of a bitch. In the past, I had escalated bids out of spite, knowing I would be outbid, no matter what. Now, I was getting my comeuppance. I ventured an absolutely last ditch bid of $260. It was a reckless thing to do, but I fully expected him to top it. He didn't. There was no backing out. The rake belonged to me. At that price, it could not be considered a bargain, but I paid the cashier in good conscience, knowing I was one step closer to making hay.

An added advantage of a wheel rake: it disassembled easily. The drizzle devolved into a downpour as I carried my new purchase piecemeal to the pickup. Umbrellas bloomed like dark flowers. People were leaving in twos and threes, leaks sprung in the auctioneer's abracadabra. Unopposed low bids held sway. A dinette set sold for ten dollars. A refrigerator went for fifteen. I couldn't resist a dollar bid for a three-legged chair. And then the auction was called off. The rain-induced giveaways had become too painful for the retired gentleman. Nevertheless, he must have been content with the price he got from me, or rather, from the man who got me to outbid him.

Barely a week had gone by when another auction notice grabbed my attention. An estate sale was being held on a Wednesday evening at six P.M., rain or shine. The advertisement gave succinct directions: "Property is located just behind the Cross Keys Farm Bureau."

It was the old tavern's turn to change hands along the infinite procession of ownership. The listing promised to include the house, its barn, assorted farm machinery, and "other items too numerous to mention." Eagerly, I fantasized about the miracle in the offing. A restoration just seemed possible. There were plenty of people with the means and ambition. I had friends who did that sort of thing, who lived in derelicts of history as they fixed them up. The question was, would a well-capitalized angel of mercy be in attendance on a Wednesday evening in Cross Keys?

I finished supper early and drove over. Vehicles were parked along both sides of the Keezletown Road. As I joined the stream of auction-goers that funneled behind the Farm Bureau, I tried to visualize a rehabilitated, refurbished Cross Keys Tavern, rightfully venerated after months of labor and tens of thousands of dollars.

My daydream was dashed in more ways than one. Just as I rounded the brick corner of the Farm Bureau, an announcement was made to the effect that the tavern and barn had been withdrawn from sale. From what I could gather, a legal snag had developed: the present occupants, deeded a lifetime right (so *that* explained their neglectful attitude), had changed their minds about vacating the premises. Now they were staying. While the real estate could be transferred to a new owner, a fair market price was unlikely. The executrix was entitled to change her mind, too.

She offered, instead, another parcel a mile down the road, an equally decrepit old place (minus the history) that belonged to the family. The crowd was clearly disappointed. People were leaving as soon as they arrived. Those who stayed were gathered around the ragtag miscellanea that filled two flatbed wagons. Lined up on the barn bridge beyond a strait of waist-tall weeds, the few pieces of farm equipment, including a moribund Massey-Ferguson tractor, resembled agrarian Titanics, sterns atilt, poised to slide forever into the depths of the earth.

I stayed because I figured there would be bidding in the twenty-five- and fifty-cent range. Junk of this provenance, in this condition, couldn't possibly fetch big money. I was eager to hear—and possibly make—bids lower than the price of a candy bar. It would bring back memories of less inflationary times.

Nowadays, most auctioneers won't exercise their vocal chords for bids below a dollar. Their strategy is to keep adding to an item until the minimum bid is elicited. The bidder ends up with the Christmas wreath, the washtub, the clothes hamper, *and* the boxful of canning jars, although only the Christmas wreath is desired. A good auctioneer is a masterful exploiter of human greed. He (to this date, I have seen no she) transfixes bidders with an eye contact that produces feelings of foolishness, bravery, and guilt rolled into one—foolishness for bothering to bid at all, bravery for competing in the dizzy spiral that flouts common sense and negative spousal reaction, guilt for prevailing and having to cart the prize home.

Barring my recent acquisition of the wheel rake, most of my experiences as an escalation-scarred veteran of a bidding war had made me secretly thankful that I lost. Our home would be overflowing with possessions of dubious usefulness—more so than it already was. I was not averse to making bids when I thought value was commensurate with desire, but, as a rule, I started backing away when bidding skyrocketed. It was one of the benefits of being habitually short of cash.

As I stood in the shadow of the old tavern, I managed a bid or two on a stoneware jug and a disk harrow, but both items went to more persistent acquisitors—people who had arrived early, cased the offerings, and made up their minds. They waggled their low-numbered bidding cards with a languor of certitude, having already amassed significant piles of treasure, and they showed no inclination to stop.

I wasn't in a competitive mood, and there wasn't a single item I really coveted. The mild evening and the opportunity to mingle with my neighbors kept me occupied. An auction aficionado of my stripe could be contented just by sharpening appraisal skills and relishing the ongoing expressions of humanity. I needed neither the jug nor the harrow. Although the auctioneer's eyes momentarily bored into mine in attempts to wrest higher bids, I shook my head and looked away. The lady who got the jug paid six times what I would have paid for it, and the gentleman who emerged triumphant with the harrow spent twice as much as he needed to, if he had taken the trouble to place a classified ad. Farmers parted with old harrows for next to nothing.

Yet it was plain to see that both bidders had been prepared to spend even more. Their bids had climbed too swiftly, like breathless commas, and their final bids rang out like exclamation points. A self-satisfied set of the jaw proclaimed their victories, as if to assert, "These bumpkins 'round here have no idea what these things are worth!"

TWENTY-TWO

As Monday, June 9 dawned at Cross Keys, only Trimble's three forward regiments faced the Union army, the bulk of Ewell's forces having decamped at four in the morning. To be the last to maintain the check was a consolation prize of sorts, an acknowledgment of gratitude from Jackson and Ewell for the autonomous gains of the day before. Tactically it made good sense, too, for Trimble's infantry was farthest from Port Republic. The tone of Trimble's report indicated that he took the new day in stride.

> Having received orders to retard the advance of the enemy on Port Republic road on the 9th, I took up our old position and remained until 9 o'clock [A.M.] when, being without artillery and finding the enemy had placed a battery to drive us out of the wood where they had sustained so fatal a repulse the day before, I slowly retired to Port Republic.

How did the soldiers of both sides react as they traversed the battleground, *their* battleground, with a history measured in minutes and hours instead of years? Around and between corpses they marched, corpses of comrades and foe. They skirted dead horses, strewn firearms, scattered personal possessions. Where the armies had so recently clashed, spewing fire and calling forth homicidal will, now there were heaps and holes and bloodstained verdure. Especially, the corpses seemed to have impressed the soldiers, for their numbers were exaggerated—counted, recounted, and magnified anew. With so many dead, it was a privilege to be alive, but among the living were those not so privileged—the wounded, who lay in diffident repose, wrenching the sympathy of passersby.

Horse-drawn ambulances and hand-carried litters had been employed during the quieter hours. The farmhouses filled with the wounded from both sides. But because of the uncertainty of the standoff, no mass burial detail had been sent into action, nor were civilians encouraged to succor to the casualties, for none could tell if the fight was truly ended. Three days later, when the Confederates were digging the mass graves for the Union soldiers (who perished in the vicinity of our new house), the farming families had had time to inspect their trampled crops, their shell-blasted woods, their dead defenders and invaders.

The impact of the battle upon the farming community could not have been anything but catastrophic, but the healing process seems to have begun at once. The tattered wheat fields bore a reduced harvest, but since it was still early June, other crops outgrew the damage done to them. Dwellings, barns, and outbuildings were patched and otherwise repaired. The soldiers from both sides who were convalescing became the focus of attention, blunting the hard feelings of their hosts into pity and love. When an invalid died, he was buried with dignity. All in all, the added privations and hardships caused by the local battle were taken into stride. There was a war on. Life wasn't going to be easy.

But on Monday morning, the quietus of the field was soon broken for Trimble's regiments. Frémont's whole army was still in place, still to be reckoned with. The old haven on the flat-topped hill was a haven no longer. Now it was a bull's-eye at which the Union gunners aimed with renewed vigor and precision, forcing the Confederate infantry to quit the woods and strike a stubborn line of retreat toward Port Republic.

> Receiving from Gen'l Jackson two messages in quick succession to hasten to the battlefield where he had engaged Gen'l Shield's army, I marched rapidly to obey this order, crossed the Bridge, burned it just before the enemy appeared, and reached the field after the contest had been decided in our favor.

Although Trimble downplayed his slow, then speeded-up withdrawal, followed by his competent firing of the North River bridge (by torching two wagonloads of very dry hay), these actions contributed enormously to Jackson's success. Again, Jackson had revised his plan; at the last moment, he decided to cancel his option to march back to Cross Keys to reengage Frémont. By burning the bridge, he could neutralize Frémont *and* throw the full weight of his forces into the battle at hand. Had Frémont been able to reach the vicinity earlier, cross the river and reinvigorate the valiant but losing battle Shields was waging, Port Republic could have been the place where the Pathfinder exonerated his lackluster performance of the preceding day. Such a scenario was never to be. Lulled by Trimble's propinquity, Frémont had been slow to begin the morning's march. Now the bridge was up in smoke, and with it, the half-baked plan to defeat Jackson.

Coincidentally, that same Sunday, June 8, Lincoln had directed Secretary of War Edwin M. Stanton to stop focusing on Jackson and start concentrating on the capture of Richmond. After the many disappointments in the Shenandoah Valley, the commander-in-chief conceded that Jackson was too elusive a quarry, a concession that news from Cross Keys and Port Republic was soon to support.

Although Frémont proclaimed Cross Keys the successful conclusion of his pursuit of Jackson, his excuse-filled messages rang hollow in Washington. His reports blamed the situation at Cross Keys on the Confederate's "position of uncommon strength," but the numbers told another story. Word was out that he had failed to coordinate his attacks; moreover, he had called them off at the very point of success. Union witnesses at Cross Keys and Port Republic told of the different Confederate regiments they had seen in each battle; it became clear that at Cross Keys, less than half of the foe had been fighting. Lincoln's disillusionment deepened, and Frémont fell further from the president's esteem.

Writing in early 1863, Emil Schalk, military commentator from New York and author of a book entitled *Summary of the Art of War*, pilloried Frémont's generalship:

> The action at Cross Keys is highly creditable to the rebel general, and to his men who fought it. The general, on the contrary, who let slip the opportunity of crushing 5,000 men with 20,000, and, what is worse, who permitted himself to be beaten under such circumstances, has certainly but very few claims to the title of "general."

Frémont did not reply to the criticism, but Lieutenant-Colonel Pilsen composed a rebuttal, circulated as a fourteen-page pamphlet, that denounced Schalk in scathing terms and presented evidence to show that Frémont had done all he could do, given the magnitude and entrenchment of the Confederate army. Pilsen argued that Jackson's entire force was available to fight at Cross Keys that Sunday (a point of some merit), even though only Ewell's division, or most of it, was manning the front.

> The hasty and stealthy manner in which he withdrew during that night (the 8th) would seem to indicate that the vigor and determination with which General Frémont pursued and attacked him had a great moral effect upon his division.

Jackson's own assessment of Frémont's ability, according to Pilsen, was demonstrated by an extract from the statements of Captain C. N. Goulding, Union Brigadier General John Pope's chief quartermaster in the field, who was taken prisoner during J. E. B. Stuart's raid at Catlett's Station in August 1862.

> Captain Goulding had several interviews with Jackson, and formed a high estimate of his capabilities. Jackson told him that during the entire war he had never been so hard pressed as he was by Frémont in the Shenandoah Valley; that he never was in such a dangerous position as at Cross Keys and Port Republic; and he freely admitted that he would have been captured, army, bag and baggage, had Frémont been reinforced or supported by McDowell.

Pilsen proceeded to state that had Frémont's pleas for reinforcement and resupply been met, the outcome at Cross Keys would have been more favorable for the North. Schalk could settle for an easy scapegoat, Pilsen said, by belittling Frémont's limited options, but the charge of ineffectuality was patently unfair.

> To censure in that matter a man who has spent a life in the civil and military service of the country, and who, besides the skill and energy he displayed in the West, in this particular campaign brought a striking example before the country, of what true zeal and ingenuity of a General can perform, while blamelessly and most vigorously accomplishing the chase of a superior enemy, after overcoming 100 miles in seven days, and every obstacle in his way, – to condemn, I say, such a man in such shameless words, having no other arguments for the denunciation than falsehoods, – this, sir, is nothing but a plain villainy, and as such, I am convinced, will be the judgement of the public.

Trimble's report continued:

> To sum up the occurrences of the day, I may state that our handsome success on the right was due to the judicious positions selected, as well as to the game spirit and eagerness of the men. The flank movement to the right, totally unexpected by the enemy and handsomely carried out by Col. Cantey, completed our success . . .

Trimble did not omit the observation that his troops were as orderly after the battle as they were before it began.

> For the bearing of all the officers (dismounted by my order, except myself and staff) and to the men I give most favorable testimony, and

cannot withhold my highest admiration of their gallant conduct and fine discipline, and after the contest, as you witnessed, every regiment was in line, as composed as if they had been on drill . . . My three Regiments, counting 1348 men and officers, repulsed the Brigade of Blenker three times and one hour after with the 13th and 25th Va. Regiments—whose conduct while observed by me was characterized by steadiness and gallantry. The other Brigade of the enemy with their Battery was driven from the field a mile and a half from the first scene of the contest.

By interjecting a note of gratitude for Colonel Walker and his two Virginia regiments, Trimble showed that he understood the value of praise in an official report. Naturally, he included his own subordinates in the encomium. Describing the actions of his battery and its protective infantry regiment, he said:

Of the heroic conduct of the officers and men of Courtney's Battery, commanded by Cap't. Courtney & Lt. Latimer as 1st Lieut, in holding their position under the incessant fire of four Batteries at one time, I cannot speak in terms which would do them full justice. The fact that they stood bravely up to their work for over five hours, exhausted all their shot and shell and continued their fire with canister to the end of the battle, speaks more in their favor than the most labored panegyric. The admirable position selected for the Battery alone saved it from total destruction—if a special Providence did not guard it from harm.

The 21st N. Carolina left to support this Battery, was exposed to the effect of the terrific fire, but under cover of the hill, happily escaped with few casualties. When the Battery was threatened with an infantry force this Regiment was called and readily took its position to repel the enemy's attack, and stood modestly ready to do its duty as gallantly as heretofore.

Then Trimble singled out, among others, a Private Long of the 21st Georgia's Company B, who, while acting as a skirmisher,

brought in 10 prisoners—5 with their arms, captured at one time—and shot an officer of Gen'l Fremont's staff, obtaining from him the enemy's order of march for that day (herewith included) . . .

The paragraphs of praise were preceded by an enumeration of enemy casualties.

On the ground where we first opened fire over 290 of the enemy was left dead. I think a moderate estimate would place the killed and wounded of the enemy on their left wing at 1740. Prisoners said that the famous 8th New York Regiment and Buck Tails [27th Pa.] whose gallantry deserved a better fate was entirely cut to pieces, their flags left on the field and secured by the 21st Geo.

Trimble totted his own casualties as twenty-five killed, seventy-five wounded, and four missing (presumably taken prisoner), "not including Col. Walker's loss which was small."

The official war records that listed only 114 Union dead did not correlate with Trimble's body count of "over 290." Were Trimble's figures accurate? Ewell himself reported to Jackson that at least 2,000 of the enemy had fallen.

Nearly a hundred and thirty years later, it was difficult, if not impossible for me to sort out the truth. Modern instances of such discrepancies abound; during the war in Vietnam, for example, body counts were subjective and often speculative. In the battles of any war, it seems casualties vary in proportion to political expediency. On the one hand, there is parsimonious grief, and on the other, there is bloated exultance. The Federal body count at Cross Keys may have been lowered, if only to allow Frémont some face-saving, but then again, Trimble's tally could have been off, although it is hard to believe it was off by much.

The turning of a full Union division by a partial Confederate brigade was what Trimble accomplished at Cross Keys. If Trimble had been given permission to carry out his final attack, Frémont's left flank might have caved in—resulting in a David-versus-Goliath rout. But if Schenck and Milroy had been allowed to continue their advances on the right, Ewell's left flank might have suffered a similar devastation.

Scholars of the battle are in agreement that Ewell succeeded in checking Frémont; what they overlook is that Ewell also checked one of his own brigadier generals, the one who did the heaviest fighting. So while the history books tout the victory at Cross Keys as the penultimate brushstroke of Jackson's masterpiece—his Shenandoah Valley Campaign—the truth was somewhat grayer. Aside from formulating and changing the grand strategy, Jackson's involvement was minimal. As for Ewell, his leadership narrowed the parameters of the fight.

Frémont had issued the military equivalent of a time out. At first, he only wanted to straighten his line of battle; then, receiving intelligence from Shields, he decided to call a halt to the battle itself. The day had gone badly, what with the losses on his left and the stubborn repulsions in the center. It was of supreme importance that Frémont join Shields with an intact army. The Pathfinder willingly acknowledged that his army had absorbed some heavy blows (by a numerically superior force, as he misconstrued), but it was by no means defeated.

The Confederate victory, if it could be called that, was mainly psychological in that it forced Frémont to call off his pursuit. Victory Hill was named for the moral inspiration it imparted to the invaded and pillaged populace. Pilsen's remonstrances notwithstanding, Frémont was stung to the point of inactivity when he realized how futile his opening gambit had been. The seemingly resilient Confederate right flank turned out to be forged of harder stuff. Then, too, he had ordered troops into battle while supports were still marching into position. But Frémont's biggest error had been to misjudge his enemy's strength—a mindset he could never shake, not even three years later, writing about the battle in 1865. It shackled his imagination and his will. There were strategies to breach the kind of defensive positioning he was up against, strategies he chose not to initiate. Instead, he settled for the brute firepower of dozens of twelve-pounders, a barrage that was kept up for hours to no real advantage.

If Frémont had not feared Jackson so, he might have used his infantry more effectively from the start. To his credit, he understood that, man for man, the Rebel outfought the Yankee, although the Rebel was usually the poorer equipped. (At Winchester, for example, Trimble had estimated that twenty percent of his men were shoeless.) Seeing the elephant was a fast way to gain proficiency as a soldier, but regional differences initially favored the Confederates, and the Valley Campaign was a telling example. As Richard Taylor stated in his memoirs,

> The first skirmishes and actions of the war proved that the Southron, untrained, was a better fighter than the Northerner—not because of more courage, but of the social and economic conditions by which he was surrounded. Devoted to agriculture in a sparsely populated country, the Southron was self-reliant, a practiced horseman, and skilled in the use of arms. The dense population of the North, the habit of association for commercial and manufacturing purposes, weakened individuality of character, and horsemanship and the use of arms were exceptional accomplishments. The rapid development of railways and manufactures in the West had assimilated the people of that region to their eastern neighbors, and the old race of frontier riflemen had wandered to the far interior of the continent. Instruction and discipline soon equalized differences, and battles were decided by generalship and numbers . . .

Taylor also told of the pathetic unpreparedness of captured Union cavalry on the long march up the Valley:

> The horse [cavalry unit] was from New England, a section in which horsemanship was an unknown art, and some of the riders were strapped to their steeds. Ordered to dismount, they explained their condition, and were given time to unbuckle. Many breastplates and other protective devices were seen . . . We did not know whether the Federals had organized cuirassiers, or were recurring to the customs of Gustavus Adolphus. I saw a poor fellow lying dead on the pike, pierced through the breastplate and body by a rifle ball. Ironclad men are of small account before modern weapons.

At Cross Keys, the march was finally over. The elusive moment to "bag" Jackson had arrived. As Frémont saw it, he had no choice but to initiate hostilities in a careful manner. Later in the afternoon, when it seemed that events might spin out of control, he opted to withdraw just as carefully.

Why was Trimble the only Confederate leader who sensed Frémont's timidity and pressed to exploit it? Again, it was a question of timing. Clearly, Trimble's ideas were at odds with Jackson's already disseminated plan for the next day. It wasn't that no one believed Trimble. Taylor, Ewell, and even Jackson were willing to listen to his proposals; they all understood that a very tangible victory lay within their grasp, if only they admitted a little more flexibility to the agenda. But such an alteration of the plan would have added unforeseen variables to a predictably stagnant situation. "You have done well enough for one day," Ewell said. It sounded like an affectionate pat on the shoulder.

An anecdote from the battle illustrates Ewell's deference to Jackson as well as a streak of romanticism that was popular during the early years of the war. Jackson had censured Ewell for giving orders not to shoot a Union officer on a white horse (Milroy on Jasper?) leading one of the fruitless attacks on the Confederate center. The picture image of heroic rider and steed struck a sympathetic vein in Ewell. He saw a reflection of his idealized self and could not bear the thought of destroying it, but later, when Jackson heard the story, he fumed,

> This is no ordinary war! The brave and gallant Federal officers are the very kind that must be killed. Shoot the brave officers and the cowards will run away and take the men with them.

Abruptly, Ewell canceled his sentimental vision, never giving another order like that again. "Old Jack" 's word was law. Likewise, to settle the question of whether or not to continue the fight, as Trimble insisted, Ewell's least painful option was to refer Trimble to Jackson himself. The resulting conference only referred the matter back to Ewell, with Jackson knowing full well what the outcome would be. As such, Jackson kept his hands clean of the affair, and in his report to Second Corps headquarters, there was no mention of the conference or its foregone conclusion.

Ewell, to his credit, drew wisdom from the situation. While sitting in front of his tent the night after the battle at Port Republic, he asked Colonel Thomas T. Munford if he remembered a recent conversation in which he (Ewell) had characterized Jackson as crazy and Trimble as doddering. Munford laughed, recollecting the caustic remarks. "I take it all back," Ewell said, "and will never prejudge another man."

> Old Jackson is no fool; he knows how to keep his own counsel, and does curious things: but he has method in his madness; he has disappointed me entirely. And old Trimble is a real trump; instead of being over cautious, he is as bold as any man, and, in fact, is the hero of yesterday's fight. Jackson was not on the field. They will call it mine, but Trimble won the fight; and I believe now if I had followed his views we would have destroyed Frémont's army.

When the soldiers in blue stopped shooting and settled in for the night, the soldiers in gray were compelled to follow suit. Frémont's quiet posture—his singularly successful initiative of the day—put the battlefield at ease. Trimble concluded his report with a reminder for posterity:

> It is but an act of simple justice to the brave men of my brigade to say that this battle was fought by them, infantry & artillery, *in fact* alone—Col. Walker's 15th and 25th Va. Reg'ts aided in the last repulse. Gen'l Taylor's Brigade not having been engaged or seen by the enemy—the infantry under Brig. Gen'l Elzey on the left of the line encountered at no time of the day more than the enemy's skirmishers as they made no demonstration on our left. The battery of B. Gen'l Steuart was in the early part of the fight but was withdrawn after a severe loss of horses, leaving Capt. Latimer's battery to contend singly with four batteries of the enemy.
> Very Respectfully,
> I. R. Trimble, Brig. Genl.

TWENTY-THREE

M<small>Y MOTLEY FLEET</small> of farm machinery was as ready as it would ever be, and I, its commodore, watched with interest as the sea of hay grew tall. All fall and winter, I had served as barn mechanic and implement restorer, and now I yearned for more active duty. The fruits of my labor were in the barn, mothballed, inert. The cutter-bar had been hitched to the tractor since late April, the combination shrouded in plastic like a secret weapon, as if to obscure it from a more formidable enemy than shitting pigeons.

One day followed the next with partly cloudy skies. Rain wasn't likely, but there was a chance. I had picked up an insidious new habit: scanning the daily weather reports. For a week, the possibility of rain had been included in every forecast like the waiver at the end of a warranty, but even the briefest of showers failed to materialize. Still, the voice of prudence suggested that I wait a couple of days. At least until tomorrow.

Too attuned to the perils of chance, I was suffering a paralysis of will. I knew that rain was the bane of hay farming. If a deluge was coming, I didn't want to be caught in it. The farmer who sold us the land had warned me that bad weather sometimes flared up unexpectedly in the shadow of the Massanuttens. "A feller has to listen to each day," he advised, and not listen too far ahead.

I was waiting for a sign from heaven. My lack of experience made me slow to understand that there was no green light. No seer would come forward and announce, "Okay, you can start making hay now." On television, in front of a map of the United States like a chalked outline of a body on a floor, the suited-up meteorologist was no more of an authority than I.

At length, there came a splendid morning that fairly shouted to my senses, "Get out and mow that goddamn field!" It happened to be the hundred and twenty-sixth anniversary of the battle. I knew I couldn't wait any longer. The farmer and his son had already made a cutting—their last, as it turned out—on most of the acreage. Only one field remained, a few acres they had skipped over for me to experiment on.

Around 11 o'clock, after the dew had lifted, I "opened" the field: that is, I began mowing concentrically from its edges. I hadn't gone around three passes before I became aware of the smell of burning metal. Aborting my progress, I discovered that the ball-jointed foot of the knife assembly was too tight in its slide. To correct the problem, I needed to replace shims I had erroneously removed, thinking there had been too much play. I should have left well enough alone. It wasn't the first time I had tried to fix something that wasn't broken.

As I bent to my task, I thought about how my self-appointed farming method fitted between the up-to-date and the old-fashioned. Ahead of me was the mower-conditioner and behind me was the two-horse mower. A modern mower-conditioner (that cutter and crusher that cruised through a hay crop so quickly) would make short work of this field. I marveled at the thought, imagining myself at the helm of a powerful new tractor, one with an enclosed cab and air-conditioning. At the other end of the spectrum, a two-horse mower would extend the work, but the experience would be a pleasant one. Or would it? I pictured myself on the bumpy mower perch, reins in hand, staring at the twin rumps of straining steeds whose tails swished away the flies.

Within an hour, I had the tractor's steering wheel back in my now greasy grip. Once again, the outlying cutter-bar combed into the standing grass, clipping as it advanced. It took careful steering to guide the bar so that it neither overlapped with nor veered from the preceding swath. Frequent glances over my right shoulder straightened my aim, and as I worked, I studiously tuned out my parched throat, full bladder, and compressed backside.

Twice in the succeeding hours I dismounted to lubricate the knife assembly with used motor oil. I also stopped a few times to unclog the guards at field corners. There was a knack to making a clogless right-angle turn: raising the mower and backing up slightly to execute a clean pivot. At one point, loose grass wound in a tight ball around the driveshaft, resulting in an extended pause while I hacked it free with a penknife. (A shield was missing, I found out later.) But when the tractor was in gear and things were going smoothly, there was a rhythmic felicity to the work. The way a seven-foot band of grass slumped continuously seemed just short of miraculous. Round and round I went, and with each pass, the acreage became increasingly groomed and sweet-smelling. Fallen blooms of red and white clover were laid in two-dimensional bouquets. Bobwhites thrummed from my path, their acceleration into flight even louder than the mower's clatter and the stuttering two-cylinder diesel.

When the entire field lay green and fragrant and flat under the baking sun, I had arrived at its very center. Already, crows were alighting to feast on the loosed banquet of insects and seed. The Bonus brothers were not far behind, having been alerted to the presence of freshly-exposed mouse and mole abodes. I climbed down to lift the cutter-bar to its traveling position, placing my fingers with the greatest of care. Then, grinning like Ike, I drove back to the barn. I could not remember when I had last experienced such an inordinate feeling of accomplishment. A sneeze or two punctuated my elation. After months of preparation, I welcomed this bout of honest-to-goodness hay fever.

In parallel swaths, the mown grass lay exposed to the sun, its chlorophyllous brilliance turning to greenish dun. The crop was becoming a tangible asset, a source of cash, a recoupment of time and effort and equipment. As I waited, I tried not to worry. I had been advised that a conscientious farmer lost sleep during drying time. There was always the chance of a stretch of inclement weather or an equipment breakdown. Every nuance of climate and good fortune would affect the finished product.

When hay dries too long it turns golden, like straw. Then it loses protein and becomes tough. If it doesn't dry long enough, it turns moldy in the bale. A test for moldiness is to throw a bale on the barn floor. Mold spores will jar loose, wafting from the bale in a sour cloud. Another test is to bend over and get a noseful. When hay smells like mildew, it is refused by finicky horses and sheep. It makes dairy cows cough. Stock cattle can be discomfited as well, but in the absence of tastier feed, they will eat it.

Hay that is rained on to the extent of a thundershower or two but dries thoroughly later on loses little in palatability and nutrition. Wet or overly thick hay can be scratched up and flung into the air by the whirling tines of a tedder to speed drying. An implement called a windrow inverter scrapes up wet windrows and flips them upside down. Drying agents in the form of chemical fogs can be sprayed from an array of nozzles at the pickup reel of a baler. Many farmers still turn wet hay the old fashioned way, with just a rake. By reversing the rake's angle, it can be made to function as a tedder, unraking, as it were, to the opposite side. In this process, hay needs to be raked several times until it redries, if the weather holds out.

The preferred method, of course, is to let the hay dry by itself, undisturbed. This is possible after a light rain, followed by steady sunshine. A gentle wind helps, too. And if luck is on the farmer's side, there is no rain at all. Yet ideal or near-ideal weather tends to elude the haymaker during these critical hours between cutting and baling. The length of time under the most benign conditions varies with the density and maturity of the crop, the humidity in the air, the slope of the land, the time of year, and a dozen other factors peculiar to a locale.

Hay cut with an ordinary field mower will not be dry enough to bale for at least three full days. The same crop cut with a mower-conditioner can be baled in a little over twenty-four hours. I have seen a chart in an agricultural publication that illustrated this time-saving difference. Along a horizontal vernier of days, the moisture content of unconditioned hay holds a steady line until the end of the second day, when it veers into a gradual curve toward desiccation. By contrast, crushed and broken hay can be represented by a line that plummets right from the first hour after cutting.

The hay that lay on our field was as unconditioned as it could be, but it was drying. The weather continued sunny and hot, yet somehow I didn't think it would last. I was in a dilly of a rush. Instead of waiting another four hours, as I should have, I started to rake. My decision was rooted in pure self-persuasion. To be in the tractor seat again was my real priority.

When was hay sufficiently dry to rake? I sought the answer through several seasons of haymaking, periodically incurring the scorn of knowledgeable hay customers. By the time the mantle of experience sat squarely on my shoulders I had learned two cardinal rules: never *make* wet hay unless making it for mulch, and secondly, never *sell* wet hay for anything other than mulch. It was wrong to fob off mulch hay for feed, and downright foolish to try to get away with it.

As the orchard grass–fescue–clover mix passes from winter dormancy to maturation, it becomes extremely sappy. Thriving on spring rains, it virtually teems with water, especially after a wet winter. An optimal first cutting is achieved right before the field goes to seed, when seed heads are fully formed and stems approach maximum height. A green field, tender and full of protein, ripples in the breeze like waves rolling toward a beach. Once cut, only the proper amount of drying will insure that its goodness is transferred to the bale.

186

The surest method to tell whether or not hay is dry is to walk out in the field and examine handfuls from a selection of locations where the hay lies thickest. The top layer will feel dry to the touch, but it is the bottom layer that counts. Checking the hay at field edges partially shaded by trees is another good indicator. Unless *all* the hay is *all* dry, a farmer wastes time and fuel by starting to rake. When mown material is completely dry to the touch, it retains fifteen to twenty percent water, yet there is no sheen or limpness to the individual blade or leaf. A dry blade of orchard grass turns chalky green and furls longitudinally into a cylinder. Clover blossoms are dark brown, even black. Formerly pliant stems turn stalklike and brittle.

Visions of a barnful of sweetly scented hay impeded my judgment. I raked the hay four hours too soon, but it was, after all, a learning experience. Being my own boss, operating my own equipment on my own field, I fell into a self-absorbed, workmanlike canter. In fifth gear, about six miles per hour, I drove along the first mown pass, pulling the hay to the left with the wheel rake as I advanced counterclockwise around the field, then reversed my direction for the second pass, again pulling the hay to the left to combine the windrows. I repeated this procedure throughout the field, one windrow from two passes.

An ideal windrow is a sinuous, loosely bunched hedge, anywhere from four feet wide to three feet tall. The hay continues to dry by virtue of its elevation above the ground, but windrows are fragile structures, easily ravaged by wind. If dust-devils (roving vortices similar to miniature tornadoes) swirl through a windrowed field, the hay will scatter as if it had never been raked.

After forming the last windrow, I shut off the tractor. Once again, I ended up at the dead center of the field, now a bull's-eye of concentric hay walls. My handiwork imparted a satisfying order and smelled (between sneezes) like Summer itself. As the shadows lengthened and the hay settled slightly, the windrows gained the impenetrability of parallel mountain ridges. From the vantage of the tractor seat, I could have been high above the Alleghenies. I wished I had a camera.

My fingers grasped for the starter switch. With the re-rattle of the doughty diesel, I pulled back on the hydraulic lever, raising the rake, and drove gingerly out of the field.

On the verge of rolling out the baler, I made a comprehensive last-minute check. Four chains and at least thirty grease fittings required lubrication. In the twine box, two spare rolls needed to be joined to the two rolls in use. There were hinges and springs to oil, and several other adjustments to account for, like chain- and belt-tensioning. Lastly, a drawbar had to be connected to the tractor's hitch, the baler tongue pinned to its center hole, and the driveshaft knuckle slipped over the splined shaft of the P.T.O.

Within thirty minutes, the fussed-over machine was descending the barn bridge behind me—a clanking, magisterial presence emerging in the yellow light of late afternoon. Both milestone and millstone, the baler seemed to be the hallmark of my fifth decade. It was my supreme farm investment, the flagship of my fleet, and now I was towing it to the proving ground. With care, I eased it between the gate posts and entered the windrowed field.

In traveling position, the baler was pulled directly behind the tractor. In working position, the baler tongue swung over and latched thirty degrees to the left, so that baling was done to the right of the tractor. A yank of a lanyard released the tongue latch, although it took some clutch-jerking to reset the latch in the offset. Having accomplished this, I climbed down to secure the lanyard, which, left loose, could entangle in the drive shaft. Then I lowered the pickup reel until its hard rubber guide wheel touched the ground. Finally, I tightened two compression springs on the bale chute that regulated the density of the bales. At this point, the only thing left to do was to climb back on the tractor and utter a benediction to ward off unforeseen calamity.

In second gear, with the P.T.O. engaged, I aligned the baler with the outermost windrow. Black smoke belched from the overwrought Kubota as the flywheel attained its recommended 540 revolutions per minute. The baler transmitted a bucking motion to the tractor; I found myself piloting a cacophonous, plodding bronco train. How different it was from swinging a pitchfork! The plunger was whipping back and forth at eighty strokes a minute, ramming clump after clump into the bale chamber. At two and a half miles per hour, the pickup reel steadily drew in the hay. There was a grating whir, followed by a *ka-thunk*. I glanced back and saw the compressed hay moving rearward along the bale chute. Two strands of twine stretched over the endless, horizontal square column. More whirring and another *ka-thunk*. Part of the column toppled to the ground. It was a bale: box-like, about a yard long and dusky green. Momentarily, I felt like a new father in a delivery room. A second bale fell. Mirabile dictu, multiple birth! The pickup reel strayed from the windrow. Enchantment was messing up my driving.

I steered the baler too sharply into the first corner, causing the driveshaft U-joints to chatter, and made a sloppy business of restraddling the windrow. Towing the baler required anticipatory steering to a degree I had never mastered. By the time the left wheel of the baler got to where the right front wheel of the tractor had been, the tractor was twenty feet ahead in unknown territory. But, in spite of my deviations, the bales fell to the ground with a clockwork regularity. My ineptitude did not alter the accumulating truth: from mountains I was creating cubicles. When the last bale was sitting on the crewcut field and twilight suffused the air, it looked as though I had created a Levittown.

TWENTY-FOUR

Washington, June 9, 1862.

Major-General Frémont:

Halt at Harrisonburg, pursuing Jackson no farther. Get your force well in hand and stand on the defensive, guarding against a movement of the enemy either back toward Strasburg or toward Franklin, and await further orders, which will soon be sent to you.

A. LINCOLN

Unaware that a battle had been fought at Cross Keys and a battle was being fought in Port Republic, the president went about the implementation of his shift in general strategy: to put the Valley offensive on hold for the time being, and concentrate upon Richmond. A similar note was sent to Shields:

Front Royal, June 9, 1862.

It being the intention of the President that the troops of this department be employed elsewhere, the major-general commanding directs that you cease all further pursuit and bring back all your divisions to Luray, and get ready for the march to Fredericksburg.

I send herewith a telegram in cipher to Major-General Frémont, which I have been directed to inclose to you for transmittal to him.

ED. SCHRIVER
Colonel, Chief of Staff.

In his report after the battle at Port Republic, Shields described his defeated advance force's flight back to Conrad's Store. Jackson had bested him, and Shields was frank enough to admit it in his reply to Colonel Schriver, Chief of Staff of the Department of the Rappahannock:

Considering the locality, which was not defensible, being liable to be turned on both flanks, and the disparity of forces engaged, it is truly wonderful that our little army was able to effect its escape. This can only be attributed to the splendid manner in which the artillery was handled and the desperate manner in which the infantry fought in its close contests with the enemy. But defeat was unavoidable. It is fortunate they withdrew when they did. My whole division in that position, or rather in that locality, would have protracted the struggle and made it more bloody, but could not have maintained the field. There is much to be regretted in this affair, but nothing which does not reflect honor upon the courage and conduct of the gallant troops engaged.

Very respectfully, your obedient servant,

JAS. SHIELDS
Brigadier-General, Commanding Division.

Nevertheless, Lincoln's order of June 9, as transmitted by Schriver, struck Shields as untimely and misinformed, for it arrived the moment his army could have operated jointly with Frémont's. Shields's complaint eventually reached the upper level of leadership, prompting a clarification from corps commander Irvin McDowell to Lorenzo Thomas, the Adjutant General of the Army in Washington. Writing on October 3, McDowell said:

With reference to the remark made by [Shields] that the order to him to cease following the enemy and return to Luray was received just "as he had planned a combined attack with General Frémont, by which Jackson was to be annihilated," I have to say that the order was given by me from the War Department by direction of the President, who at the same moment wrote a similar order to General Frémont, it being not considered expedient to continue the chase after Jackson up the valley, which could bring on nothing decisive for us, and it being greatly the desire of the President and myself that the forces under my command should as speedily as possible return to Fredericksburg to move on Richmond. Both the condition of General Shields' division and that of the roads and rivers, as represented by him, indicated anything than the success he anticipated.

Frémont, on the other hand, withdrew from the vicinity of Port Republic of his own free will. Lincoln's telegram had not reached him. On the afternoon of the ninth and the morning of the tenth, his troops made a show of felling timber on the bank of the North River, as if to construct a bridge to cross in pursuit of Jackson, but the labor was soon halted. At the time, Frémont also sent a scouting party of cavalry under the command of a Major Haskell, of his staff, down the river to ascertain Shields's whereabouts. The party, in Confederate mufti, successfully forded the river seven miles below, and met up with the remnants of Carroll's command, which informed Haskell that Shields was complying with Lincoln's orders. A few days later, the communication link between Shields and Frémont was reopened with the following message:

> Headquarters Shields' Division,
> Luray, June 12, 1862.
>
> Maj. Gen. John C. Frémont:
> My advance guard was driven back on the 9th after a sanguinary engagement of four hours. I re-inforced it, and determined, in connection with you, to renew the attack the next morning. After handing the dispatch to your messenger, a peremptory order reached me from Washington directing me to get my command together and return at once to this point, preparatory to marching to Fredericksburg. I never obeyed an order with such reluctance, but no option was left me. The mismanagement of one of my generals left the route open to Jackson. He failed to burn the bridge at Port Republic, according to orders, and the result has been the defeat of his small command and the escape of Jackson. Here I found orders to remain till Banks is in position at Front Royal. The moment he is there I am to march to Catlett's Station to report to Fredericksburg, thence to Richmond . . .
> I have the honor to be, your friend and obedient servant.
>
> JAS. SHIELDS
> Major-General, Commanding Division.

But Haskell had already returned with the news of Shields's retreat. In the apologia of 1865, Frémont stated,

> With the receipt of the intelligence brought by Major Haskell I regarded the movement against Jackson as closed. Whatever of the original objects of my mission I had been enabled to accomplish was now fairly fulfilled. That the retreat of the rebel leader had been conducted with skill and ability is what no just enemy can deny him; but had he been less favored by circumstances of weather and by the absence of combinations beyond my control, though easy enough to have been made during Jackson's earlier pursuit, it is for consideration whether he would have been able even to reach the [North River] and still less to cross that river with or without a bridge to invite his transit . . .
> The withdrawal of Shields had left my command an isolated body far in advance of all other troops, and all expectation of aid or concert of action with others was now cut off. My troops had been long with-

out proper food or shelter; their march had been exhausting, and I had expended their last effort in reaching Port Republic. I determined, therefore, to fall back at once upon my supplies, and accordingly during a day of stormy rain I marched my command back to Harrisonburg.

At Harrisonburg on that Tuesday evening, two days after the battle at Cross Keys and at least two days before Shields's message arrived from Luray, Lincoln's telegram was received. For once, the commander-in-chief directed the Pathfinder to go exactly where he already happened to be. The coincidence didn't last long, though, for Frémont felt too exposed in Harrisonburg, a town "22 miles from the enemy's main railroad line at Staunton, and approached by nine different roads." He wrote to Lincoln:

> Headquarters Mountain Division,
> Harrisonburg, June 11, 1862.
> (Received June 12. 10 A.M.)

> Your dispatch of yesterday morning finds me here withdrawing upon Mount Jackson, a strong, defensible position behind the Shenandoah and the key to the surrounding country. General Shields' withdrawal after his action of the 9th, together with the condition of my troops made this move imperative. Will you allow me to halt at Mount Jackson instead of Harrisonburg, which is not a line of defense, and exposes me to be cut off from my supplies and communication? My troops are much distressed for want of supplies, which are far in the rear and come up very inadequately. We are greatly in need of surgeons and ambulances.

> J. C. FRÉMONT,
> Major-General.

With what must have been a long sigh of resignation, Lincoln acquiesced.

> Washington, June 12.

> Major-General Frémont:
> Yours, preferring Mount Jackson to Harrisonburg, is just received. On this point use your discretion, remembering that our object is to give such protection as you can to Western Virginia. Many thanks to yourself, officers, and men for the gallant battle of last Sunday.

> A. LINCOLN.

Seeing that Lincoln was giving an inch, Frémont tried to take a mile. Having acquired permission for the "defensible position" of his choice, he now went whole hog by demanding the recruitment of more men, as well as the absorption of the commands of Sigel and Banks into his own. He estimated Jackson's troop strength at 38,000. Frémont's requests, which implied continuing paranoia about Jackson, were induced, in part, by Colonel Thomas Munford, who had assumed command of the Rebel cavalry following the death of Ashby. Munford was maneuvering on the fringe of the retreating Union army in such a way that Jackson's entire force seemed to be present—although the Confederates had withdrawn southeast of Port Republic to Brown's Gap, in the foothills of the Blue Ridge. Munford's activity quite confounded Frémont, occasioning a panicky flow of telegrams to Washington.

On June 14, Stanton wired Frémont the following brief message to set matters straight:

> General Sigel is under command of Major-General Banks. Major-General Banks will co-operate with you, but he is commander of a separate corps, and does not come under your command.

With entreaties, corrections, cajolery, and droll humor, Lincoln also countered Frémont's missives. Commenting on the estimate of Jackson's strength, Lincoln telegraphed on June 15:

> My Dear Sir:
> . . . We have no indefinite power of sending re-enforcements; so that we are compelled rather to consider the proper disposal of the forces we have than of those we could wish to have. We may be able to send you some dribs by degrees, but I do not believe we can do more. As you alone beat Jackson last Sunday* I argue that you are stronger than he is today, unless he has been re-enforced, and that he cannot have been materially re-enforced, because such re-enforcement could only have come from Richmond, and he is much more likely to go to Richmond than Richmond is to come to him. Neither is very likely.

The president went on to state the reason for his new thinking, and the subsequent shift in strategy.

> I think Jackson's game—his assigned work—now is to magnify the accounts of his numbers and reports of his movements, and thus, by constant alarms keep three or four times as many of our troops away from Richmond as his own force amounts to. Thus he helps his

---

*Frémont never admitted that he had lost. Lincoln may have been talking tongue-in-cheek.

friends at Richmond three or four times as much as if he were there. Our game is not to allow this.

Lincoln's astuteness went beyond the perception of many of his generals, but Frémont, in particular, was increasingly immune to strategic reasoning. At Mount Jackson, he concentrated his energies on rebuilding the destroyed trestles on the railroad to Strasburg. Then, Mount Jackson itself became too dangerous to defend. In 1865, Frémont wrote:

> Significant demonstrations of the enemy, who had been reported largely re-enforced, taken in connection with the still isolated position at Mount Jackson, induced my farther withdrawal down the valley to Strasburg, and subsequently to Middletown, where I arrived with my command June 24, effecting a junction with the forces of Generals Banks and Sigel.
>
> The tents and baggage left at Petersburg on the 27th May, having been brought forward to Middletown, and camps and hospitals established at healthful points, having due regard to positions of defense, the troops of my command were made comparatively comfortable, and the sick began to improve. For the first time since they had started on the campaign the men received full rations.

At rest in camp, Frémont happily succored to his army, believing himself to be on the threshold of even greater expeditionary feats. He had no idea that Lincoln's patience had run out. The apologia ended:

> While thus occupied in preparing my corps for active service, which telegrams from the War Department were preparing me immediately to expect, I received from the Secretary of War the President's order of June 26, which placed my own and the corps then with me under the command of Major-General Pope.
>
> Having the conviction that consistently with a just regard for the safety of my troops and what was rightfully due to my personal honor I could not suffer myself to pass under the command of General Pope, I asked to be relieved from the duty to which I had been assigned under him. On the 27 of June, having been relieved of my command by direction of the President, I proceeded to New York to await further orders.
>
> Respectfully, your obedient servant,
>
> J. C. FRÉMONT,
Late Major-General, U.S. Army.

For the remainder of the war, the Pathfinder was never entrusted with another command. In 1890, a few months before he died, he was reinstated into the army as major general, with pay on the retired list.

As Confederate Major R. L. Dabney, preacher to the Stonewall Brigade, witnessed Frémont's impotent shelling from across the North River at Port Republic, he filed away impressions which were later formalized in his writings about Jackson.

> The ambulances, with their merciful attendants, were driven away, and the wounded fled precipitately from their cots. The design of this outrage was obvious; it was supposed that the humanity of General Jackson, would prompt him to demand by flag of truce, an unmolested opportunity to tend the wounded; and on that request, the Federal General designed to found a pretext for claiming, in his despatches, the command of the field and the victory; which he knew belonged to Jackson. But the latter was as clear-sighted, and as determined, as he was humane. No flag of truce, no request was sent. Thanks to the affectionate zeal of the soldiers, all the Confederate dead and wounded had been already removed; and they were just proceeding to extend the offices of humanity to their enemies, when this treacherous interruption occurred. So that the only result of Frémont's savage generalship was, that his own suffering comrades lay under the drenching rain, until he retired to Harrisonburg. By that time, many had died miserably of hemorrhage, exhaustion and hunger, whom their generous enemies would have rescued; and not a few of their dead, with some, perchance, of the mangled living, were partially devoured by swine before their burial!

To fall prey to man-eating pigs was an apt fate for those who fought against Jackson, the "General of transcendent abilities." Dabney continued:

> It was as General Jackson was returning on this day from the pursuit of the routed Federalists, that he first saw their diabolical explosive rifle-balls. A soldier presented him several which he had found in the dust of the road, unexploded. On examination they were found to be composed of two pieces of lead, enclosing a cavity between them, and cemented together by pressure. The hollow space was filled with fulminating powder, which was intended to explode by percussion, upon the impact of the ball against the bone of the penetrated body. Thus the fragments of lead would be driven in various and erratic

directions through the mangled flesh, baffling the surgeon's probe, and converting the wound into a mortal one.

Through the proselytizing of Jackson, Dabney, and others, a growing sense of Christian zeal pervaded the Confederate army, and to a lesser extent, the Confederacy itself. Because of its success, Jackson's mission in the Shenandoah Valley became synonymous with the smiting of infidels, and an "ever-kind Providence"—not solid generalship, nor dogged devotion to duty—was held to be responsible. God sympathized with the South. God had singled out the South to win. Jackson's public piety and humble demeanor gave no indication that he relished the personal glory that was rendering his name synonymous with the righteous crusade.

Before dawn on the twelfth of June, with the trains of captured supplies headed safely over the mountains, the Confederate army quitted the confining foothills of Brown's Gap and bivouacked on an open plain several miles to the southwest, at Mount Meridian, not far from Weyer's Cave. The rain had stopped. Having no reason to fear the separately withdrawn Union forces, Jackson's men relaxed. Their camp was situated in a chain of leafy groves between two rivers, and Dabney described the scene with a Biblical cadence:

> In this smiling paradise they solaced themselves five days for their fatigues, the men reposing under the shade, or bathing in the sparkling waters of the Shenandoah, and the horses feeding in the abundant pastures.

On Saturday, June 14, the commanding general proclaimed a day of thanksgiving and prayer "for the purpose of rendering thanks to God for having crowned our arms with success, and to implore his continued favor." Jackson wrote his wife, Mary:

Near Wier's [sic] Cave, June 14th.

> Our God has thrown his shield over me in the various apparent dangers to which I have been exposed. . . . my earnest prayer is that our ever kind Heavenly Father will continue to crown our arms with success, until our independence shall, through his divine blessing, be established.

The army remained at Mount Meridian until June 17, when the order came from Lee to march toward the Chickahominy River and Richmond. Promptly, the troops decamped, commencing a debilitating march of one hundred and thirty miles in the hottest weather. Arriving in unfamiliar territory and physically exhausted from lack of sleep, Jackson made a series of ineffectual thrusts and fatigue-induced errors, for which he was not remembered. The inspired victories in the familiar purlieus of the Shenandoah Valley were a part of history that would never repeat itself.

TWENTY-FIVE

In the barn, by flashlight, I read the bale counter. One hundred and fifty-three bales — not bad for a first try. It was a quantity I could pick up from the field by myself. The following morning, as soon as the dew lifted, I hitched up "Ol' Swayback," as I had nicknamed the hay wagon, and went to work. One trip was all it would take.

The bales were on the heavy side. They all weighed the same, because their size and density had been determined by preset adjustments to the baler (density was controlled by the two springs holding down a bar that functioned as a brake in the bale chute, and size was governed by a trip mechanism linked to the revolutions of a spiked wheel pressed against the hay as it moved rearward). Ideally, the bales would have weighed about thirty-five pounds apiece, but because the hay hadn't dried completely, they seemed ten pounds heavier. A bale should feel light for its bulk and compress slightly when its twine strings are forcibly pulled. These bales felt dense and unyielding.

Bales are lifted most successfully by their strings. Bale hooks, curved iron hooks that snag into the hay like carrying handles, aren't used much anymore. The thought of wielding a meat hook in close proximity to the pantlegs makes most farmers wince. Grasping a string in each hand, I began carrying the bales one at a time to the wagon. Over distances of fifteen feet or fifty, what mattered was that both strings bore the weight of the bale, lest one string be inadvertently pulled off. A bale with a missing string will open up like an accordion. As I became adept at handling bales, I learned the trick of a splayed, one-handed grasp, pulling both strings toward each other in a single valise-like grip. This method enabled me to carry two bales at a time over short distances, although it brought to mind the image of a suitcase-laden traveler walking to a taxi stand from the far end of a railway platform.

When a bale is tossed or thrown with precision, it lands without roll-

199

ing end over end, so as not to cause excessive ablation. Sisal twine is remarkably strong, and knots rarely untie. When a kicker flings bales twenty feet in the air, and later, when the jumbled wagon load is dumped prior to stacking, every bale survives. If a bale breaks, it is almost always the result of an imbalance in the bale itself—one string is looser than the other, or the hay on one side less compressed.

A bale is a prickly, itch-inducing entity, a bundle of roughage that takes up a well-defined block of space and causes, as my dictionary puts it, "a sudden violent spasmodic audible expiration of breath." As such, baled hay is destined for rapid handling. On my maiden voyage with the hay wagon, I got off to a running start. Anticipating the many stops, as well as the long carries, I began at a pace more suitable for a person half my age. By pre-grouping several bales, then driving to them, I worked my way around the field, saving a little time and energy, but still pushing myself too hard. Jumping off and on the tractor, jumping on and off the wagon, I wore myself to a frazzle.

By the time the sun was getting hot and my legs and arms were giving out, I had lifted every bale and was headed for the barn. There was never a sweatier, more hay-begrimed wretch of a novice. I had tried to do too much too quickly, and now I didn't give a damn if I never saw another bale of hay, nor did I care about the so-called hallowed ground of the stupid battlefield upon which I toiled.

Well, an enforced rest and a prolonged draught of water began to revive me. I sat on the barn floor with my back against a tractor wheel and watched the swallows dart through the doorway. To follow their winged freedom from the puddle of my despair took me outside of myself. I surrendered to the therapy of the barn, and as contemplative minutes ticked by, my thoughts were redirected beyond self-pity.

I glanced about the dark interior at the tall oak studs, the strakes of weatherboard, and the vaulting, rough-sawn barn frame. The orange tractor and its long, aromatic wagon load were intruders from the world of light. I, too, was an anomaly from the sunny field. The underside of the roof, an infinitude of pewter, spread behind the gridwork of stringers and steeply pitched rafters. I imagined a pigeon's-eye view: the equipment clutter, cloacal targets one and all. Above my head, the somber volume spread to the left and right in the empty mows. Bales could be stacked to the ridge board in mows like these, and still there would be room over the main floor to hangar a small blimp.

Abstractly, I thought about volume and displacement, and that led me to think about the wagon load. Mentally, I carried the hundred and fifty-three bales, one by one, to the left mow and stacked them in a cube. The work went easily; in fact, the bales weighed nothing at all. I was almost finished when a very real wasp droned by, inches from my nose. I stood up in a daze, my drowsing vanquished.

Common sense told me that the stacking of hay was best undertaken when the barn was ventilated to the maximum and my clothing was ventilated to the minimum. Accordingly, I opened the barn doors on the cantilever side and buttoned my shirt cuffs. No matter how gently the bales were handled, they would release a continuous residue. I had already seen (and shoveled) a knee-deep, fifty-year accumulation. But common sense could not supply every answer. I really had no idea how to stack the bales correctly, which, as I learned later, was to crisscross them loosely to create gaps for air circulation. I thought they could be lumped together any old way, so I stacked them tightly one alongside the other, like sardines in a tin. Two weeks later, the bales in the center of the stack went moldy.

Nothing deflates the ego of a harvest-weary hay farmer faster than the smell of mold. The fragrance of newly put-up hay is its own reward. During that first summer on my own, a weekend of rain came on the heels of a second cutting. On Monday, the sun returned. On Tuesday, I reraked the fields at intervals, then baled. As I was loading the wagon, I noticed the bales were heavier than usual. Rained-on but redried hay would be heavier, I reasoned, because it compacted more. It was stiffer to the touch and slightly gray, but still viable winter feed for cattle. Not a week had gone by, though, before I noticed that the topmost bales in the mow were actually bubbling with fermentation. The hay was hot to the touch and frothed with a creamy scum. I removed the hot bales in the nick of time. If fermentation had gone unchecked, the whole stack could have spoiled, or worse, smoldered into flame.

All hay cures to some degree when it is put up—a concluding desiccation on the cellular level that takes about two weeks, during which time the barn doors are left open in the daylight hours for extra ventilation. The drier the hay before baling, the shorter the curing period. When hay is fully cured, the headiness of its fragrance mellows. Satisfactorily cured bales retain feed value up to ten years, as long as the bales stay dry and well ventilated.

Still, the ravages of moisture are difficult to evade if the condition of the barn or the attentiveness of the farmer deteriorates. That was one of the advantages of a well-made haystack standing in a field—it took care of itself. Nowadays, when hay stored in a barn gets wet, there are ways to keep it from spoiling. Granulated salt can be sprinkled on the bales to draw out dampness. Drying agents and fungicides can be sprayed. Considering the ups and downs of hay farming, and the uncertainties of weather, doctored hay is not uncommon, but I can state unequivocally that the hay from our forty acres is always served up straight. If I wind up with a bad batch, as I sometimes do, I sell it for an appropriate use, or don't sell it at all.

With my poorly stacked first harvest in a corner of the mow, I backed out the empty wagon, unhitched the tractor, and closed the barn doors. I should have left the doors open. I should have restacked the hay. Somewhat shakily, I had completed the process. No, it wasn't the best of hay, but I was able to sell it to a cattle farmer who ran short of feed over the winter. The next year and the next, aside from an occasional weather disaster, I made better hay, and a lot more of it—between three and four thousand bales. Once or twice, I even managed to achieve excellence, much to the delight of horse owners, who are my pickiest customers. Three years later, I entered a quarter bale for judging in the Rockingham County Fair and won a first premium in the mixed hay category. Even then, I was just learning.

TWENTY-SIX

THE HANDS-ON generalship that afforded Trimble such sure gains when he personally led his front line into battle at Cross Keys was to retire him at Gettysburg, a scant thirteen months later, with a leg amputation followed by his capture as a prisoner of war.

Beginning in mid-summer 1862, he kept a diary in a leather-bound notebook measuring four by five inches. The diary was inherited by his grandson, who saw to its publication in 1922.

After the Battle of Cross Keys, Trimble continued to serve as a brigade commander in Ewell's division, though he chafed openly at Ewell's ill-considered directives. He was on the long march to Richmond with Jackson, and in July he took part in the Seven Days' Campaign against McClellan. On August 9, near Culpeper, about four miles north of Robinson's River, Trimble led three regiments forward against a Union battery, but lost twenty crucial minutes when Ewell's batteries began shelling the ground he intended to charge over. The result was a situation similar to that during the battle at Cross Keys: in the confusion, the Union guns were limbered up and withdrawn out of reach. In his diary, Trimble wrote:

> Had we not been delayed by waiting for our fire to cease, we should have captured this battery – & I am sorry we did not advance at the risk of hurt from our own artillery.

Later in the month, in an exploit highly commended by Jackson, Trimble took Manassas Junction, a Federal matériel depot. The laconic diary entry read: "August 26 night. I with 2 Regts. captured Manassas Junction and 8 pieces artillery – *vast stores, etc.*"

Two days later, in gratitude for this prize of war, Trimble was awarded his first divisional command, coinciding with Jackson's own elevation to head of Corps. But the day after, at Second Bull Run, the new division commander was hit in the leg by one of the recent refinements in rifle ammunition that Major Dabney had found so diabolical, "an explosive ball which broke the bone & inflicted a bad wound." Trimble convalesced at Front Royal, in the home of a Mrs. Cloud, "a lady and her daughters of great dignity & loveliness of character." He stayed with the Cloud family until October 15, when, still convalescing, he was moved southwest to Staunton, seventy miles up the valley, where he was quartered with the Opie family.

> Nov. 16. Bone of leg has knit, & wound nearly closed, but boils have broken out on ankle & prevent me from using crutches & restoring the circulation in the leg.

As a proud afterthought, he added:

> N.B.—On 22nd Sept. Genl. Jackson recommended me for promotion—stating that "the capture of Manassas by two small regiments after a march of 30 miles was the most brilliant exploit of the war." Many prisoners, 100 horses & 8 pieces of artillery were taken & retained.

Jackson's letter of recommendation had been a mixture of praise and censure:

> I respectfully recommend that Brig. General I. R. Trimble be appointed a Major General. It is proper in this connection to state that I do not regard him as a good disciplinarian, but his success in battle has induced me to recommend his promotion..

Was this a veiled reference to Trimble's maverick effectiveness at Cross Keys? Fiercely independent then, the old brigadier's example undoubtedly fostered a sense of independence in his troops, and this may have irked Jackson.

By December 11, increasingly chipper, though still convalescent, Trimble recorded:

> My wound mending slowly, inflammation of lower leg increases & abates alternately. Dec. 13th—a small piece of bone taken from the leg above the fracture—can't yet walk without crutches.

On December 17, he left Staunton for Charlottesville, settling the bill (in inflated Confederate dollars) with Mr. Opie for a hundred dollars per month of rent while "self, wife, Frank & Alfred" were lodged at the Opie residence. In Charlottesville, a Dr. Garnett called on him and recommended laudanam and lead water washes for his leg, which had become dangerously inflamed from calf to instep.

25th. Christmas day—wife went to church—having received letters from home & word that all were well, we pass this holy day in quiet happiness, thankful truly for the goodness & mercies of God toward us—for which we ever feel grateful.

But the comforts of hearth and family could not keep Trimble away from his command.

Jan. 10th. Reported for duty in consequence of a letter from Genl. Jackson, proposing for me to join the army & occupy a room, taking command of his Div. until a march, where my place in the Div. could be filled temporarily. My wound not well, but I can sit up all day & write, read & converse.

Jan 25th. Rec'd orders to join Genl. Jackson at F'burg [Fredericksburg].

Jan 28. Left Charlottesville for the Army—& reached Genl. Jackson's Hdqrs. same day—2 days with him.

Jan 31. Order placing me in command of Jackson's old Div.

Feb 1. Assumed command—and issued an address to the men.

Feb 12th. Mounted my mare for the first time in more than five mos., rode 5 miles without pain or inconvenience.

At Fredericksburg, Trimble was back in the army and back in the saddle, but the winter of 1862–63 was severe. The roads were bad, if not impassable. As division commander, he had to oversee the distribution of dwindling rations. There was sickness in both men and horses. A significant part of his new duties required the granting of extensive furloughs during the long weeks of inactivity. Moreover, it was up to Trimble to order the execution of deserters. On top of all this, he had to fight for his promotion, which had been opposed in the Confederate senate by a personal enemy, Louis Trezevant Wigfall, the truculent former U.S. senator from Texas who had negotiated Major Robert Anderson's surrender of Fort Sumter.

A stultifying amount of paperwork crossed Trimble's desk daily, and the brevity of his diary entries attested to the tedium.

[Feb.] 17th Heavy Snow

18th Fair & warm

19th Rain

21st Heavy snow storm.

22nd, 23rd, 24th. Snow still lies—great difficulty in hauling forage & rations—packing without saddles resorted to. Many horses dying daily in Div. for want of food and disease—Strict orders given to provide better shelter & grooming for all animals—troops still working on roads to Guinea's Station.

On April 13, 1863, as spring was leavening the hardship of the previous months, Trimble came down with a bad cold that kept him at death's door for several weeks. On April 27, he was moved to Richmond, where better medical attention could be given. As he recuperated, he made notes on the battles he should have been fighting, particularly the two-day battle at Chancellorsville, in which General Paxton of his own division was killed, and fellow generals Jackson, A. P. Hill, and Heth were wounded. (Jackson, whose arm was amputated, died not many days afterward of pneumonia.) By Trimble's sixty-first birthday, he was still unwell, but struggling each day to better his health.

Monday, May 18th '63 —Continued to improve rapidly, riding out daily—started at 6 A.M. for Shocco Springs, Warren Co. N.C. and reached Warrenton at 7—a long journey for an invalid & rather too much for me—however I felt refreshed by a sound night's sleep & started at 6 for the Springs by stage—arriving at Breakfast, which was eaten with a good appetite and probably too much—ate dinner at 2—probably before breakfast was digested, for at 6 P.M. felt sick & threw up undigested food, at night had some fever, but it passed off by morning—It may be that the sudden stopping of my iron and quinine, which was left in Warrenton, had some effect on my stomach.

A little over a month later, Trimble rode through Maryland with Robert E. Lee's army to rejoin General Ewell, now Corps Commander, in Carlisle, Pennsylvania. On June 30, Trimble received orders to march his division to Gettysburg. His diary for the next few days was a detailed account—and critique—of one of the largest and bloodiest battles of the Civil War.

July 1st, Wednesday at 1 P.M. engaged the enemy on his left flank, on the Middletown road, the hills west of town occupied by him. Genl. Hill's corps had been engaged an hour before in his front on Cash Town road—Genl. Ewell's Corps (Rhodes Div.) drove the enemy along the ridge South & when our flank attack joined Hill, the Feds abandoned their position and fled to Gettysburg & Cemetery Hill . . . We took this day and next 7,000 prisoners. The fighting ceased 3 P.M. Genl. Ewell saying he did not wish to bring on a hurried engagement without orders from Lee.

This was the same hesitancy, the same refusal to take the initiative that Ewell had displayed at Cross Keys, and it aggravated Trimble to no end.

This was a *radical error*, for had we continued the fight, we should have gotten in their rear & taken Cemetery Hill & Culps Hill, a rocky and woody eminence ½ mile to the east of Cemetery Hill. This would have given us the command of the position . . . As it was the enemy had full time on Wednesday night to throw up works & be joined by two other corps and on Thursday noon they occupied Culps Hill, erected defenses there & thus made perfect their position—having inaccessible hills on each flank & Cemetery Hill in the center.

The veteran topographer and tactician knew the consequences of Ewell's delay. Still, the Confederates stayed in the fight, inflicting what damage they could.

On Thursday Longstreet got up & gained considerable advantage over the enemy's left and drove them. Johnson and Early's div. attempted [in] the evening to drive the enemy from his position on his right, but found him too strongly defended by triple lines. Friday it was decided that Longstreet shd. make a vigorous assault on the enemy's left. After a furious cannonade of 2 hours this attack was made, our troops marching over open fields (exposed at every step to a most destructive fire) for a mile. This distance broke down the men and exhausted & ranks thinned, they only reached the enemy lines in small numbers and were repulsed—the error was in charging over so broad a space. Had the troops marched at night to mile of the works & charged vigorously by daybreak we [might] have carried the lines on the enemy's left.

The action Trimble described was more popularly known as Pickett's Charge, a failed advance that resulted in thousands of ill-afforded casualties and ultimately forced Lee to fall back to the other side of the Potomac. Pickett's Charge was regarded as Lee's costliest mistake in the war—an act of will with no grounding in reality, a reckless gamble that churned on and on like a meat-grinder, cutting down the brave and determined Confederate troops as they marched toward an impenetrable Union stronghold.

Earlier that day, Trimble heard that Generals Heth and Pender had been wounded in the charge. The valorous Trimble applied to Lee for one of the leaderless divisions.

> He put me in command of Pender's. I took command at 12, went into the fight on the extreme left at 12 & after the terrible artillery fire ceased at 2 made the charge on the batteries. I took in 2 N.C. Brigades, Prince's & Lane's, as the supporting force. We marched ¾ mile under a terrible fire, passed the first line & reached a point some 200 yards from the breast works—here the men broke down from exhaustion & the fatal fire & went no further but walked sullenly back to their entrenchments. It was a mistake to charge batteries & lines over so great a distance, every yard exposed to a hot fire—Had we marched at night to mile of the works it is I think certain we could have carried them. As it was the enemy admit they 'shook in their shoes.'

Even Trimble's bellowing charisma could not hold the brigade together. The attack was pointless, suicidal. He was in the thick of it. Those few hours of glory, if they could be called that, hastened the end of his active military career.

> I was shot through the left leg on horseback near the close of the fight & my fine mare after taking me off the field died of the same shot—Poor Jinny, noble horse, I grieve to part thus with you.
>
> My leg was amputated by Drs. McGuire, Black & Hays Saturday A.M. but the surgeons saying my leg would become inflamed by moving in the ambulance & erysipilas ensue—I decided to fall a prisoner—was taken to Mr. McCardy's house in Gettysburg & treated with the most tender kindness for two weeks when I was removed by *orders* to the Seminary Hos. ½ mile west of town.

In extreme pain, Trimble opted for survival. It was better to live a prisoner than die a hero. Trimble's practicality, and perhaps his mistrust of further treatment at the hands of Confederate physicians, overruled his allegiance. It was not an easy choice to make. The conscientious captain usually went down with his ship. Trimble's decision may have been a tacit admission of the losing war he now perceived the Confederacy to be waging. He lay in Gettysburg from July 3, the day he was wounded, to August 19. Weakened but healing steadily, he got his first taste of the deprivations due a prisoner of war.

> Augt. 20th—taken to Balto. in a miserable rough burden lime-car and laid on straw. Stood the trip well & placed in Hospital, Lexington St., clean and comfortable.

Augt. 23rd. Moved in to Ft. McHenry—no one allowed to see us or communicate with us.

Augt. 30th. Applied to be permitted to attend church in the Fort Chapel—the favour denied.

While a prisoner at Fort McHenry during the dog days of the Maryland summer, Trimble wrote a wrathful "Reflections on the War," an essay of several thousand words crammed into his diminutive diary, the premise of which was defiance to the death for the Southern Cause. He could sense the coming victory—total, irrevocable Union victory—yet he railed against the inevitable.

Can you ask us of the South to forget our wrongs, wade through this river of blood & clasp in friendship the hands of those who have just stricken us to death? but lately desecrated & made our homesteads—hallowed for centuries by every sacred tie & tender memory—scenes of desolation—can you think us so lost to every manly virtue as to believe we would aid you to reconstruct a Union and cement its fabric with the purple current of our children [?]

To such a proffer made in mocking or insincerity, we have but one wide & deep respond from every plain, hill & valley of our land—No. *Never, never, never!* Every instinct of humanity repels and every proud sentiment of honour, abhors such baseness.

As Trimble composed this baroque invective—never intended to be read by anyone—he was effecting a salutary accomplishment, a purging of the bile that his wounds and two and a half years of military privation had built up. It was an important step in his physical and emotional recovery. Con brio, he flung his words at the North, as though he were dressing down a recalcitrant junior officer.

Our connection with you never had, from the early settlement of the colonies till now, any bond but that of political interest. Your bigotry & hatred of everything southern drove us from you . . . Let the calm verdict of a future age be awarded on the merits of this contest. The South has no fears for her reputation either on account of the wisdom of her statesmen or the valour of her soldiers—If she perish, she can go down to the grave of nations, with the proud boast that she has abundantly nourished with her blood the seeds of Liberty, which will spring up & bear fruit to bless mankind in coming time . . .

The whole land [the South] shall be to you a curse and the favour of a just God shall rest upon it; *never.*

The "Reflections" ended on that peevishly underlined adverb. He had spoken his piece. Having exorcised the burning rhetoric from his heart, he was content to grumble in his diary about more mundane matters.

> September 3rd—having declined to pay for our board, when every privilege has been taken from us—we now receive food, if food it can be called, from the hospital—chunks of dark beef in a greasy tin can, two slices of bread steeped in spilt coffee and two tin cups of dark liquid for coffee, is our meal—no butter, no vegetable, no salt or pepper no condiment to seduce the appetite, to devour such trash—but for Balto. ladies we should starve or become skeletons by inches. Leg measured for an artificial one—to be done in 3 weeks.

Trimble hoped to be included in a prisoner exchange, but instead he was moved at the end of September to Johnson's Island, a Federal prison on Lake Erie, near Sandusky, Ohio. It was about as elite a prison as could be expected. Incarcerated there at the time were 1500 Confederate officers and 600 privates. By 1865, 3,000 officers would be held there as prisoners of war.

> All draw rations & purchase other articles which make a good table, costing 2 to 3$ a week—10 barracks in a lot of 2 acres, are allotted to prisoners 8 in a room, Govt. provide bunks & straw mats, no servants allowed.

While at Johnson's Island, Trimble eased himself back into the world of commerce. Yankee businessmen contacted him about bridge patents he held and other railroad matters. The diary entries became erratic, most of them grousing about the food and the shabby treatment of officers.

> About the 10th of Nov. the sutler was turned out of the yard to bring us [officers] down to soldiers fare—in retaliation for alleged starvation [of Union prisoners] in Richmond. We now have rough soldiers rations and scant at that—with not wood enough to cook over two meals a day & often but one—we get good bread—but fat salt pork, neck, shins & other refuse of beef (no whole quarters, only eatable when boiled)—Rice (no vegetable) vinegar, salt—sugar & coffee. The fare is so rough that the Vicksburg & Port Gibson officers, reduced to starvation point in those places during the siege, eat rats, which they say are equal to frogs or chicken. They say disgust to rats is all a mere prejudice as the Ashanter chief in Africa said when he ate his grandmother . . .

The return of Trimble's sense of humor was a milestone in his self-rehabilitation. After a snowstorm in January 1864, he joined his fellow prisoners in a rollicking three-day snowball fight—snow being a novelty to the officers from the deep South. On crutches, with a rolled up newspaper for a spyglass, Trimble joined in the high jinks by commanding from a stairway landing at one end of a barracks.

In all other respects, the drab prison life at Johnson's Island was enervating.

> Every week attempts are made to escape by some one, always a failure except in Charley Grogan's case who got off very cleverly and is in Rich—

> I have begun using my artificial leg, but still use crutches until the stump hardens.

> April 22 '64. Today 156 sick and wounded officers went off for exchange—my name was put down among them by the surgeon, but from some influence, it was stricken off & I retained here—It was a disappointment, but I bear up in the prospect of a general ex. soon—Special exchanges have given much discontent here & considered unjust to those of *longer* capture & of *more* conspicuous service.—the Sutler for some weeks has been restored here & permitted to sell, at high rates, stationary—tobacco, potatoes & cabbage, as also apples & dried fruits—but potatoes per bbl. $1.25, apples bbl $8.00, other things in proportion.

> I have heard from inmates of the larger rooms containing over 60 persons that during the winter they had to take turns going to bed & sitting by stoves to keep warm, 1/3 at stoves, 1/3 in bed, and 1/3 running about the room or dancing to protect themselves from freezing—

During the winter of 1864, the prisoners met clandestinely to organize a mass escape. Over the previous winter, according to one incarcerated Confederate, Captain L. W. Allen, whose diary covered a period from November 1863 to March 1864, a four-part plan had been drawn up to facilitate the exodus:

> I. Get out of the Enclosure.
> II. Capture the Garrison.
> III. Escape from the Island.
> IV. Return to the South.

As ranking officer, Trimble was designated commander-in-chief of the escape committee, which debated the pros and cons of various means before concluding that all of them were impossible. The most promising idea (once the garrison walls were breached) had been to walk over the frozen lake in the dead of winter. Noting that the thermometer often registered twenty to thirty degrees below zero, Captain Allen, also of the committee, said,

> Large numbers have been planning to get away on the ice, but the weather is too *intensely cold* to hope that Southerners can possibly stand the severity . . .

The committee reluctantly agreed that outside help would be their only hope. It never came.

Trimble's diary trickled along with intermittent commentary, including tabulations of prisoners who died. His last entry, in the spring of 1864, noted that he had been a prisoner at Johnson's Island—he kept referring to it as "Fort Johnston"—for seven months.

In early April, 1865, Trimble's name was finally included on an exchange list. By now fully recovered and adept in the use of his artificial limb, he was on his way to Virginia to resume his command when he heard of Robert E. Lee's surrender.

Eventually, Trimble returned to Baltimore, where, with characteristic energy, he redirected himself to the duties of a railroad executive. He lived to the ripe age of eighty-five and died at home on January 2, 1888. He never revisited the battlefield at Cross Keys.

TWENTY-SEVEN

———

In 1962, in preparation for the centennial of the battle, a local man named Casper Hinkle constructed a tabletop replica that featured soldiers in motion and real gunpowder explosions. Hinkle had lived in a farmhouse to the east of us, along Route 708, just across the wooded ravine.

I learned of the replica quite by accident, while paying a visit to the farmer who sold us the land. He and I were seated in his parlor, talking about neighbors past and present (the farmer's memory was a storehouse of local genealogy), when I happened to mention the name of Casper Hinkle, which I had seen on a plat of an adjoining parcel.

"Old Man Hinkle, you say? He was the one who built the working model of the battle."

My ears perked up. Here was new grist for the mill, but try as I might, I could not jog my neighbor's memory beyond a few broad observations. Hinkle had been "kinda different." In his replica, there had been "lotsa little soldiers runnin' 'round, gettin' blown to bits." Upon overhearing this stunted recollection, the farmer's wife yelled from the kitchen that one of Hinkle's daughters lived in a nearby community.

Subsequently, I spent the greater part of an afternoon in Mount Crawford, five miles southwest of Harrisonburg along the Valley Pike, at the home of the widowed daughter, where I was shepherded through an impressive collection of memorabilia, including snapshots and newspaper clippings, which told the story of Casper Hinkle's creative genius.

He had been deceased but a few years, having almost reached his ninety-eighth birthday. The last two years of his life had been spent in a residential home—not a nursing home, his daughter emphasized—in which he was cheerfully headed toward his own centennial until the flu, then pneumonia, overtook him. He had worked as a shoemaker, a paper hanger, and a house painter, but above all, he was a dedicated tinkerer—

a fixer of anything and everything. As his daughter put it, "He just had a lot of ideas in his head."

In his spare time, he conceived a mechanical city in miniature to exhibit as a traveling road show. Busy City, as he called it, was begun in 1938 and took five years to finish. During the twenty years it was taken to carnivals, fairs, and town squares in a dozen states, from New Jersey to Georgia, it was annually revamped and improved. Hinkle constructed his city on a six-by-eight-foot plywood table, the underside of which was even more of a marvel to some viewers, for it consisted of six line shafts, seventy-eight belts, sixty pulleys, nine motors, and over two thousand feet of electrical wire. Topside, portraying "nearly every phase of American life today and yesterday," as the handbill boasted, Hinkle had crowded everything he could think of. There were railroads, highways, steamboats, a drawbridge, a sawmill, a farm with a milking parlor (on the outskirts of the city), a church with a working organist, and three hundred realistically painted figurines engaged in diverse activities from ambulance-driving to zookeeping. The action-packed tableau never failed to draw a crowd. Admission was a quarter.

Busy City was installed on a flatbed truck, replete with a covered viewing platform and an array of folding billboards advertising it as "The Biggest Little Show on Earth." From June to September, Hinkle and his wife were on the road with the exhibit, living in a homemade trailer they towed behind. By the mid-1960s, it was estimated that 300,000 people had seen the mechanical city in one form or another.

Between tours in his seventy-third year, Hinkle began working on his replica of the neighborhood battle. As a boy, he had listened to the war stories of an uncle who had been a Civil War veteran. Flavor, not factuality, was Hinkle's chief intent, although he incorporated as many features of the local terrain as a scaled-down seven-by-nine-foot battlefield could hold. Governed by a complicated timing mechanism, seven hundred toy soldiers marched and fought. Twenty miniature field pieces were wired to small charges of steel wool and black powder, producing forty-eight explosions which caused soldiers to fall and lines of engagement to shift. A tape recording added realistic battle din.

In an interview with a news reporter for the *Richmond Times-Dispatch*, Hinkle was asked why the preponderance of soldiers on his sawdust and water-putty topography wore blue. There were more than twice as many Yankees as Rebels fighting, he replied. His uncle, the Confederate veteran, had drilled those proportions into his head.

The miniature armies were readied for their inaugural battle in the driveway of the Hinkle home on a Sunday after church in early June. To prepare for the seventeen-minute simulation, Hinkle had worked ninety-eight days and used an impressive three thousand feet of wire. Invitations had gone out to friends, neighbors, and kinfolk. To shade the battle and better dramatize the explosions, a gravesite canopy was rented from a funeral home. A snapshot taken that afternoon showed the audience in its Sunday best, standing three deep around the square canopy with "Kygers Service" stenciled along its crenate edge. The flatbed containing the shuttered Busy City was parked to one side. In the foreground, the tail fin of a '57 Chevy intruded like a chrome ramp.

The battle went off without a hitch. As pulleys and wheels whirred below, cannon fired and officers on horseback spurred forward. Regiments advanced and retreated, foot soldiers fell prostrate in fields of simulated wheat and corn, or woods of green cotton. Onlookers young and old stood transfixed. A few were shocked out of their wits by the larger explosions. An eyebrow or two may have been singed.

Hinkle had rigged his replica for reloading and replay, fully intending to display it before a wider audience. During the centennial summer and two or three summers later, he towed it to regional lawn parties and weekend fairs where it was viewed free of charge. Youngsters heralded its arrival with whoops of joy, but in a larger sense, the public's attention had turned toward television and tail fins. Despite the tabletop battle's entertainment value, it was regarded as a history lesson, and a recondite one at that. It never drew the crowds as Busy City had. Upkeep was a painstaking process, and Hinkle, who wasn't getting any younger, had gained enough experience as a showman to know when to fold the tent. Besides, he couldn't help but notice a cool whiff of disapproval from members of his church who felt that the celebration of so violent an event was un-Christian and uncalled for.

Although the exact fate of the miniature battle was unknown, Hinkle's daughter assumed it had been broken up and hauled off to the dump. Busy City suffered a slightly more respectable dismemberment; when Hinkle's wife took ill and could no longer travel with him, he dismantled the exhibit and set up part of it in his living room. The rest was distributed among his grandchildren.

I am balanced on the cusp between agriculture and history. Every step I take seems to reverberate on the empty husk of time, and time itself often stops when I find myself thinking about that long-ago Sunday in June. Somewhere in excess of sixteen thousand soldiers gathered here for the purpose of annihilating each other, and now I am rolling farm machinery over the ground.

I did not come here to farm, but farming fits me like a second skin. It connects me to those who worked this land both before and after it became a battlefield, and even as I struggle to prove myself as an artist, another part of me is preoccupied with the means and exigencies of the next harvest.

But when the hay is in the barn, and the unhitched equipment sits idle and statuesque until the next cutting, I walk alone over the trimmed fields and try to visualize an eternity of growing seasons. My mind goes backward in time, back before the advent of mechanized agriculture, when the waving, unkempt grasses were scythed, and if not scythed, then grazed, and if not grazed, then left to bloom and wither by the hand of God. Then I think about the present. Through all the churning of my seasonal occupation with the hay—the fixing, the driving, the lifting, the selling—and through all my consumption of fossilized remains that have been alchemized into gasoline, diesel fuel, lubricating oils, and grease, there remains one constant: the mysterious seed pushing up through the soil toward the sun.

The battlefield is a constant of a different order. It is a permanent scar on the face of the American experience. It was an open wound, a chasm of destruction, for a full day and part of the next morning, and then it healed over. To the east, the neighbor whom I never met entrusted himself with the construction of a simulacrum. By some strange directive of fate, I am entrusted with the real thing. This is certain: I will never throw it away.

AFTERWORD
TO THE 2017 EDITION

[In early 2011 I penned the following document, an op-ed piece for The Washington Post *that was never published. It makes a fitting conclusion to this new edition of the book.]*

QUESTION: when is property no longer your property? Answer: when you haven't owned it for seventeen years and are staring at it across a barbed wire fence.

This was my experience recently in Cross Keys, Virginia, where I used to own a forty-acre hay farm that turned out to be situated at the epicenter of a Civil War battlefield.

The Battle of Cross Keys, the penultimate clash in Stonewall Jackson's Shenandoah Valley campaign, was fought on June 8, 1862, and is singled out for uniqueness because of the wily tactics of a 60 year old Confederate field commander, Brigadier General Isaac R. Trimble, who led his relatively small force to unexpected victory over a much larger Union presence.

Now, after so long an absence, I'm looking at the rolling hay fields that I still practically know by heart, having driven tractor-drawn farming equipment over and over them for a period of ten years, and walked them countless times.

It is an accessible battlefield to reconnoiter. With a map or guidebook in hand, armed with an elementary knowledge of the battle's particulars, most visitors can figure out what happened and where, and in the process gain that spooky, spiritual thrill which often accompanies tours of battlegrounds from any era. The Cross Keys battlefield is easily walked, easily understood, and as others have said, one of the "prettiest" battlefields in Virginia.

Mindful of all this before I sold and moved away from my farm, I placed a preservation easement on the forty acres *in perpetuity* with the Virginia Outdoors Foundation (VOF) in 1994—the first easement of its kind in the Cross Keys area. This initiative on my part did not come without a price. The farm became instantly devalued and difficult to sell, because an encumbrance of this sort runs counter to typical notions of rural property ownership. In the place of limitless options for agriculture and agribusiness, there were strictures: no building or structure could be erected without permission of the VOF, no residential development, no commercial industry, and most importantly, *no disturbance to the topography*. Much of the wording of the easement seemed to be aimed directly at me, the owner, as if I was likely to be the first offender.

After two years of unsuccessful listings with realtors, I wound up selling the farm at auction, barely breaking even on my original investment. I was quite satisfied, however, knowing that I had done the right thing by preserving this historic acreage for all time.

Or so I thought. Fast-forward to fourteen years later: the current landowner decides to build a horseback riding ring, more than an acre in size, breaching a ravine along the property line—basically filling it to a height of twelve feet and leveling off the top. Staffers at the VOF grant it approval. Giant yellow machines—scraping pans, bulldozers, loaders, excavators—are brought in to do the work. The resulting flatness, considerably wider than the ring itself, looks like the deck of an aircraft carrier.

As I stare at it from across the fence, I cannot think of a more incongruous intrusion upon the gently rolling terrain. There was obviously leftover soil, too, which got graded into an adjacent hillock like an oversize ski mogul. The ring itself has been packed with many truckloads of fine gravel, and board fence delineates its boundaries. Today, it is a "tasteful" fait-accompli, not easily visible from the road—a private facility for serious horsemanship.

But there's more. What the staffers at the VOF and the landowner didn't realize—and apparently never bothered to find out—is that this particular ravine figured prominently in the 1862 battle, for it lies at the heart of the area where the Union troops advanced to meet the hidden Confederate line and were repulsed with frightful casualties. In other words, the ravine and its surroundings are as hallowed as hallowed ground gets. And now the ravine is no more.

So I'm standing there, looking across the barbed wire at this desecration that's already four years old. Apparently, nobody did anything to try to stop it (*I* certainly wasn't notified). Two adjectives, *heedless* and *thoughtless,* come to mind. I can hardly believe my eyes. As Grantor, I feel betrayed, and I also feel a sense of shame. In the intervening years, I moved on with my life, never doubting that the easement had teeth and was enforceable. Besides, I was under the impression that 1860s battlegrounds were all but sacrosanct in the public's consciousness.

At this point, I can only make a plea, on behalf of all Americans, that the full measure of my preservation easement be honored. I'd like to see the Virginia Outdoors Foundation and the current landowner admit what I think is an egregious error, and immediately make amends. That same squadron of heavy equipment—scraping pans, bulldozers, loaders, excavators—should be brought back to undo the desecration, so the ravine is no longer bridged by twelve feet of fill dirt. If it were returned to its original state, visitors to the Cross Keys battlefield, now and in the future, will be able to better visualize the attack and subsequent slaughter that transpired on a sunny late-spring day one hundred and fifty years ago.

APPENDIX A

A Compilation of Additional Battle Reports

Headquarters, Army in the Field,
Camp near Port Republic [sic], June 8, 1862–9 P.M.
(Received June 10, 9:30 A.M.)

The army left Harrisonburg at 6 this morning, and at 8:30 my advance engaged the rebels about 7 miles from that place, near Union Church. The enemy was very advantageously posted in the timber, having chosen his own position, forming a smaller circle than our own, and with his troops formed in masses. It consisted undoubtedly of Jackson's entire force. The battle began with heavy firing at 11 o'clock, and lasted with great obstinacy and violence until 4 in the afternoon. Some skirmishing and artillery firing continued from that time until dark. Our troops fought occasionally under the murderous fire of greatly superior numbers, the hottest of the small-arm fire being on the left wing, which was held by Stahel's brigade, consisting of five regiments. The bayonet and canister shot were used freely and with great effect by our men. Loss on both sides very great. Ours very heavy among the officers. A full report of those who distinguished themselves will be made without partiality. I desire to say that both officers and men behaved with splendid gallantry, and that the service of the artillery was especially admirable. We are encamped on the field of battle, which may be renewed at any moment.

J. C. FRÉMONT,
Major-General.

Hon. E. M. Stanton,
Secretary of War.

Hdqrs. Third Div., Valley Dist., June 16, 1862.

Major: I have the honor to submit the following report of the 8th instant at Cross Keys between the division commanded by me and the forces under Major-General Frémont:

217

I was ordered on the 7th by the general commanding to occupy the advance, and my division encamped for that night near Union Church. The enemy made a reconnaissance in the afternoon, and going forward I found General Elzey drawing up his own and General Taylor's brigades in position. I at once determined to meet the enemy on the ground selected by General Elzey.

On the morning of the 8th the enemy advanced, driving in the Fifteenth Alabama, Colonel Cantey, from their post on picket. The regiment made a gallant resistance, enabling me to take position at leisure. The camp-fires left by the regiment—no tents or anything else—were the camps from which the enemy report to have driven us. At this time I had present Elzey's, Trimble's and Steuart's brigades, short of 5,000 men, Taylor's having been ordered to Port Republic . . . General Trimble's brigade was posted a little in advance of my center on the right, General Elzey in the rear of the center, and General Steuart on the left; the artillery was in the center. Both wings were in the woods. The center was weak, having open ground in front, where the enemy was not expected. General Elzey was in position to strengthen either wing.

About 10 o'clock the enemy felt along my front with skirmishers, and shortly after posted his artillery, chiefly opposite mine. He advanced under cover on General Trimble with a force, according to his own statement, of two brigades, which were repulsed with such signal loss that they did not make another determined effort. General Trimble had been re-inforced by the Thirteenth and Twenty-fifth Virginia regiments, Colonel Walker and Lieutenant-Colonel Duffy, of General Elzey's brigade. These regiments assisted in the repulse of the enemy. General Trimble in turn advanced and drove the enemy more than a mile, and remained on his flank ready to make the final attack.

General Taylor, with the Eighth Brigade, composed of Louisiana troops, reported about 2 P.M., and was placed in rear. Colonel Patton, with the Forty-second and Forth-eighth Regiments and Irish Battalion, Virginia Volunteers, also joined, and with the remainder of General Elzey's brigade was added to the center and left, then threatened. I did not push my successes at once, because I had no cavalry, and it was reported, and reaffirmed by Lieutenant Hinrichs, topographical engineer, sent to reconnoiter, that the enemy was moving a large column 2 miles to my left. As soon as I could determine this not to be an attack I advanced both my wings, drove in the enemy's skirmishers, and when night closed was in position on the ground previously held by the enemy, ready to attack him at dawn . . .
Respectfully,

R. S. EWELL,
Major-General.

Maj. R. L. Dabney, Asst. Adjt. Gen., Valley District.

Headquarters, Mountain Department,
Port Republic, June 9, 1862–noon, via Martinsburg.
(Received June 12, 8 A.M.)

There was no collision with the enemy after dark last night. This morning we resumed the march against him, entering the woods in battle order, his cavalry appearing on flanks.

General Blenker had the left, General Milroy the right, and General Schenck the center, with a reserve of General Stahel's brigade and General Bayard's. The enemy was found to be in full retreat on Port Republic, and our advance found his rear guard barely across the river and the bridge in flames. Our advance came in so suddenly that some of his officers remaining on this side escaped with the loss of their horses. A cannonading during the forenoon apprised us of an engagement, and I am informed here that General Jackson attacked General Shields this morning, and after a severe engagement drove him down the river and is now in pursuit. I have sent an officer with a detachment of cavalry to open communication with General Shields, and in mean time [am] preparing to bridge the river, having no pontoon.

This morning detachments were occupied in searching the ground covered by yesterday's action at Cross Keys for our remaining dead and wounded. I am not fully informed, but think 125 will cover our loss in killed and 500 in wounded. The enemy's loss we cannot clearly ascertain. He was engaged during the night in carrying off his dead and wounded in wagons. This morning upon our march upward of 200 of his dead were counted in one field, the greater part badly mutilated by cannon-shot. Many of his dead were also scattered through the woods, and many had been already buried. A number of prisoners had been taken during the pursuit.

I regret to have lost many good officers. General Stahel's brigade was in the hottest part of the field, which was the left wing from the beginning of the fight. The brigade lost in officers 5 killed and 17 wounded, and one of his regiments alone—the Eighth New York—had buried 65. The Garibaldi Guards, next after, suffered most severely, and following this regiment the Forty-fifth New York, the Bucktail Rifles of General Bayard's and General Milroy's brigade. One of the Bucktail companies has lost all its officers, commissioned and non-commissioned. The loss in General Schenck's brigade was less, although he inflicted severe loss on the enemy, principally by artillery fire. Of my staff I lost a good officer killed, Capt. Nicolai Dunka. Many horses were killed in our batteries, which the enemy repeatedly attempted to take, but were repulsed by canister fire.

Generally I feel myself permitted to say that all our troops, by their endurance of this severe march and their splendid conduct in the battle, are entitled to the President's commendation. The officers throughout behaved with a gallantry and efficiency which require that I should make particular mention of them, and which I trust will receive the particular notice of the President. As soon as possible I will send a full report, but in this respect I am unable to make any more particular distinction than that pointed out in the description of the battle.

Respectfully,

J. C. FRÉMONT,
Major-General, Commanding.

Hon. E. M. Stanton.

BATTLEFIELD

🪰

Hdqrs. Second Corps, Army of Northern Virginia,
April 14, 1863

. . . This attack of General Shields [Carroll's incursion] had hardly been repulsed before Ewell was seriously engaged with Frémont, moving on the opposite bank of the river. The enemy pushed forward, driving in the Fifteenth Alabama, Colonel Cantey, from their post on picket. This regiment made a gallant resistance, which so far checked the Federal advance as to afford to General Ewell time for the choice of his position at leisure. His ground was well selected, on a commanding ridge, a rivulet and large field of open ground in front, wood on both flanks, and his line intersected near its center by the road leading to Port Republic. General Trimble's brigade was posted on the right, somewhat in advance of his center. The batteries of Courtney, Lusk, Brokenbrough, and Raine in the center; General Steuart's brigade on the left, and General Elzey's brigade in the rear of the center, and in position to strengthen either wing. Both wings were in the wood.

About 10 o'clock the enemy threw out his skirmishers and shortly after posted his artillery opposite to our batteries. The artillery fire was kept up with great animation and spirit on both sides for several hours. In the mean time a brigade of Federal forces advanced, under cover, upon the right, occupied by General Trimble, who reserved his fire until they reached the crest of the hill, in easy range of his musketry, when he poured a deadly fire from his whole front, under which they fell back. Observing a battery about being posted on the enemy's left, half a mile in front, General Trimble, now supported by the Thirteenth and Twenty-fifth Virginia Regiments, of Elzey's brigade, pushed forward for the purpose of taking it, but found it withdrawn before he reached the spot, having in the mean time some spirited skirmishing with its infantry supports. General Trimble had now advanced more than a mile from his original position, while the Federal advance had fallen back to the ground occupied by them in the morning . . .

T. J. JACKSON,
Lieutenant-General.

🪰

Headquarters Mountain Department,
Harrisonburg, Va., June 10, 1862.
(Received June 12, 4 P.M.)

In my dispatch of yesterday I omitted to state that Colonel Cluseret's brigade, consisting of the Sixtieth Ohio and Eighth Virginia, afterward supported by the Garibaldi Guard, formed our advance, and commenced the battle of Cross Keys by sharp skirmishing at 9 o'clock in the morning. During the day they obtained possession of the enemy's ground, which was disputed foot by foot, and only with-

drew at evening, when ordered to retire to a suitable position for the night. The skill and gallantry displayed by Colonel Cluseret on this and frequently former occasions during the pursuit in which we have been engaged deserve high praise.
Respectfully,

J. C. FRÉMONT,
Major-General, Commanding.

Hon. E. M. Stanton,
Secretary of War.

🐾

Hdqrs. Third Div., Valley Dist., June 16, 1862

. . . As before mentioned, the credit of selecting the position is due to General Elzey. I availed myself frequently during the action of that officer's counsel, profiting largely by his known military skill and judgement. He was much exposed. His horse was wounded early in the action, and at a later period of the day was killed by a rifle-ball, which, at the same time, inflicted upon the rider a wound that forced him to retire from the field. He was more particularly employed in the center, directing the artillery. General George H. Steuart was severely wounded, after rendering valuable aid in command of the left.

I had Courtney's, Brockenbrough's, Raine's, and Lusk's batteries. The enemy testifies to the efficiency of their fire. Captain Courtney opened the fight, and was for hours exposed to a terrible storm of shot and shell. He and Captain Brockenbrough have been under my observation since the campaign opened, and I can testify to their efficiency on this as on former occasions. The loss in all the batteries shows the warmth of the fire. I was well satisfied with them all.

. . . I append a list of casualties, showing 42 killed and 287 killed, wounded, and missing. I buried my dead and brought off all the wounded except a few, whose mortal agonies would have been uselessly increased by any change of position. Some of the enemy's wounded were brought off and arrangements made for moving them all, when I was ordered to another field. There are good reasons for estimating their loss at not less than 2,000 in killed, wounded, and prisoners. On one part of the field they buried 101 at one spot, 15 at another, and a house containing some of their dead was said to have been burned by them, and this only a part of what they lost. They were chiefly of Blenker's division, notorious for months on account of their thefts and dastardly insults to women and children in that part of the State under Federal domination.

The order of march of General Frémont was found on a staff officer left in our hands. It shows seven brigades of infantry, besides numerous cavalry. I had three small brigades during the greater part of the action, and no cavalry at any time. They [the Federals] made no bayonet charge, nor did they commit any particular ravages with grape or canister, although they state otherwise. Colonel Mercer and the Twenty-first Georgia tried to close with them three times, partly succeeding in overtaking them once. That officer is represented to have handled his regiment with great skill, and, with the Sixteenth Mississippi, Colonel Posey, was the closest engaged.

Brigadier-General Trimble, Seventh Brigade, had the brunt of the action, and is entitled to most thanks . . .

Respectfully,

R. S. EWELL,
Major-General.

Maj. R. L. Dabney, Asst. Adjt. Gen., Valley District.

⚜

[Inclosure No. 3.]

Mountain Department, Headquarters in the Field,
Harrisonburg, Va., June 8, 1862.

Order of march.

ADVANCE GUARD.

1. Colonel Cluseret's brigade.
2. The pioneers of all brigades, as also the ax-men of every regiment, to start at 5 A.M.
3. Fourth New York Cavalry.
4. General Stahel's brigade, with Bucktail Rifles as flankers, at 5:30 A.M.

MAIN COLUMN.

5. Cavalry, under command of Colonel Zagonyi, at 5:45 A.M.
6. General Milroy's brigade, at 6 A.M.
7. General Schenck's brigade, at 6:15 A.M.
8. General Steinwehr's brigade, at 6:30 A.M.
9. General brigade train, at 6:45 A.M.

REAR GUARD.

10. General Bayard's brigade.

Each regiment to be accompanied by its ambulances and a sufficient number of wagons to carry their cooking utensils.

The train will move in the order of brigades.

All horses unable to perform service to be left at this place until further orders.

By order of Major-General Frémont:

ALBERT TRACY,
Colonel and Assistant Adjutant-General.

✵

Hdqrs. Second Corps, Army of Northern Virginia.
April 14, 1863

. . . General Taylor, of the Eighth Brigade of Louisiana troops, having arrived from the vicinity of the bridge at Port Republic, toward which he had moved in the morning, reported to General Ewell about 2 P.M. and was placed in rear. Colonel Patton, with the 42nd and 48th Virginia Regiments and 1st Battalion of Virginia Regulars, also joined, and with the remainder of General Elzey's brigade was added to the center and left, then supposed to be threatened. General Ewell — having been informed by Lieutenant Hinrichs, of the Engineer Corps, who had been sent out to reconnoiter, that the enemy was moving a large column on his left — did not advance at once, but subsequently ascertaining that no attack was designed by the force referred to, he advanced, drove in the enemy's skirmishers, and when night closed was in position on ground previously held by the enemy. During this fighting Brigadier-Generals Elzey and Steuart were wounded and disabled from command.

This engagement with Frémont has generally been known as the battle of Cross Keys, in which our troops were commanded by General Ewell. I had remained at Port Republic during the principal part of the 8th, expecting a renewal of the attack. As no movement was made by General Shields to renew the action that day, I determined to take the initiative and attack him the following morning. Accordingly General Ewell was directed to move from his position at an early hour on the morning of the 9th toward Port Republic, leaving General Trimble, with his brigade, supported by Colonel Patton, with the Forty-second Virginia Infantry and the First Battalion of Virginia Regulars, to hold Frémont in check, with instructions, if hard pressed, to retire across the North River and burn the bridge in their rear. Soon after 10 o'clock General Trimble, with the last of our forces, had crossed the North River and the bridge was destroyed . . .

I am, general, very respectfully, your obedient servant,

T. J. JACKSON,
Lieutenant-General.

Brig. Gen. R. H. Chilton,
A.A. and I.G. Hdqrs. Dept. of Northern Virginia.

✵

Headquarters Army in the Field,
Mount Jackson, Va., June 12, 1862.

I arrived at this place today. My officers have been so much engaged with marching duties since the battle of the 8th, at Cross Keys, that full reports of that engagement have not been made to me. Still, wishing to give you a fuller account of that battle than that contained in my telegraphic dispatch, I make the following statement:

The forces under my command left Harrisonburg on the 8th instant, the advance consisting of the Eighth West Virginia and Sixtieth Ohio, being under the command of Colonel Cluseret, aide-de-camp, who was temporarily supported by the Thirty-ninth New York Volunteer Regiment of General Stahel's brigade.

At 9 A.M. the skirmishers of the advance discovered the enemy most advantageously posted in the woods at Cross Keys, on the road to Port Republic. A spirited bayonet charge was immediately made by the Garibaldi Guard, and his right driven back in some confusion. The main body of the army now coming up, General Stahel, commanding the First Brigade, of General Blenker's division, supported by the Third Brigade, General Bohlen commanding, entered the woods on our left with the Eighth, Forty-first, and Forty-fifth New York Volunteers and the Twenty-seventh Pennsylvania Volunteers. After an obstinate contest of three hours, during which the bayonet was used to extricate one of our batteries from more than three regiments of the enemy, and after some desperate struggles, in which canister-shot was used to repel him from an attempt to take Johnson's and Schirmer's batteries, the brigade (Stahel's) withdrew from the wood in good order, taking up another position under the support of Bohlen's and Steinwehr's brigades.

Meanwhile, on the right, Brigadier-General Milroy, with the Twenty-fifth Ohio, the Second, Third, and Fifth West Virginia, supported by the brigade of General Schenck, drove the enemy steadily forward until the withdrawal of General Stahel's brigade and the near approach of night prevented any farther advance. Colonel Cluseret, commanding the advance, maintained his position throughout the day, steadily resisting the attempts of the enemy to turn his flanks, until, at the approach of night, he was ordered to take position on the right wing. The enemy's force was so largely superior that he was enabled to attempt turning both flanks, and massed overwhelming forces against the brigade of General Stahel, on our left, with the obvious design of interrupting our line of communication. The plan was frustrated by the coolness and courage of our men.

Our troops slept on their arms through the night of the 8th, expecting to renew the contest at an early hour the following morning. The enemy, however, retreated during the night, leaving behind on the field of battle the most of his dead and many of his wounded. His loss in killed, wounded, and missing cannot be less than 1,200. More than 200 dead were discovered in one field alone and buried by our men . . .

Respectfully,

J. C. FRÉMONT,
Major-General, Commanding.

Hon. E. M. Stanton,
Washington, D.C.

Headquarters Valley District,
Near Gordonsville, Va., July 28, 1862.

. . . I rode over [from Port Republic] toward Cross Keys, where the battle had been raging between the forces of Major-General Ewell and Major-General Frémont since about 10 A.M. I found our batteries posted in good positions on a commanding ridge to the left of the road. Their fire had been directed by Brigadier-General Elzey up to the time he was wounded, and I found them holding their ground well, and delivering their fire with accuracy and spirit. Those engaged were the batteries of Captains Courtney, Lusk, Brockenbrough, Rice and Raine, while those of Cutshaw and Caskie were held in reserve. As I got up I found Captain Courtney's battery withdrawing from the field, as also a part of of Captain Brockenbrough's, having exhausted their ammunition. Upon inquiry I found the other batteries getting short of ammunition, and as the ordnance train had taken a different road from the one intended, and was a considerable distance away, I slackened their fire to correspond with that of the enemy.

Some of these batteries suffered a good deal from the enemy's fire of small-arms, but all held their ground. At one time those of Captains Rice and Raine had to be withdrawn to the rear for a short distance for this reason. Captain Raine's battery was particularly well and gallantly managed, he having his horse shot, and serving a gun himself when short of cannoneers. The enemy's fire soon ceased and his guns withdrew from the field. None of our guns or caissons were lost or injured in this affair . . .

Most respectfully, your obedient servant,

S. CRUTCHFIELD,
Colonel and Chief of Artillery, Valley District.

Capt. A. S. Pendleton,
Assistant Adjutant-General, Valley District.

Hdqrs. Schenck's Brigade, Mountain Department,
Camp at Mount Jackson, Va., June 12, 1862

I have the honor to report the part taken by the Ohio Brigade in the engagement at Cross Keys on the 8th instant.

It was about 1 P.M. when I arrived near the point of the road leading to Port Republic, where the advance guard had already come upon the enemy. A staff officer, after indicating the position where my cavalry was to be left in reserve, informed me that I was to pass into the field and take position on the right, forming my line of battle and placing my batteries so as to support Brigadier-General Milroy, whose brigade preceded mine in the march and was already getting into line. I was entirely without knowledge of the ground, but immediately proceeded to find the best position I could, according to these instructions, in the direction indicated.

I turned my artillery (De Beck's and Rigby's batteries) into and across the fields, supported by infantry, throwing the body of my infantry into the line of battle and extending it in the rear of Milroy's brigade. As I advanced, however, upon the open ridge first pointed out as probably the best on which to establish my batteries, about one-fourth of a mile from the main road by which our column arrived, I discovered that I was brought into the rear of a line of woods through which Milroy was passing, also to the right. These woods at the same time concealed the enemy and the character of the ground he was occupying, while they afforded no eligible position for placing my guns so as to reach him. I became satisfied, too, from the character of the ground beyond, as it now opened to us, that the enemy would seek to extend the line of his forces on his left, so as, if possible, to outflank us. I hastened, therefore, to press forward to the right to anticipate any such movement, and to occupy an extended ridge of higher ground half a mile farther to the south, which I found gave me a more commanding range and advanced me farther to the point . . . This position placed my brigade on the extreme right wing, which I occupied for the rest of the day . . .

Reaching the farther position, which I had selected, I found the line of woods extended still to the right and shutting in our front. An examination of these woods by companies of the Seventy-third and Thirty-second, immediately thrown forward as skirmishers, discovered the enemy concealed there in force and still endeavoring to extend himself to the left, with the evident object of turning our right, as I had expected. A few shells thrown into the woods on that side by De Beck's battery checked this movement and drove back the rebel infantry farther to our left . . .

I believed that the moment for attacking and pressing the rebels successfully on this wing had now arrived, and I brought forward the Thirty-second to advance also in the woods and form on the Seventy-third, extending thus the line to the right, and intending to order a charge which should sweep around the enemy's left flank and press him back toward our sustaining forces on the left. Never were troops in better temper for such work; but just as the Thirty-second was marching to the front for this purpose, leaving only the Seventy-fifth in the rear to cover the battery, I received the order of the general commanding to withdraw slowly and in good order from my position and go to the relief of the left wing, composed of the brigades of Blenker's division. I felt reluctant to obey, because I was satisfied that the advantageous and promising position and condition of my brigade could not have been known at headquarters. I held my place, therefore, and sent back instantly to ascertain whether the emergency was such as to require me with all haste to retire. The order came back repeated. To prevent my being followed and harassed by the rebels while falling back I then began to withdraw my infantry, moving them carefully by the flank toward the left until I could uncover the enemy's line sufficiently to enable my battery to throw shot and shell into the woods. This done, I returned the Thirty-second to the support of the battery and commenced drawing off the whole of my force to the left along the same lines in which I had advanced them. Here, again, however, I was met by a messenger from the general commanding, informing me that if I thought I could hold my ground I might remain, but stating that Milroy's brigade, my supporting force on the left, had also been directed to retire, I stopped and threw the artillery again into battery at a point a few rods in the rear of the place which it had at first occupied and ordered a number of rounds of quick, sharp firing into the woods occupied by the rebels. The severe effect of this firing was discovered the next day by the number of rebels found lying on that part of the battle-field; but while thus engaged Captain Piatt, my assistant adjutant-general, ascertained for me that General Milroy, under the order he had received, was rapidly withdrawing his brigade, passing toward the left, and so I had to follow him or be left separated from all the rest of the forces. I returned, however, only to the ridge (half a mile to the left) which I had at first occupied, and there remained, in pursuance of orders, encamped for the night. My other battery (Rigby's) which I understood had been very effectively engaged during the action on the left, was here returned home. It was now perhaps 5:30 or 6 o'clock.

Late in the evening the enemy from the opposite point opened a brisk fire upon our camp and upon Hyman's battery, occupying the point of a hill at our left with what seemed to be a battery of two 6-pounders. This was probably a cover to his retreat, but he was replied to with so quick and hot a return by Hyman, Rigby, and De Beck that his fire was very soon silenced and, as afterward ascertained, both his guns dismounted. Subsequently a company of skirmishers from the Seventy-third had an encounter with skirmishers of the rebels in the woods immediately in front of us, in which we had 1 man killed and another man wounded; but otherwise we rested undisturbed until called to march in pursuit of the enemy again in the morning . . .

I am, very respectfully, your obedient servant,

ROBT. D. SCHENCK,
Brigadier-General.

Col. Albert Tracy, Asst. Adjt. Gen.

🎖

Hdqrs. Forty-Second Regiment Virginia Vols.,
Camp near Port Republic, Va., June 15, 1862.

. . . Between 8 and 9 o'clock of the morning of the 8th instant the Forty-second Regiment received orders from headquarters to load their wagons, form quickly, and proceed from their encampment, which was about 1 and ½ miles from Port Republic, on the Harrisonburg road. The regiment was promptly conducted to the heights near Port Republic, and stationed on the left of the road in an open field in rear of our batteries, and in view of the retreating enemy on the opposite side of the Shenandoah River. We retained that position until about 1 o'clock, in hearing of heavy cannonading and musketry in our rear, when I was ordered by Colonel Patton to move my regiment quickly in that direction. I accordingly promptly put my regiment in motion, and conducted them back along the Harrisonburg road to a church [the Dunker church, now Mill Creek Church of the Brethren, east of the battlefield], a distance of 3 miles, where I was met by Colonel Patton, and received orders to throw my regiment in line of battle to the right of the road and march them in quick-time in the direction of the firing, which I accordingly did, and, after marching them several hundred yards, I received orders to conduct my regiment to the left of the position occupied by our batteries. I accordingly placed myself at the head of the regiment and conducted it through an open field a distance of half a mile in rear of our batteries, under a heavy fire of shells and Minié balls from the enemy.

On reaching the woods I was met by Captain Nelson, of General Ewell's staff, who conducted us a short distance to General Ewell, by whom I was ordered to place my regiment in position on the brow of the hill to the left of our batteries, which position we occupied about a half hour, many shells and Minié balls passing over us. We were then conducted by Colonel Patton about 300 yards farther to the left, and formed on the left of the First Virginia Battalion, when I threw out two companies of skirmishers, commanded by Captain Dobyns. We marched for a short distance, then changed direction to the right, proceeding down quite a steep hill crossed a small stream, about which place there were traces of repeated and heavy skirmishing on both sides — our skirmishers, as I have been informed by the captain in command, at one time driving back an entire regiment of the enemy, the casualties of which upon our side have been given in a report which I have heretofore had the honor of submitting.

Shortly after crossing the stream the Seventh Louisiana Regiment passed in our rear and formed on our left. We continued our march in the direction of the road, a short time before reaching which, a sharp fire from the enemy drove in our skirmishers, and we halted, which was then about dark. We remained in this position until a little before daybreak the next morning, in full view of the enemy's camp-fires and in the hearing of their voices . . .

Respectfully, your obedient servant,

J. B. MOSELEY,
Major, Twenty-first Regt.,
Comdg., pro tempore, 48th Regt.

Col. John M. Patton,
Commanding Second Brigade.

꙰

The brigade received orders to march on the 8th at 6:15 A.M., and marched at that time from their camping ground in the following order: Fifty-fourth Regiment New York Volunteers, commanded by Colonel Kozlay; Battery I, First New York Artillery, commanded by Captain Wiedrich; Seventy-fifth Pennsylvania Volunteers, commanded by Lieutenant-colonel Mahler; Fifty-eighth New York Volunteers commanded by Colonel Krzyzanowski; Seventy-fourth Pennsylvania Volunteers commanded by Major Hamm. Ambulances and ammunition wagons followed in the rear of the brigade. Receiving orders to hurry on the column, I passed the train in front of my brigade and arrived near the place where the engagement should take place, immediately in rear of the First Brigade. Here I received orders to form the battalions in columns, to support the First Brigade, commanded by General Stahel. This order was executed at once, and the brigade at the point A (see diagram) [missing] was put in motion in the following order, the battalions being in double columns, closed in mass: On the right the Fifty-fourth Regiment, followed by the Seventy-fifth; in the center (on the road) the battery of Captain

Wiedrich; on the left the Fifty-eighth Regiment New York Volunteers, followed by the Seventy-fourth Regiment Pennsylvania Volunteers.

At the point B a staff officer of General Stahel requested me to order the column forward to support the First Brigade. The Fifty-eighth Regiment, being nearest on hand, was immediately ordered forward, formed in line of battle, and marched to the point C, the direction given by General Stahel. The Seventy-fourth was then ordered forward to the point D, on the left of the Fifty-eighth Regiment, and formed in line of battle. The battery was ordered to form at the point E on elevated ground. Receiving the indication that a force of two regiments with some cavalry was concealed in the wheat field (at point F) and tried to outflank me on the left, I immediately ordered the two regiments in reserve to the left to check the enemy's movements. I regret to say that at that time I received no communications at all as to what was going on on my right, where part of the First Brigade had taken position.

Meanwhile, as is shown in the report of Colonel Krzyzanowski, the Fifty-eighth marched gallantly ahead, supported by a section of Captain Schirmer's battery, which disabled the enemy's pieces placed on a hill on the right of the regiment (point G). The Fifty-eighth met the enemy and drove him back at the point of the bayonet. Being in danger of being cut off by two columns advancing on the right, and also by the enemy's force placed on the left, the regiment had to retire, Captain Schirmer's battery having previously retired. The regiment, being without any support, fell back behind Captain Wiedrich's battery in good order.

Meanwhile the Seventy-fourth Regiment had proceeded in line of battle toward the wheat field (at point D). Here General Blenker ordered to send only two companies of skirmishers ahead, he supposing the New York Eighth Regiment to be in front, the main body of the regiment following slowly. At the outskirts of the woods (at point H) our skirmishers met the enemy suddenly again, concealed in a wheat field and protected by fences, as appears in the report of Major Hamm, in the strength of two regiments. Major Hamm, being in danger of being outflanked on the left and overpowered by the superior strength of the enemy, was forced to retire, which he did slowly. He then received orders from me to move to the left toward the woods to give the battery of Captain Wiedrich a full sway. This battery soon opened fire and did fearful execution. Before the battery was brought in action the Seventy-fifth Regiment Pennsylvania Volunteers was ordered to advance and relieve the Seventy-fourth Pennsylvania Volunteers. It had already the skirmishers deployed, when the order was given to fall back in a small ravine to give the artillery an opportunity to fire.

The Fifty-fourth Regiment New York Volunteers, Colonel Kozlay, was ordered to the left to deploy in the woods. Captain Schirmer's battery on my right having already retired, he (Captain Schirmer) gave the command to Captain Wiedrich to retire also, against my positive order to remain. The battery then retired.

At this moment a battalion of the enemy deployed in line of battle on the hill opposite our position. The battery then came into action again, pouring grape shot into the line of the enemy, which forced him to retire. After few shots, the battery was again ordered by Captain Schirmer to retire, which order was obeyed. Meanwhile the Fifty-fourth Regiment New York Volunteers was ordered to the left into the woods ready to support part of the Seventy-fourth, which was on the extreme left deployed in line of skirmishers. After the battery had retired a retrograde movement of the Seventy-fifth and Fifty-fourth Regiments was visible. They retired slowly about 100 paces when they were ordered to a halt. The Fifty-fourth, being in front, was ordered to deploy at once, which order was executed in the woods (at J). A second regiment of the enemy appearing on the outskirts of the woods, the Fifty-fourth regiment opened fire. After a few shots the enemy retired and did not molest us any longer. General orders being given to fall back, the movement was executed in complete order by my entire command . . .

[HENRY BOHLEN,]
Brigadier-General, Commanding.

🙰

Headquarters, Fourth Brigade,
June 14, 1862.

. . . On the morning of the 8th General Elzey ordered me to take my own (Thirteenth Virginia) and the Twenty-fifth Virginia Regiment, Lieutenant-Colonel Duffy commanding, and proceed to the right of our lines to prevent an attempt to turn that flank. We moved by the right flank until I thought we were on the enemy's extreme left, and then, sending two companies forward, under the command of Lieutenant-Colonel Terrill, as skirmishers, we advanced in line across the cleared ground and through the wood beyond without encountering the enemy.

When the skirmishers reached the skirt of the woods, near Ever's house they reported a large body of the enemy close at hand. I halted my command, and going forward to reconnoiter, found a large force of infantry, probably a brigade, and a battery in a wheat field, about 400 yards from our position. Finding myself entirely separated from our troops on the left, and perceiving the enemy were moving a regiment through the woods to our right, I deemed it best to withdraw to the woods and await the coming of other troops. I did so, and encountered General Trimble's brigade advancing on our left. General Trimble informed me that he was going forward to charge the enemy's battery, and directed me to advance on his right. This I did, again sending Colonel Terrill forward with the skirmishers. He soon encountered the enemy's skirmishers that had followed us into the woods. After a brief but active skirmish they were driven back with the loss of several killed and wounded, among the latter an aide of General Blenker.

We again moved forward, under cover of Ever's house and barn, until ordered by General Trimble to move more to the right, so as to leave the house and barn on my left. In moving by the right flank to gain this position we received a heavy volley of musketry from a Yankee force on our left, which wounded several of the Twenty-fifth Regiment, and almost at the same instant the right of the Thirteenth Regiment came into full view of a battery of three pieces, supported by three regiments of infantry, and not more than 400 yards in front. The battery opened a well-directed and heavy fire with grape, which, owing to the unexpected nature of the attack, caused some confusion, but, order having been restored, the troops advanced steadily to the front to a fence 50 yards farther in advance. Finding General

Trimble's brigade was detained by a force on our left, I ordered the men to lie down and fire. This they did with such effect as to twice drive the enemy from one of their guns. The fire of the enemy was galling, and seeing no further good could be accomplished by remaining longer in my position, I moved again by the right flank to the cover of a wood and halted. About this time the enemy fell back and I was ordered to remain in my position. About sundown I was directed by General Trimble to join him on the left, which I did, and remained with his brigade until ordered back to camp about 10 o'clock at night. The men and officers of both regiments were exposed to a terrible fire for a few moments, and behaved to my entire satisfaction . . .

Respectfully, your obedient servant,

J. A. WALKER,
Colonel Thirteenth Virginia Vols.,
Comdg. Fourth Brigade.

Maj. James Barbour,
Assistant Adjutant-General.

Mount Jackson, June 12, 1862.

On arriving near the battle-field the Third Brigade, commanded by General Bohlen, formed in order of battle, with the battery in the center, which order was given by General Bohlen. After forming, the brigade advanced about half a mile, when the battery was ordered by General Blenker to break off from the road to the left in an open field. After arriving in said field General Bohlen ordered the battery to take position near and to the left of a road on high ground and shell a piece of wood in front and to the right of the battery. After forming in battery Captain Schirmer arrived, and ordered the battery to the right side of the road to assist his battery, and after coming to action front again Captain Schirmer ordered the battery to its former position, but a little farther ahead. After coming to action front again the battery fired a few rounds in the woods in front by order of General Bohlen.

Presently, after firing these few rounds, a regiment made its appearance in front of us in a wheat field, when Captain Schirmer ordered the battery to limber to the rear and take the position first selected by Generals Blenker and Bohlen. The Fifth-fourth Regiment was then ordered by General Bohlen to the left in the woods, to keep the said regiment from outflanking us. Having arrived at our old position we came in battery again and continued our fire, without one man flinching, until Captain Schirmer ordered us to limber to the rear and retire, as Lieutenant Jahn, commanding Schirmer's battery, was obliged to retreat. When the battery was limbering to retire General Bohlen came up and ordered me to stay and keep up the fire, but Captain Schirmer insisted on retiring, and as I had received orders from General Blenker a few days before that all orders form Captain Schirmer should be obeyed the same as before, I withdrew with my battery, against the protest of General Bohlen.

Respectfully, your obedient servant,

M. WIEDRICH,
Captain, Comdg. Battery I, First Regiment N.Y. Arty.

Headquarters Eighth Brigade,
June 11, 1862.

. . . On the morning of the 8th I received orders to march the brigade to Port Republic to assist in repelling the attack commenced on the bridge at that point by Shields' forces. When within 1 and ½ miles of the bridge the column was halted, by order of Major-General Jackson, to await further orders. These were shortly received—in effect to return to the front and act as a reserve to the troops there engaged against Frémont. Here the brigade became separated, two regiments, the Seventh and Eighth Louisiana, being ordered to Major-General Ewell to the support of a battery in the center or on the left of our line, while I marched the remaining two regiments and Wheat's battalion to the right to support General Trimble's brigade, then much pressed. The display of force caused the enemy to retire still farther from the position to which he had been driven by the vigorous charge of Trimble's command.

The brigade, though not actually in action on this day, was much exposed to the enemy's shell, and suffered a loss of 1 private killed, 1 officer . . . and 7 privates and non-commissioned officers wounded . . .

Respectfully, your obedient servant,

R. TAYLOR,
Brigadier-General.

Major Barbour,
Assistant Adjutant-General, Third Division.

Fifth-Fourth Regiment New York State Vols.,
June 11, 1862.

General: I have the honor to report that on the 8th of June, about 3 or 4 miles on the other side of Harrisonburg, I was ordered to deploy my regiment into double columns and to proceed on the right of the road leading to Port Republic, parallel with the Fifty-eighth Regiment, who were marching on the other side of the road. Arriving in a small open field I was ordered to cross the road and to proceed with my double columns and take a position on a small bare hill on the left of the Seventy-fifth Regiment, which was posted there in double columns. Before I occupied the position assigned to me (and having many difficulties in marching on account of fences and morass which lay before me and which I had to cross), I rode myself on the top of the hill to choose a suitable position for my columns. When on the top of the small hill on my right the Seventy-fifth Regiment already began to move backward, as the fire of the enemy was very severe upon us. Under these circumstances I could not bring my forces on the top of the hill without an unnecessary great loss, and I had ordered them to stay in a little valley, as it is seen in the annexed diagram [missing], on the side of the same hill, ordering my men to stand for a minute on the side of the hill which covered them against the fire of the enemy. I hardly stood there two minutes when I received orders to retreat after the Seventy-fifth Regiment, whom I had protected with my double columns against the advancing forces of the enemy.

I hardly marched with my regiment 40 paces when I met General Blenker alone riding through the column, and suggested to him that there is a regiment of the enemy whom we could take prisoners. He at once gave me orders not to retreat, but flank the regiment and proceed into the woods. By a flank movement I at once directed my regiment and marched into the woods, deployed the columns into a line of battle, and opened a severe fire upon the approaching enemy. This fire put the enemy into great confusion, and they gave up not only their object to flank us but began to run before our advance and fled on the other side of the open field. Seeing that the enemy was retreating, I gave directions at once to change direction to the right in order to inflict a more severe chastisement on them, but before I could accomplish this I received orders to withdraw, and I have retreated in good order and without the least confusion.

My officers and men behaved themselves, though exposed to severe fire of the enemy, admirably and bravely. I had in the engagement present 373 men (officers, non-commissioned officers, and privates), and had the misfortune to lose 2 brave soldiers, who were killed, and 3 wounded. I beg also to state that through the engagement I received a great many conflicting orders, coming from staff officers unknown to me, which I disobeyed. I have also to report that by our fire we have also prevented two regiments of the enemy to advance upon our batteries, who were only stopped by our flank fire, and have suffered by it a considerable loss of lives, while my regiment was protected against the fire of the enemy in the woods, excepting about 100 paces where I had to cross the open field in my retreat. My men were unwilling to retreat, and I was the last who retreated, because I was not supported by other regiments. My men were eager to fight, and if not withdrawn the enemy would have been at this point repulsed. I was not followed by them. My flank fire stopped the enemy's advance.

I am, general, yours, most respectfully,

E. A. KOZLAY,
Colonel, Commanding Fifty-fourth Regiment New York Vols.
Brig. Gen. H. Bohlen,
Commanding Third Brigade.

Hdqrs. Fifty-Eighth Regt. New York Vols.,
Mount Jackson, June 12, 1862.

I have the honor to submit to you the following report in regard to the engagement of June 8:

After the arrival of my regiment near the field of battle to the left of the battery of the First Brigade, I received your orders to move to the right, when Brigadier-

General Stahel asked me to come up to his assistance. I at once formed my regiment into line, being in column by division, and advanced to the place indicated by General Stahel. I was at that time in the middle of a large rye field, skirted by woods immediately on the right of the battery and in front of my regiment, into which direction I moved in line up to and just beyond a fence at the outskirts of these woods, looking for the troops I was to assist and for the enemy. On the right of my position was another open field, on the opposite side of which I saw a column move by the flank toward the left of our lines, and upon a hill I perceived a battery opening fire toward our right. In order to find out whether I was on the left I sent one company out as skirmishers to keep up the connection on that side and by throwing them a little forward to give information of the enemy's advance.

Directly after this Captain Schirmer came up, and seeing the battery he told me if I would protect him with my regiment he would bring up a couple of guns and open fire upon the enemy's battery. He did so, and soon silenced the latter, when the enemy engaged my skirmishers, who slowly retired toward the regiment for the purpose of giving my men a chance to fire. Captain Schirmer now withdrew his guns and soon the whole regiment was engaged. Keeping up a constant fire, which told greatly among the enemy's lines, I now gave the command to charge bayonets, and succeeded in driving them back about a hundred yards.

To my greatest dismay I noticed at this instant two regiments coming out of the woods on the right of the enemy's battery, and having no reserve to fall back on I thought it imprudent to remain any longer, and consequently gave the command orders to retire while a heavy musketry fire was poured upon my men. I retired behind the battery of Captain Wiedrich, who now opened a heavy fire upon the enemy.

I remain, general, your obedient servant,

W. KRZYZANOWSKI,
Colonel, Commanding Fifty-eighth New York Volunteers.

General H. Bohlen,
Commanding Third Brigade.

※

Hdqrs. Seventy-fourth Regt. Pennsylvania Vols.,
Camp near Mount Jackson, June 12, 1862.

On Sunday, at 2:30 o'clock P.M., June 8, 1862, the Seventy-fourth Regiment Pennsylvania Volunteers was formed in line of battle by General H. Bohlen, and remained such for ten minutes, when General L. Blenker in person gave Lieut. Col. J. Hamm the order to detail the right and left companies . . . General L. Blenker ordered the companies to proceed without reserve, remarking at the same time that these skirmishers of the Seventy-fourth Regiment Pennsylvania Volunteers were ordered only to protect the wounded of the Eighth Regiment New York Volunteers; also saying to be very careful and not to fire, as the Eighth Regiment New York Volunteers was ahead of the Seventy-fourth Regiment. This order was rehearsed several times to the adjutant of the regiment, Lieut. F. Klenker, in hearing of the different companies . . . The skirmishers, after having gone forward, found themselves about 20 paces from the enemy, and had such volleys of balls discharged at them that Maj. F. Blessing found it necessary to order the skirmishers to fall back toward the left, and order Captain Huestmann to send the artillery forward to play upon the enemy.

The regiment being close by, the skirmishers ahead of us received torrents of musket-balls into them, whereupon Lieut. Col. J. Hamm ordered the regiment to fall back to the next fence, 20 paces to the rear, to take a good position, the regiment having returned the fire of the enemy very briskly. General H. Bohlen then ordered the regiment, through Captain Chandler, to fall back toward the left, the enemy's forces being discovered to be entirely too strong for us; also allowing the artillery to have full range at the enemy. Maj. F. Blessing's horse was shot from under him during the engagement. The falling back was conducted in the best possible order, without confusion. Roll call was held upon arriving at camp, and but 6 were missing, not accounted for at the time.

Very Respectfully,

J. HAMM

Lieut. Col., Comdg. Seventy-fourth Regt. Pennsylvania Vols.

General H. Bohlen,
Commanding Third Brigade.

Hdqrs. Seventy-fifth Regt. Pennsylvania Vols.,
Mount Jackson, June 1 [?], 1862

Having been informed that serious charges have been made in regard to the conduct of the regiment which I have the honor to command, in the engagement of Sunday last, by General Blenker, it is due to the honor of my regiment that I should report the part that we took in the action. While in the support of the Seventy-fourth Regiment Pennsylvania Volunteers and Fifty-fourth New York Volunteers, on the extreme left of the line, I was met by General Blenker and ordered to the front, advising me at the same time to be very cautious not to fire, as the Thirty-fifth (former number of the Seventy-fourth) was right in our front, and the Eighth New York were removing their wounded from the woods on our right. Arriving on the top of a knoll I perceived that the Seventy-fourth engaged a superior force, and seeing that their line of skirmishers were falling back I halted and immediately ordered my two flank companies to relieve them, which left me only four companies, about 150 men in all, having previously detached two companies by order of General Bohlen for the support of Captain Wiedrich's battery. At the same time, in order to shelter the reserve from the galling fire which was being poured into us, I ordered them to fall back a few paces, to take advantage of the sloping ground until the moment for action should arrive. The enemy at this time making an attack to outflank us, we, in concert with the Fifty-fourth New York, were ordered to the left, to deploy in the woods.

The Fifty-fourth were in advance of us, and had opened their fire just as we arrived on the ground. At this moment our battery was obliged to retire from the attack of a force that deployed from the woods, which General Blenker led me to suppose were occupied by the Eighth New York, and before I was able to fire I received the order to fall back. I deny totally that my regiment ran away, as charged by General Blenker, and will say for them that they behaved themselves worthy of a better opportunity.

I have the honor to be, respectfully, yours,

F. MAHLER,
Commanding Seventy-fifth Pennsylvania Volunteers.

General H. Bohlen,
Commanding Third Brigade.

Headquarters Maryland Line,
Camp on Mountain, June 11, 1862.

. . . On the 8th of June my regiment was engaged in the center, on the left, and supporting the Baltimore Light Artillery. Soon after getting into position, I was attacked by a regiment slightly to my left. I changed position and drove them back. In a short time another regiment came up, and got behind a fence some 300 yards from me. This place they obstinately held for an hour. I could not charge them, not having 175 men in ranks, and having to cross a branch, a ravine, and a fence. At last, however, I drove them out, leaving some dead and quantities of arms, accouterments, and blankets. Soon after, another regiment was brought up the road, a little to my right, but my men dispersed them rapidly.

No other attack was made on this point during the day. The enemy had a piece of artillery, some 800 yards distant, the whole time, playing on me with grape, but when our rifles sent the last attacking regiment back, it retired. A demonstration was before that made on my left, but the force retired without affecting anything. About 4 to 5 o'clock my ammunition gave out, and the guns became so hot and foul as to be seriously impaired. Major-General Ewell then ordered me back for a new supply, and my regiment did not get into action again. There was no move made on my wing after I left, for I came back myself, and, under General Ewell's orders, pushed Colonel Patton's and Colonel Hays' commands forward on our extreme left.

Our loss was severe. Brig. Gen. George H. Steuart, in command on the left, and of my regiment and battery, was shot, toward the close of the engagement, in the shoulder, severely, but not dangerously . . .

Your obedient servant,

BRADLEY T. JOHNSON,
Colonel First Maryland Regt., Comdg. Maryland Line.

Maj. James Barbour,
Assistant Adjutant-General, Third Division.

Camp near Port Republic,
June 9, 1862.

Dear Sir: In obedience to orders I yesterday morning reported with my command to Brigadier-General Stahel, commanding First Brigade, General Blenker's division, and was by him detailed to support Captain Buell's battery of his brigade, and accordingly I accompanied it to the front, where one of our batteries had already engaged the enemy. After waiting for a short time under cover of a wood the rattle of small-arms in advance showed us where our infantry had engaged them, and directly we were ordered to cross the strip of woods on our right and engage the enemy. The movement was executed promptly, and immediately upon our emerging from the wood we attracted the attention of the enemy, who threw a few shot and shell at us, one of which struck Private John McElhaney, of Company C, inflicting a severe wound in the leg; another struck a member of Company A, Twenty-seventh Regiment Pennsylvania Volunteers (which was deployed along a fence in advance of us), blowing him to fragments. Fortunately our course led us down into a ravine under cover, and another hollow at right angles with it enabled the battery to advance across the entire field and take up a position with their caissons well under cover. I placed my command in the first-mentioned hollow, and ordered the men to lie down, which was done in good order, but a few minutes' observation convinced me that I was too far to the right and too nearly in the range of our guns for safety. Accordingly I moved the command more to the left and down the hollow, and again ordered them to lie down. Most of the shells flew over us, but one burst right in our midst, wounding Private Edmond Debeck, of Company G, and tearing the pants of Lieut. T. B. Winslow, of same company.

In the mean time the rattle of musketry steadily advancing toward our position told me that the enemy were gaining ground upon the other side of the wood, and presently orders came to fall back and bring off the battery. The Twenty-seventh formed in column by division and [Company] I formed in line of battle upon their left, in which positions we advanced into the wood at a double-quick, and owing to a high fence which we had to clamber over entered it in some confusion, the Twenty-seventh still on my right and the battery coming up on my left. We found it already occupied by the enemy, and received a volley, which killed 1 and wounded 5 of Company I, of my command. We immediately opened upon them, driving them out of the wood at the point of the bayonet. The battery also unlimbered two pieces and double-shotted them, but so eager were the men and so rapid the firing that I could not rally the men in time to allow the guns to play without endangering our own men. So soon as possible I rallied my command, and the Twenty-seventh having also retired in rear of the guns, we waited to give them a taste of grape, but the brush was too dense to allow us to see them, and we came on. Upon emerging from the wood we were opened upon by our own batteries, who had retired and taken up a position some distance in the rear. The prompt display of the flag of the Twenty-seventh Regiment soon put a stop to that, with the loss of one or two horses by the battery, and we came in bringing in our wounded.

Where all behaved so well it would be invidious to mention names, and hoping that we may always acquit ourselves as well in future, I have the honor to subscribe myself yours, respectfully,

HUGH MCDONALD,
Captain, Commanding Kane Rifle Battalion.

Brigadier-General Bayard,
Commanding Brigade.

APPENDIX B

Union Forces

The following is a detailed listing of Frémont's forces as they approached Cross Keys on the morning of June 8, 1862.

Leading the column was the Advance Brigade of Lieutenant-Colonel Gustave P. Cluseret, consisting of the 60th Ohio Infantry Regiment led by Colonel William H. Trimble, the 8th (Western) Virginia Infantry Regiment led by Lieutenant-Colonel Lucien Loesner, reinforced by parts of the 39th New York Infantry (Garibaldi Guard). Next in the column was Colonel Christian F. Dickel's 4th New York Cavalry. Then came Brigadier General Julius Stahel's First Brigade, composed of the 8th New York Infantry Regiment led by Colonel Francis Wutschel, the 41st New York Infantry Regiment led by Colonel Leopold von Gilsa, the 45th New York Infantry Regiment led by Colonel George von Ausberg, the 27th Pennsylvania Infantry Regiment led by Colonel Adolphus Buschbeck, and three artillery batteries: an unattached unit commanded by a Captain Dilger, Battery "C" of (western) Virginia commanded by Captain Frank Buell, and the 2nd New York Battery commanded by Louis Schirmer. Brigadier General Henry Bohlen's Third Brigade came next, including the 54th New York Infantry Regiment led by Colonel Eugene Kozley, the 58th New York Infantry Regiment led by Colonel Vladimir Krzyzanowski, the 74th Pennsylvania Infantry Regiment led by Lieutenant-Colonel John Hamm, the 75th Pennsylvania Infantry Regiment led by Lieutenant-Colonel Francis Mahler, and Battery "I" of the First New York Artillery commanded by Captain Michael Wiedrich. Next in column was Brigadier General Robert H. Milroy's Brigade, consisting of the 25th Ohio Infantry Regiment led by Lieutenant-Colonel William P. Richardson, the 2nd Virginia Infantry Regiment led by Major James D. Owens, the 3rd Virginia Infantry Regiment led by Lieutenant-Colonel Francis W. Thompson, the 5th Virginia Infantry Regiment led by Colonel John Zeigler, Battery "G" of the Virginia Artillery commanded by Captain Chatham T. Ewing, Battery "I" of the 1st Ohio Artillery commanded by Captain Henry F. Hyman, and Captain Aaron C. Johnson's 12th Ohio Battery. Then came Brigadier General Robert C. Schenck's Brigade, consisting of the 32nd Ohio Infantry Regiment led by Lieutenant-Colonel Ebenezer H. Swinney, the 55th Ohio Infantry Regiment led by Colonel John C. Lee, the 73rd Ohio Infantry Regiment led by Colonel Orland Smith, the 82nd Ohio Infantry Regiment led by Colonel James Cantwell, the 1st Battalion Connecticut Cavalry led by Captain Louis N. Middlebrook, Battery "K" of the 1st Ohio Artillery commanded by Captain William L. DeBeck, and an independent battery commanded by Captain Silas F. Rigby. In reserve was Brigadier General George D. Bayard's Brigade, which included the 13th Pennsylvania Infantry Regiment led by Captain Hugh McDonald, the 2nd Maine Battery commanded by Captain James A. Hall, the 1st New Jersey Cavalry led by Lieutenant Joseph Karge, and the 1st Pennsylvania Cavalry led by Colonel Owen Jones. The rear guard following the ambulances and ammunition trains was the Second Brigade (Steinwehr's) under the command of Colonel John A. Koltes. It consisted of the 29th New York Infantry Regiment led by Lieutenant-Colonel Clemmons Soest, the 68th New York Infantry Regiment, the 73rd Pennsylvania Infantry Regiment led by Lieutant Colonel Gust A. Muhle, and the 13th New York Battery under the command of Captain Julius Dieckmann.

APPENDIX C

Confederate Forces

The following is a detailed listing of Ewell's division during its defensive stance at Cross Keys, June 8, 1862.

Brigadier General George H. Steuart's Second Brigade consisted of the 1st Maryland Infantry Regiment led by Colonel Bradley T. Johnson, the 44th Virginia Infantry Regiment led by Colonel W. C. Scott, the 52nd Virginia Infantry Regiment led by Lieutenant-Colonel James H. Skinner, the 58th Virginia Infantry Regiment led by Colonel Samuel H. Letcher, and the Baltimore batteries of Captains John A. M. Lusk and J. B. Brockenbrough. Brigadier General Arnold B. Elzey's Fourth Brigade was composed of the 13th Virginia Infantry Regiment led by Colonel James A. Walker, the 25th Virginia Infantry Regiment led by Lieutenant-Colonel Patrick J. Duffy, the 31st Virginia Infantry Regiment led by Colonel John S. Hoffman, the 12th Georgia Infantry Regiment led by Colonel Z. T. Conner, plus Captain Charles I. Raine's Battery. Brigadier General Isaac R. Trimble's Seventh Brigade included the 15th Alabama Infantry Regiment led by Colonel James Cantey, the 21st Georgia Infantry Regiment led by Colonel J. T. Mercer, the 16th Mississippi Infantry Regiment led by Colonel Carnot Posey, the 21st North Carolina Infantry Regiment led by Colonel W. W. Kirkland, and the Virginia (also called Courtney's or Latimer's) Battery, commanded by Captain A. R. Courtney. Later in the day, Jackson ordered Richard Taylor's Eighth Brigade to return from the vicinity of Port Republic, as well as Campbell's Brigade (second of Jackson's division), under the command of Colonel John M. Patton. Taylor's brigade consisted of the 6th Louisiana Infantry Regiment led by Colonel Isaac G. Seymour, the 7th Louisiana Infantry Regiment led by Major David B. Penn, the 8th Louisiana Infantry Regiment led by Colonel H. B. Kelly, the 9th Louisiana Infantry Regiment led by Colonel Leroy H. Stafford, as well as the Louisiana Battalion (infantry) led by Major C. R. Wheat. Campbell's Brigade included the 1st Virginia Infantry Regiment

241

(Irish Battalion) led by Major John Seddon, the 21st Virginia Infantry Regiment led by Lieutenant-Colonel R. H. Cunningham, the 42nd Virginia Infantry Regiment led by Lieutenant-Colonel William Martin, and 48th Virginia Infantry Regiment led by Lieutenant-Colonel Thomas S. Garnett. Held in reserve, these two brigades added 2,500 and 800 soldiers, respectively, to Ewell's forces. There were no significant cavalry.

HISTORICAL AND
BIBLIOGRAPHICAL SOURCES

Allan, William. *History of the Campaign of Gen. T. J. (Stonewall) Jackson in the Shenandoah Valley of Virginia*. Philadelphia: J. B. Lippincott, 1880. Reprint. Morningside Bookshop, Dayton, Ohio, 1974.

Angle, Paul M. *A Pictorial History of the Civil War Years*. New York: Doubleday, 1967.

Ashcraft, John M., Jr. *31st Virginia Infantry*. Lynchburg: H. E. Howard, Inc., 1988.

Avirett, James B. (Rev.). *The Memoirs of General Turner Ashby and His Compeers*. Baltimore: Selby and Dulany, 1867.

Benson, R. T. (Col.). *Disposition of Union and Confederate Forces Engaged at Cross Keys* (Aerial Map of Cross Keys Battlefield), 1962(?). Materials in possession of the Harrisonburg-Rockingham Historical Society, Harrisonburg, Virginia.

Boatner, Mark M., III. *The Civil War Dictionary*. New York: David McKay, 1959.

Botkin, B. A. *A Civil War Treasury of Tales, Legends and Folklore*. New York: Random House, 1960.

Brent, William B. *Geology and Mineral Resources of Rockingham County*, Bulletin #76. Charlottesville: Virginia Division of Mineral Resources, 1960.

Brice, Marshall Moore. *Conquest of a Valley*. Charlottesville: University Press of Virginia, 1965.

Catton, Bruce. *Terrible Swift Sword; The Centennial History of the Civil War*, Vol. 2. New York: Doubleday, 1963.

Chase, Agnes. *Grass: The Yearbook of Agriculture, 1948*. Washington: U.S. Department of Agriculture, 1948.

Chenoweth, Joseph Hart. *Diary* and *Letters* (to his mother, Nancy Ann Chenoweth), 1862. Manuscript in possession of the Virginia Historical Society, Richmond.

Cohn, Douglas A. *Jackson's Valley Campaign*. Washington, D.C.: American Publishing Co., 1986.

Cullum, George Washington. *Biographical Register of the Officers and Graduates of the United States Military Academy*. New York: Government Printing Office, 1868.

Dabney, R. L. (Rev.). *Life and Campaigns of Lieut.-Gen. Thomas J. Jackson*. Richmond, Virginia: Sterling and Albright, 1865. Reprint. Sprinkle Publications, Harrisonburg, Virginia, 1983.

Douglas, Henry Kyd. *I Rode With Stonewall*. Chapel Hill: University of North Carolina Press, 1940. Reprint. Fawcett Publications, New York, 1961.

Downer, Edward T. *Stonewall Jackson's Shenandoah Valley Campaign, 1862*. Lexington: Stonewall Jackson Memorial, Inc., 1959.

Evans, Gen. Clement A., ed. *Confederate Military History: A Library of Confederate States History, in 12 Volumes, Written by Distinguished Men of the South*. New York: Thomas Yoseloff, 1962.

Forbes, Edwin. *Thirty Years After, An Artist's Story of the Great War*, 2 vols. New York, 1890.

Freeman, Douglas Southall. *Lee's Lieutenants: A Study in Command. Vol. 1, Manassas to Malvern Hill*. New York: Charles Scribner's Sons, 1942.

Harding, Joseph F. *Memoir about Joseph H. Chenoweth, 1862*. Manuscript in possession of the Virginia Historical Society, Richmond.

Henderson, G. F. R. (Lieut.-Col.). *Stonewall Jackson and the American Civil War*, Vol. 1. London, New York and Bombay: Longmans, Green, and Co., 1898.

Holbrook, Stewart H. *Machines of Plenty; Pioneering in American Agriculture*. New York: Macmillan, 1955.

Holt, John Lee. *I Wrote You Word: The Poignant Letters of Pvt. Holt*. Edited by James A. Mumper. Lynchburg, Virginia: H. E. Howard, Inc., 1991.

Jackson, Thomas J. *Letter to Headquarters, Valley District, September 22, 1862*. Manuscript in possession of the Virginia Historical Society, Richmond.

Johnson, Allen, ed. *Dictionary of American Biography*, Vol. 1. New York: Charles Scribner's Sons, 1957.

Kellogg, Sanford C. *The Shenandoah Valley and Virginia, 1861–1865: A War Study*. New York: Neale Publishing, 1903.

Kennedy, Frances H., ed. *The Civil War Battlefield Guide, the Conservation Fund*. Boston: Houghton Mifflin, 1990.

Lee, Alfred Emory. *The Battle of Cross Keys: Campaigning in the Mountain Department*. New York: The Magazine of American History, Vol. 15, 1881.

Lee-Jackson Quarterly Review, Vol. 6, No. 2. Charlottesville, Virginia: The Lee-Jackson Foundation, 1977.

Long, E. B. *The Civil War Day by Day; An Almanac, 1861–1865*. New York: Doubleday, 1971.

Martin, David G. *Jackson's Valley Campaign, November 1861–June 1862*. New York: W. H. Smith, 1988.

Martin, Samuel J. *The Battle of Cross Keys: Old Bald Head, Broken Wheat Stalks and a Matter of Coddling*. Berryville, Virginia: Virginia Country, January/February 1987.

McDonald, Archie P. *Make Me a Map of the Valley: The Civil War Journal of Stonewall Jackson's Topographer*. Dallas: Southern Methodist University Press, 1973.

McDonald, William N. *A History of the Laurel Brigade: The Ashby Cavalry of the Army of Northern Virginia and Chew's Battery*. Baltimore: Kate S. McDonald, 1907. Reprint edition. R. W. Beatty, Ltd., Arlington, Virginia, 1969.

McPherson, James M. *Battle Cry of Freedom, The Civil War Era*. New York: Oxford University Press, 1988.

Milhollen, Hirst D., and James R. Johnson. *Best Photos of the Civil War*. New York, Fawcett Books (Publication #487), 1961.

Milroy, Robert H. *Letters to His Wife, Mary Jane Armitag Milroy, 1862* (Manuscript in possession of the Library of Congress). Union Master Notebook, U.S.M.C. Jackson's Valley Campaign Staff Ride, 1989.

Moore, James (Dr.). *June 1862 Civil War Battles of Harrisonburg, Virginia, including Cross Keys and Port Republic*. Harrisonburg: William Arey, undated.

National Encyclopaedia of American Biography, Vol. 4, 1892–1906. New York, 1906.

Osborne, Jack. Resident Engineer (Ret.), Virginia Department of Transportation, Harrisonburg Office. Telephone conversation, April 1990.

Phisterer, Frederick. *New York in the War of the Rebellion*, 2nd Ed. Albany: Weed, Parsons, 1890.

——. *New York in the War of the Rebellion, in Six Volumes*. Albany: J. B. Lyon, 1912.

Pilsen, John (Lieut.-Col). *Reply of Lieut.-Col. Pilsen to Emil Schalk's Criticisms of the Campaign of the Mountain Department, Under Maj.-Gen. J. C. Frémont*. New York: privately published, 1863.

Randolph, William Fitzhugh. *Randolph Family Papers, 1862*. Manuscript in possession of the Virginia Historical Society, Richmond.

Robertson, James I., Jr. *Stonewall in the Shenandoah. The Valley Campaign of 1862*. *Civil War Times Illustrated*, Vol. XI, No. 2. May 1972.

Shenandoah Valley Civil War Round Table, Harrisonburg, Va. Welcomes Winchester Civil War Round Table to our Civil War Battlefields. Harrisonburg: 1964.

Smith, Richard B. (Col.). *Talk Delivered to Civil War Round Table of Wilmington, Delaware, 4 November 1987*. Copy in author's possession.

The South in the Building of the Nation, Vol. 12, 1909–1913. Richmond, 1913.

Southern Historical Society Papers, Vols. VII, X, XXVI, XIX, XXXVII. Richmond, 1879–1906.

Springer, Francis W. *Jay Johns of Old Virginia*. Southern Partisan, Fall/Winter issue 1986/1987.

Steward, John F. *The Reaper*. New York: Greenberg, 1931.

Tanner, Robert G. *Stonewall in the Valley, Thomas J. "Stonewall" Jackson's Shenandoah Valley Campaign, Spring 1862*. New York: Doubleday, 1976.

Taylor, Richard. *Destruction and Reconstruction, Personal Experiences of the Late War*. New York: D. Appleton, 1879.

Terrell, Isaac Long. *Old Houses in Rockingham County: 1750 to 1850*. Verona, Virginia: McClure Press, 1970.

Thompson, William Fletcher. *The Image of War; The Pictorial Reporting of the American Civil War*. New York: T. Yoseloff, 1960.

Tracy, Albert (Col.). "The Journal of Colonel Albert Tracy, March–July, 1862." *Virginia Magazine of History and Biography*, Vol. LXX, 1962.

Trimble, I. R. "The Civil War Diary of General Isaac Ridgeway Trimble." *Maryland Historical Magazine*, Vol. XVII, No. 1, March 1922.

———. *Report to Maj. Gen. Ewell on the Battle of Cross Keys, June 11, 1862.* Copy of original in possession of the Harrisonburg–Rockingham Historical Society.

U.S. War Department. *The War of the Rebellion: A Compilation of the Official Records of the Union and Confederate Armies.* Series I–Vol. XII–in Three Parts. Part I– Reports: Ch. XXIV, Operations in Northern Virginia, West Virginia, and Maryland. Washington: Government Printing Office, 1885.

———. *Atlas to Accompany the Official Records of the Union and Confederate Armies,* 4 vols. 1891–1895. Reprint (1 vol.). New York: Fairfax Press, 1983.

Wayland, John W. *A History of Rockingham County, Virginia.* Dayton, Virginia.: Ruebush-Elkins Company, 1912.

———. *Stonewall Jackson's Way: Route, Method, Achievement.* 1956. Reprint. Dayton, Ohio: Morningside, 1984.

Warner, Ezra J. *Generals in Blue: Lives of the Union Commanders.* Baton Rouge: Louisiana State University Press, 1964.

———. *Generals in Gray: Lives of the Confederate Commanders.* Baton Rouge: Louisiana State University Press, 1959.

Wert, Jeffrey D. "The Valley Campaign of 1862." Richmond: *Virginia Cavalcade,* Vol. XXXV, No. 1. Summer 1985.

The West Point Atlas of American Wars, Vol. I, 1689–1900. U.S. Military Academy, West Point. Department of Military Art and Engineering, Chief Editor, Col. Vincent J. Esposito. New York: Frederick A. Praeger.

Wiley, Bell Irvin. *The Life of Johnny Reb.* Baton Rouge: Louisiana State University Press, 1943.

Wiley, Bell Irvin, and Milhollen, Hirst D. *They Who Fought Here.* New York: Macmillan, 1959.

Williams, Kenneth P. *Lincoln Finds a General: A Military Study of the Civil War,* Vol I. New York: Macmillan, 1950.

Williams, T. Harry. *Lincoln and His Generals.* New York: Alfred A. Knopf, 1952.

Worsham, John H. *One of Jackson's Foot Cavalry.* New York: Neale, 1912. Reprint. New York: Time-Life Books, 1982.